THE INNOCENT EYE:
PRIMITIVE AND NAIVE PAINTERS IN CORNWALL

AF378289

THE INNOCENT EYE

Primitive and Naive Painters
in Cornwall

Alfred Wallis and Bryan Pearce

Mary Jewels and others

Marion Whybrow

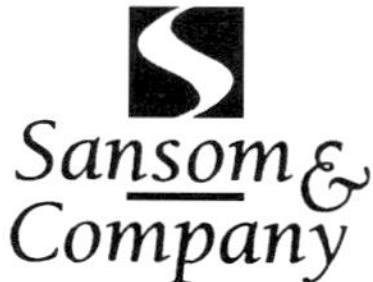

Sansom &
Company

First published in 1999 by Sansom & Company Ltd.,
81g Pembroke Road, Bristol BS8 3EA

© Marion Whybrow

ISBN 1 900178 96 6

British Cataloguing-in-Publication Data
A catalogue record for this book is available from the British Library.

*For Mum and Dad, brothers and sisters,
Harold, (me), Joan, Barney, (Patricia
and Gary) twins (Margaret and Shirley)
and Janet.*

All rights reserved. No part of this publication may be reproduced,
stored in a retrieval system, or transmitted, in any form or by any
means, electronic, mechanical, photocopying, recording or otherwise,
without the prior permission of the publishers.

Typeset by Mayhew Typesetting, Rhayader, Powys
Printed in Great Britain by WBC Print, Bridgend

CONTENTS

Introduction   6

Alfred Wallis and the Hand of God   9
Bryan Pearce: A Sense of Order   23
Techniques, Themes and Topics   38

Alfred Wallis 1855–1942   53
Bryan Pearce 1929–   75

Other Artists, Other Visions   91
Mary Jewels 1886–1977   93
Profiles: Bob Bourne – Fred Yates   129

Bibliography   153
Acknowledgements   156
Index   157

Introduction

There is a tendency to use the terms 'primitive' and 'naive' indiscriminately when writing about apparently unsophisticated paintings, and often the words seem interchangeable. But if any two artists illustrate the difference between the terms, they are Alfred Wallis and Bryan Pearce. Both drew their inspiration from the town of St Ives in which they lived and painted. There the resemblance ends. Their subjects may be similar but their styles, techniques, materials and life experiences differ. However, in some societies the words 'primitive' and 'naive' are considered derogatory and dismissive. Indeed the terms act against the work when considering it for critical acclaim or serious recognition. The Latin word 'nativus' is a far better description, translating as inborn, natural and original. Other words chosen to substitute the English terms are 'intuitive' and 'idio-syncratic'. Both allow for the wide variety of individual work in this field and are empathetic with the nature of the paintings.

Wallis and Pearce both exceeded society's expectations. This can be unforgivable and can lead to alienation because it is easier to sympathise with others' afflictions, especially in those already labelled as failures, rather than celebrate victory over adversity. They were both misunderstood and Wallis in particular experienced a degree of ostracisation. People generally are disarmed and wary of those who achieve success. Barbara Hepworth understood this only too well. In a letter dated January 1964 she wrote, 'The ordinary artist expects the world to be hostile and he also expects a certain amount of persecution. Henry Moore has had his bronzes broken. My big carving has recently been disfigured with black paint all over up in the North. Epstein's work was tarred and feathered. In addition, the world likes to think the artist is a bit mad. Whereas, we think we are pretty sensible.'

As with most genuinely intuitive artists, born not made, Wallis's and Pearce's styles are their own and like other artists in this field they were unable to copy or be influenced by academic work. Such artists now appear to be gaining recognition, their works bought by collectors from the few galleries who specialise in this painting phenomenon. However, there are still few 'natural' artists in national collections.

Primitive or naive artists, as they are at present categorised, rarely appear in books recording the development of art. Their history is not part of the mainstream. They are therefore in a class of their own and this is probably to their advantage. They are true to themselves and have an unshakeable belief in their own vein of art, not doubting its validity, and not wishing to achieve a style acceptable to the mainstream. They follow their own dream, obsession or eccentricity.

'Art from the heart' is an apt description of their work. One can see the analogy in jazz, where an untutored musician picks up an instrument and with an attuned ear, but with no knowledge of notation, can improvise on a melody and compose wonderful music. Such musicians have long been recognised and have earned their place in the world of music, whereas acceptance has been slow to materialise for painters.

George Melly, authority on jazz and collector of naive art, and well placed to comment, has said that authentic naive painting 'must be compulsive, primitive and childlike'. These qualities are in abundance in Wallis and Pearce. Wallis is compulsive and primitive, Pearce compulsive and childlike. They painted their pictures as though their lives depended on it. Pearce tamed his frustrations and his inability to comprehend the ordinary every day affairs of life which other people take for granted. He coped by perfecting his painting to a degree which satisfied him, and his creativity freed him from his limitations. And truly, Wallis only just maintained his sanity. His great compulsive love in recording his life and his memories, with the natural every day materials to hand, helped keep the demons at bay.

Alan Bowness put it succinctly in *The Listener* in 1968: 'he [Wallis] is as essential to English painting, and particularly to the circle of Ben Nicholson and the artists who've gone to work in Cornwall, as Rousseau was to Picasso and his friends.' Naive painting, he noted, was a discovery of the twentieth century and suggested that naive or primitive artists make an appearance in the history of painting when art becomes too precious, too clever and someone with a natural gift overturns everyone's preconceived notions of art and makes them rethink and return to a pre-Renaissance naturalness.

Martin Gayford echoed this sentiment when writing in the *Sunday Telegraph* in 1992: 'It is easy to see how liberating Wallis's paintings must have been to the avant-garde of the 1930s and '40s . . . With the French customs man, Douanier Rousseau, Wallis ranks as one of the two primitive painters who really count in 20th-century art.'

However, Patrick Heron in *The Changing Forms of Art*, compared Rousseau unfavourably with Wallis, describing his paintings as a 'sentimental suburban clerk's daydream . . . Wallis, fisherman and rag-and-bone merchant, was a much more interesting artist: the reality of the sea's white menace to the huddled dark-green headlands, and of the matchwood boats that did not always cheat it, was his imaginative and his actual world in one. His images have a profounder source than Rousseau's; their content is far more urgent and mysterious; and, strangest of all, their design and the texture of their paint has far more to say to us today.'

With Bryan Pearce, the sheer simplicity of his forms and the magic of his colours speak of love so honestly portrayed that it pierces the hearts of those open to these qualities. His paintings contain magical symbols which are daily recreated as a constant reappraisal of his world, 'expressed he knows not how,' proving an enriching experience for the onlooker.

Perhaps it was Wallis who paved the way for the acceptance of Pearce and his painting style many years later. Pearce was hampered by a limited education, resulting from brain damage, and was less capable of conversation than Wallis. However, his comfortable background provided many advantages. What is certain is that both had a struggle to overcome their own limitations and those which society placed on them.

The paintings of Wallis and Pearce reflect the essence of their lives and their unique understanding of their world. Their works show no evidence of sophisticated painting techniques, knowledge of perspective, spatial orientation or proportion, but they each have an innate feeling for design, an honesty of approach to their work, and a love of their subject matter. Each painted according to his life's history and each triumphed through adversity, to creativity, and to recognition.

Writing this brief study of the contrasting lives and work of these two noted St Ives artists has encouraged me to look at kindred spirits working in the area, notably the much under-rated Mary Jewels. This book concludes, therefore, with brief profiles of a selection of other intuitive painters who have done so much to enrich the artistic life of the region.

Marion Whybrow

Alfred Wallis and the Hand of God

Alfred Wallis's paintings are experiences. He had been to sea, felt the power of a huge ocean tossing a boat into the air, climbed a tidal wave and dipped into holes created by the swirling waters. He had been cold, wet, exhausted and work-weary. He had felt the heavy hand of God and the power of nature. He had explored his world and feared it.

Wallis painted with the materials to hand, ship's paint, oddments of card, wood or tea-chests, his table, plates, a cup, the walls, a door or other domestic items. But he was restricted, not only by money to buy materials, but by the limited expectations of his class, education and religion. At that time, a working man could not be seen trying to attain anything above his station in life. However, he ignored ridicule and carried on painting. He lived, ate, slept and painted in one room; surrounded by his life's experience he painted with an impassioned recall of places and events. The chaos of his life was brought to order by his compulsive painting habit.

Wallis was at a loss after the death of his wife. 'Think I'll do a bit of painting. Think I'll draw a bit,' he told friends Edwards the watchmaker and Armour the antique dealer, for whom Wallis worked on occasions. His two friends encouraged him.

When Wallis began to paint seriously 'for company' in 1925 he was 70 years old. Self taught, he wrote letters to Jim Ede, assistant curator of the modern collection at the Tate Gallery, London, who had bought a large number of his works. In a letter of 1936, he explained 'i never see any Thing i send you now it is what I have seen Before i am self Taught so you Cannot like me to Thouse That have Been Taught Both in school and paint i have had To learn my self i never go out To paint nor i never show Them from your friend alfred wallis.' This was to distinguish him from the 'gentlemen' artists whose studios were close by his cottage and who submitted work to the Royal Academy. Unlike the 'plein air' painters, Wallis worked in his living room on a flat table top and surrounded himself with his paintings. These icons represented his life, signifying his identity.

Once Alfred had started, painting became a compulsion. He painted every day, producing perhaps several paintings in a day – except on the Sabbath, when

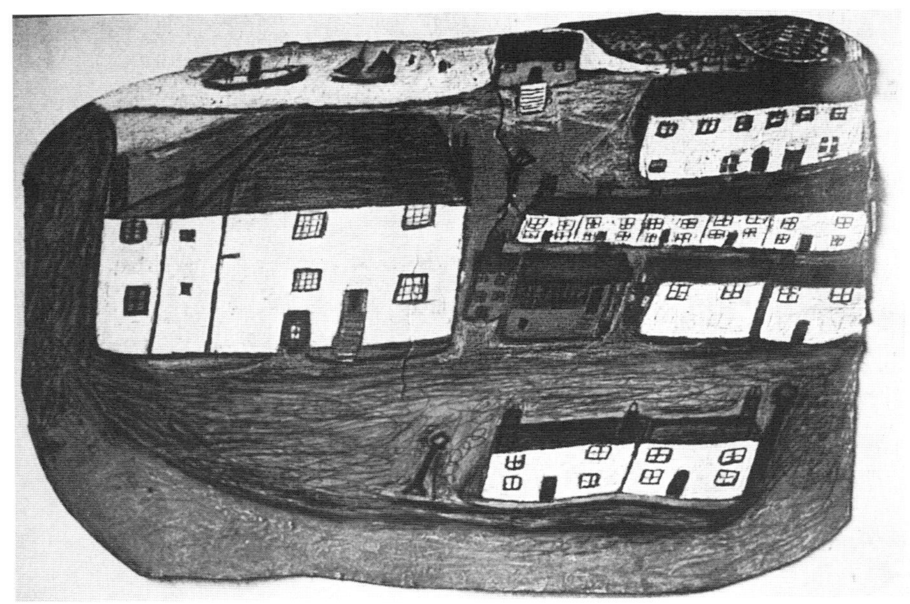

Alfred Wallis: *House in Porthmeor Square, St Ives* [courtesy Dr Roger Slack].

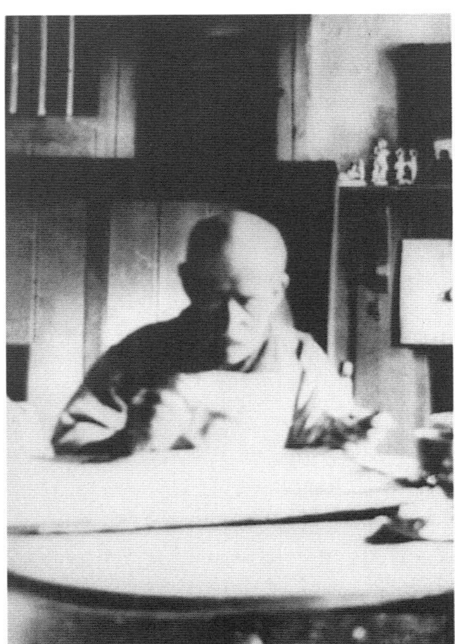

Alfred Wallis in his
cottage at 3 Back Road
West, St Ives.

he restrained his urge to paint, covered his pictures with newspapers and read from the large family bible, his one Sunday activity. He searched for left-over household and ship's paints and demanded scraps of card from another friend, Mr Baughan, who had a grocer's shop in the Digey. He cut, tore and shaped the pieces of card to fit the subjects of his design, no matter what rough edges would remain. This was something unheard of by the 'real' artists, but for Wallis to paint was the important factor, not the presentation. Some of his pictures were painted on the backs of Great Western Railway posters, or on advertisements.

He painted the herring and mackerel boats that once crowded the harbour of St Ives when a man could step from boat to boat to arrive at Smeaton's Pier from the slipway. He remembered his days at sea as a young man and painted three-masted sailing ships and early steam ships, and he began to record the little town of St Ives where he and his wife Susan, from their arrival in the 1880s, lived the rest of their lives. He painted the island, the pier with its two lighthouses, seine boats in the harbour, the houses and Godrevy lighthouse standing sentinel in St Ives Bay. He included everything that had shaped his daily life, painting as though all these things were history, regarding even his present conscious existence as part of his previous life, 'as it used to be'.

The story of how Wallis was 'discovered' is now part of the folklore of the modernist art movement in St Ives. Ben and Winifred Nicholson and Christopher Wood were staying with friends at Feock, and on a day trip to St Ives in August 1928, Nicholson and Wood passed Wallis's cottage and looked inside. They were astonished by what they saw. Nicholson wrote an account in *Horizon* a year after Wallis's death. 'Not only was it the first time I saw St Ives, but on the way back from Porthmeor Beach we passed an open door in Back Road West and through it saw some paintings of ships and houses on odd pieces of paper and cardboard nailed up all over the wall, with particularly large nails through the smallest ones. We knocked on the door and inside found Wallis, and the paintings we got from him then were the first he made.'

After seeing Alfred painting in his cottage, and with such humble materials, Ben did several paintings and drawings of Porthmeor beach, capturing an immediacy that he felt was present in the paintings of the little old chap. It is perhaps not claiming too much to suggest that Wallis became something of a mentor to both Nicholson and Wood.

The often repeated story of Wallis's discovery prompted Andrew Lanyon to comment in one of his satirical studies on the arts colony. The caption to a painting showing Wallis peering out of his window observing two figures making their way along the beach, reads: 'Alfred Wallis noticing Nicholson and Wood ages before their discovery of him.'

One of those first paintings Nicholson bought was *Schooner and Lighthouse*, for which he paid two shillings and sixpence. Many years later, in 1958, the painting was given to the sculptor Denis Mitchell, when Ben left St Ives to live with his third wife, Felicitas Vogler, in Switzerland. When he came across Wallis, Nicholson was in the process of refining and simplifying his own work. He found the child-like vision appealing. 'Nicholson perceived in Wallis's work a sense of the painting as an object and enjoyed the stress he placed naturally and possibly unknowingly on materials,' but in using the word 'unknowingly' Jeremy Lewison may not have allowed for Wallis's natural integrity. One remarkable thing about Wallis is his conscious use of materials to suit his design. This is what Nicholson admired.

Nicholson's interest in naive painting can be traced to the Italian Primitives and the work of Henri Rousseau which was exhibited at the Lefevre Gallery, London, in 1926. Wallis's work was, if anything, an affirmation of his already adopted idea to simplify and achieve a directness of vision, rejecting his father's academic stance. William Nicholson was a fine painter, but Ben was not looking for excellence, nor to assuage his father's criticism of his exploratory work.

Another artist, Cedric Morris, claimed to have known about Wallis before the historic meeting. He had lived briefly in Cornwall and was a frequent visitor in the 1920s. In 1926 he was elected a member of the Seven & Five Society, of which Ben was a founder, and may very possibly have mentioned the retired seaman painting his seascapes at the cottage in Back Road West, so that when the two protagonists arrived in St Ives it may have been consciously to seek out Alfred Wallis. Jeremy Lewison notes in the catalogue to the Ben Nicholson exhibition at the Tate Gallery in 1993, that the Nicholson archive contains an issue of *Cahiers d'Art* which is illustrated with a number of works depicting boats and childlike houses: 'Given the context of the interest in "primitivism" and children's art and that Nicholson had a copy of this article, when he and Wood "discovered" the fisherman painter Alfred Wallis in St Ives in 1928, their response to the quality of his work must have been somewhat preconditioned.' Whatever the exact sequence of events, it was Ben Nicholson's advocacy that put Wallis's paintings on the artistic map.

Christopher Wood was said to have admired the poetic quality of Wallis's paintings. Winifred Nicholson also noted this particular quality, writing in *Unknown Colour*: 'They are painted with the imagination of a poet and the restraint of colour and sense of movement of a master. His work is true naive and of the utmost sincerity . . . Ail his painting is expressive as only great and simple painting is. His work had great influence on the work of both Kit and Ben.' Jim Ede felt Wood was 'nurtured and illumined by his meeting with Wallis'.

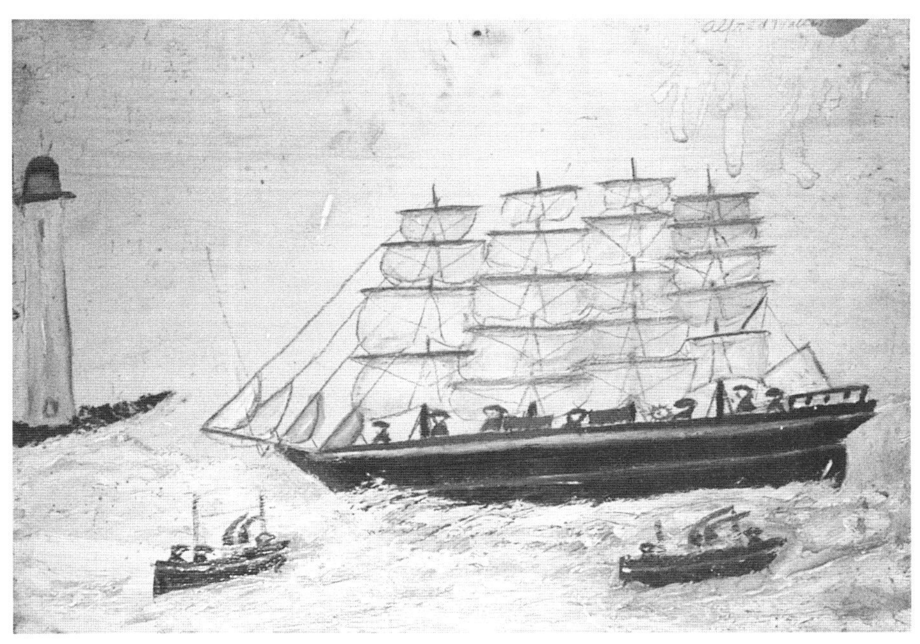

Alfred Wallis: *Four-masted schooner*. [courtesy Dr Roger Slack]

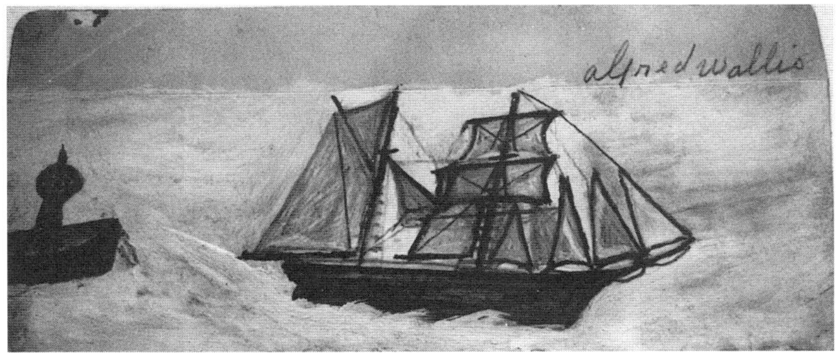

Alfred Wallis: *Schooner leaving harbour*. [courtesy Sims Gallery]

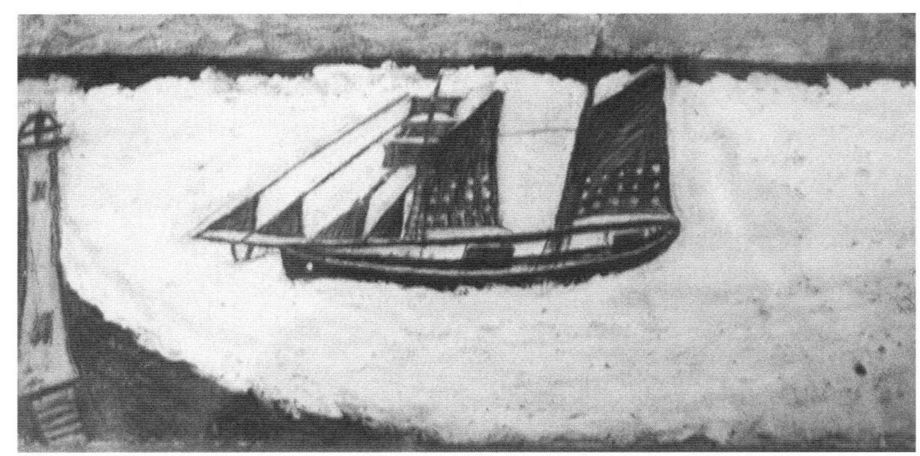

Alfred Wallis: *Schooner and lighthouse*. [courtesy Jane Mitchell]

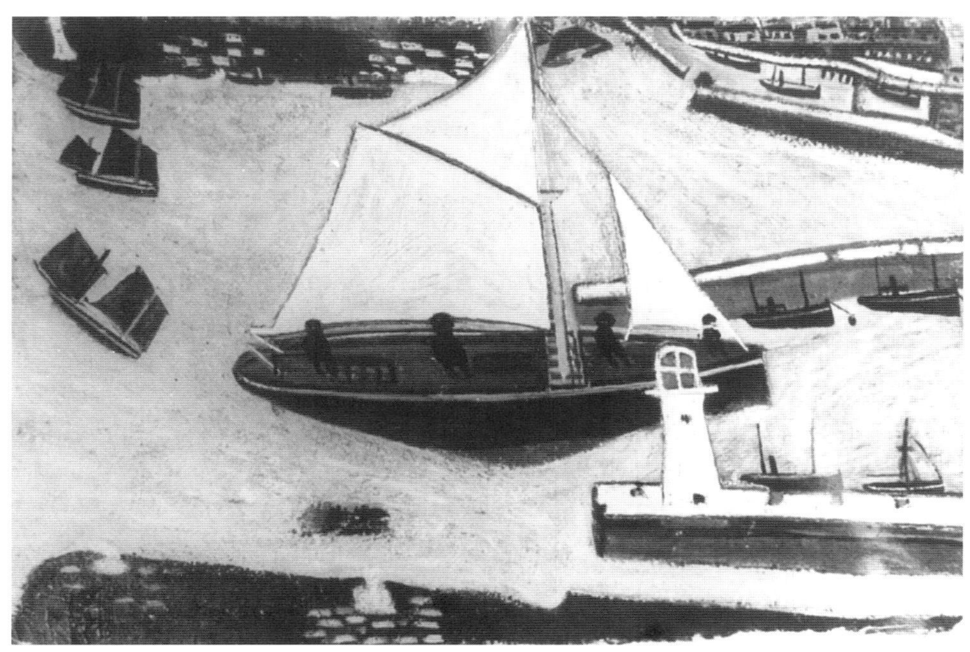

Alfred Wallis: *Penzance*. [courtesy Reg Watkiss Collection]

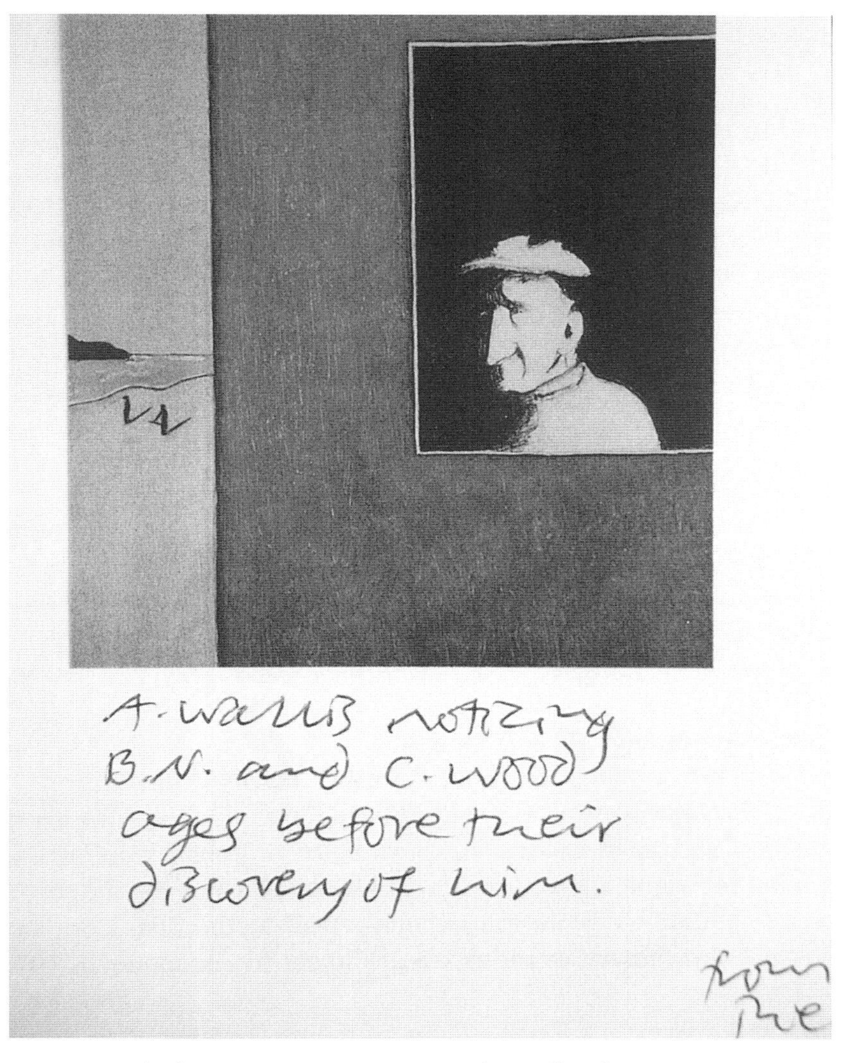

Andrew Lanyon's comment on the Wallis 'discovery'.

After Ben and Winifred had gone back to London, Kit Wood stayed on in St Ives, taking a room overlooking Porthmeor beach and close to Wallis's cottage. 'Admiral Wallis I often see,' he wrote to Winifred, 'I took him some baccy and a few papers last evening. He showed me the lovely boats Ben sent him. I think he appreciated them as he had noticed much the same construction as in his own pictures. He said when he came to my house that they looked as well as anything – "Draw 'em off."'

From London Ben sent Alfred a book of boats, probably that to which Kit Wood referred. This would have been a gift, but Alfred always liked to pay his way. He wrote to Nicholson on 5 December 1928: 'Sir I Receved The Book all Right and I think it a fine one i serpose i shall pay you som Day you Can Take it out of The last pictures i sent what it Cost mind you Take it out i shall Be Displeus if you do not so mind and Take it out opin you all well from your friend alfred wallis Respets to all will you be home over The Christmas i serpos it will of no use To Rit nor send any Thing Till after you Come Back.'

Nicholson also gave Wallis boxes to paint on. In a letter in 1929 Wallis says he received the box and he had painted a boat on one side and another vessel on the other, adding 'my paint is don and gon thick so the one on each end you can do yourself.'

But for Nicholson's promotion of Wallis, and the introduction of his work to other artists and collectors, Wallis might well have died in obscurity, along with other naive painters of his humble background. Certainly, much of his work would have been destroyed. Edwin Mullins has described him as the only British primitive painter to possess 'a touch of genius' and agreed that 'but for a handful of admirers his achievements could easily have died with him in the workhouse.' Wallis suffered from the drawback of many working class people who aspire to reach beyond their destiny, and found himself at odds with his society, considered 'mad' by adults, and made fun of by local children.

In an interview recorded by Dr Roger Slack, who spoke to relatives of Wallis's in the 1960s, Emily Woolcock said, 'We used to laugh at it really because mother used to say: "Well that's just like a child's picture. Always boats, nothing but boats." And every time, practically, I went in he used to say: "There you are, carry this home." I used to carry them home and mother used to say to me: "Well don't, for heaven's sake, Emily, bring any more of them in. Throw them in the dustbin." I've had scores of them. I've only got one today.'

Barbara Hepworth understood Wallis's predicament and wrote to Roger Slack in 1964: 'the minute Wallis began to paint, he put himself on the side of a new group which naturally meets with hostility, and he alienated himself from the normal friendships around him. Whilst he entered this world of aesthetic values with unerring instinct, he had no worldly sophistication to meet the hostility which this preoccupation of his gave rise to within his immediate neighbourhood. No wonder he loved people like Ben Nicholson, Christopher Wood and Adrian Stokes.'

Wallis considered he was not a 'real artist' – not a 'gentleman artist' – like those who occupied the Porthmeor Studios, just ten yards from his house in Back Road West. His paintings, which he seldom titled, were never dated, except by the people who bought them. He also said that only one or two people had collections of his paintings and 'I does no harm to no one.' In some indefinable subconscious way, he believed in himself.

Wallis, indeed, was capable of giving advice: 'You don't want to use too many colours,' he advised Ben Nicholson, and to Jim Ede he wrote 'I do not put collers what do not Belong I think it spoils the picturs Their have been a lot of paintins spoiled by putin collers where they do not Blong.' For *Flying Scud, Newlyn*, a fishing boat on which he is thought to have worked, Wallis used an old envelope. He has left most of the buff background unpainted, allowing two thirds of the colour to play a major role in the make-up of the picture; thus following his own advice of not putting colours where they do not belong. This was the informed choice of an artist who knew the effect he wanted to achieve.

Nicholson noted the tones he used, 'lovely dark browns, shiny blacks, fierce greys, strange whites and a particularly pungent Cornish green'. He would give paintings to Nicholson and others, saying, 'These are for you to take off from.' Perhaps he meant they were to act as a source of inspiration which indeed they were to many of the artists, especially Ben, who remarked, 'his imagination is surely a lovely thing – it is something which has grown out of the Cornish earth and sea, and which will endure.'

Barbara Hepworth, remarking on the relationship of Ben and Alfred in a BBC radio broadcast in 1968, recalled that 'when we called his whole face lit up at the sight of Ben and he always asked us in and we stood there, just within the door, because there was nowhere to sit. It was such a tiny, tiny room and between us and Wallis lay this very big table spread out with all his boards, some he was working on, all his paints – tin after tin of the best ship's paints, which he believed in – and brushes, and in his right hand he held the brush; in his left hand was an enormous open bible. He and Ben would talk in a rather desultory way as one friend who's just bumped into another friend and knows he's on even ground.'

The first one-man show after Wallis's death in 1942 was held at the Penwith Society's gallery in Fore Street in 1959. This was a celebratory exhibition with works loaned by Hepworth, Kate Nicholson, Denis Mitchell, Wilhelmina Barns-

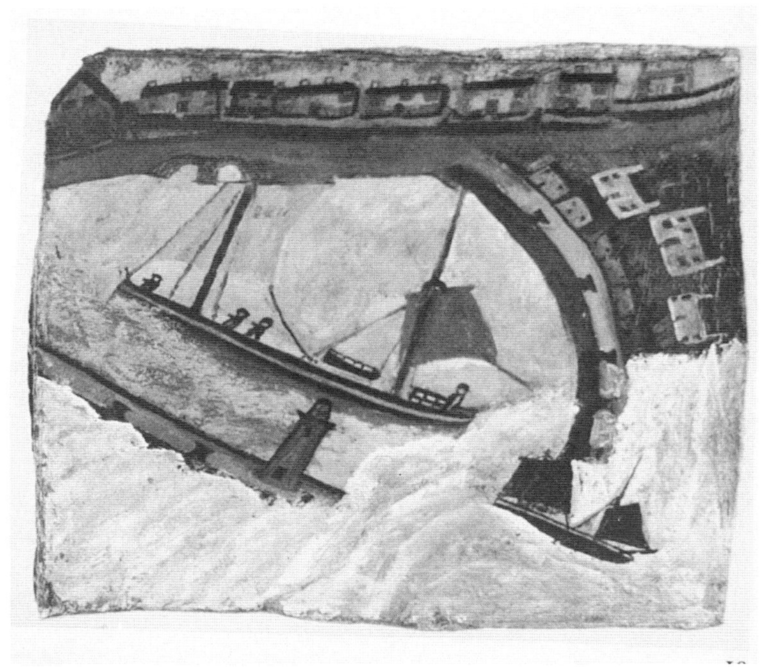

Alfred Wallis: *Sailing into harbour.*

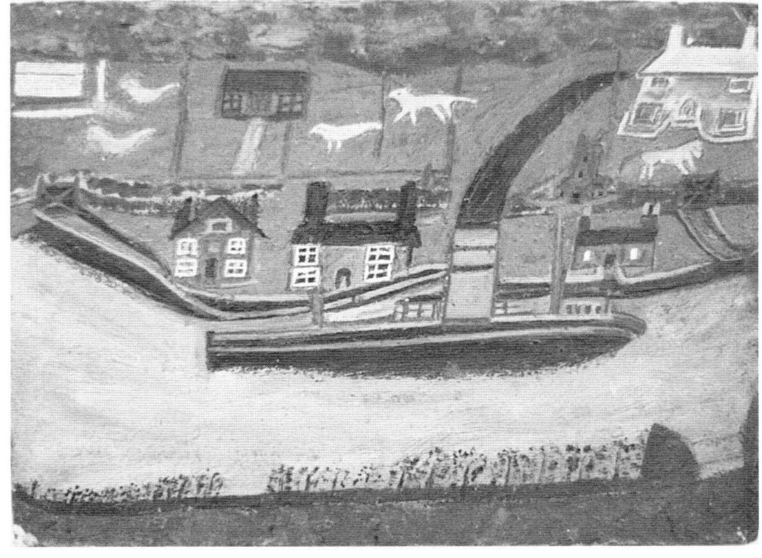

Alfred Wallis: *A river fall.* [courtesy Dr Roger Slack]

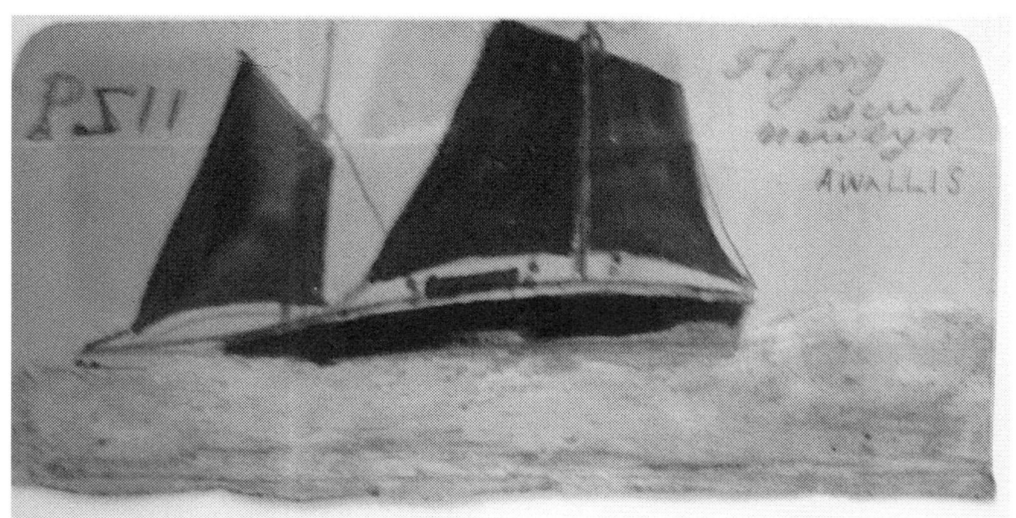

Alfred Wallis: *Flying Scud*.

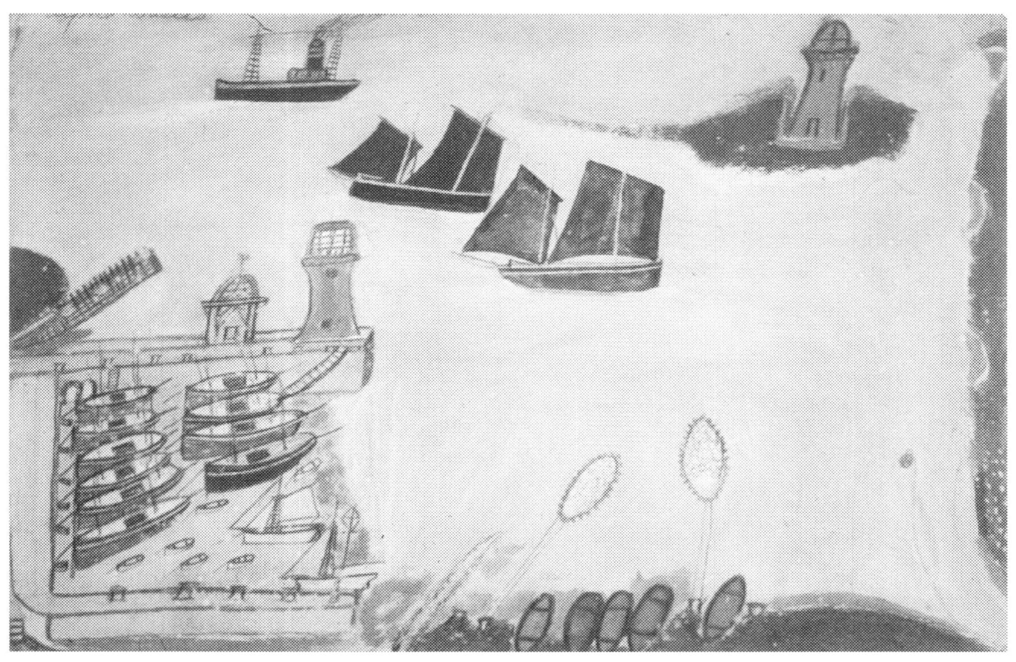

Alfred Wallis: *St Ives Harbour, Godrevy and seine boats*.

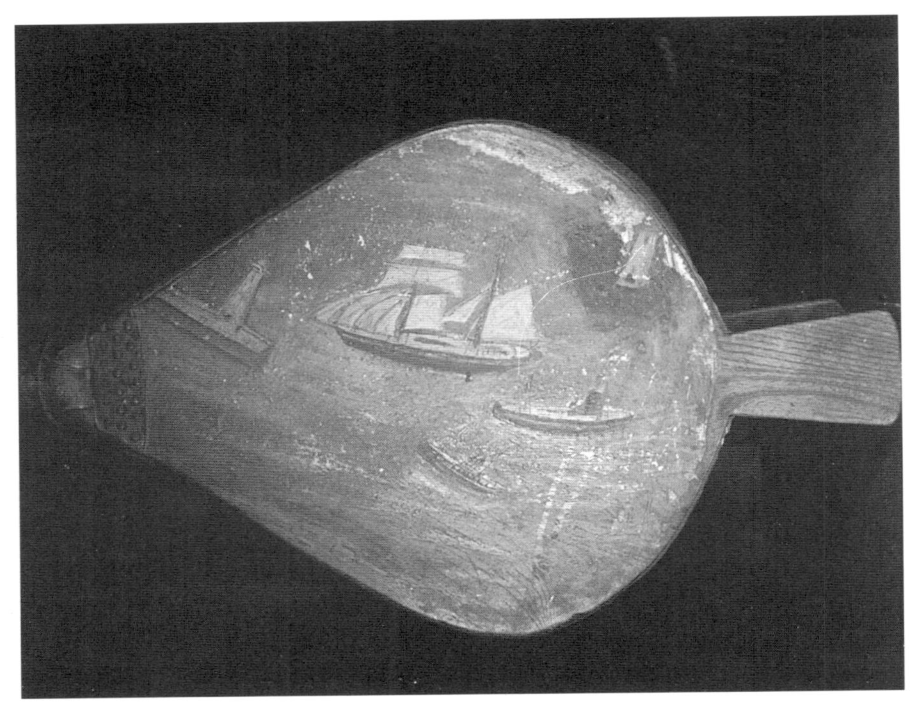

Alfred Wallis painting on bellows. [courtesy Dr Roger Slack]

Graham and others. Family and neighbours were amazed at such an honour and Alfred himself would doubtless have been shocked. A further one-man show was held at the Penwith Gallery's new premises in Back Road West in 1967, a hundred yards from his cottage. The paintings came from the collection of his coterie of friends and artists who supported him and bought his work: Jim Ede, Winifred Nicholson, Margaret Mellis, Margaret Gardiner and Barbara Hepworth, among others. Enlarging on this in 1968 Alan Bowness, with the support of the Arts Council, mounted 177 pictures at the Tate Gallery, London, which travelled to York, Aberdeen and Kendal art galleries. Peter Lanyon's work was exhibited at the same time, four years after his death in a gliding accident. Lanyon was a great admirer of Wallis whose influence can be detected in Lanyon's colours, especially the salty greys and tumbling whites and what became known as a St Ives green; and the speedy application of colour which gives a feeling of vitality and energy to both men's work.

William Feaver wrote of Peter Lanyon in *Cornwall*, published in 1983 by Alison Hodge, that Lanyon was seeking new ways of organising the space in a picture. 'He learned from Alfred Wallis, the St Ives primitive, how to dispense with conventional perspective. If you ignored it, the pressure to represent scenes as peep shows disappeared.' Wallis would not have been able to say that he ignored perspective in his work, or even to have understood what perspective was. It took an educated artist to unravel, explain and define Wallis' unique way of working.

The 1968 Tate exhibition featured work on scraps of material to show how Alfred Wallis painted on any objects he could find: a painted bellows, large stoneware marmalade jars, wooden boxes, pieces of wood given to him by Adrian Stokes, pots, and two sketchbooks, which were bought by the artists and given to Wallis while he was in Madron poorhouse. One of these, owned by Denis Mitchell, contained 34 pencil and blue crayon drawings. The other, owned by Margaret Mellis, held nineteen oil and wash paintings.

> No relevance here for perspective, impressionist tricks
> Learned at the Slade, the glorification of light.
> You knew the stink of fish and smear of tar, the cutched sails
> Drying stiff in the raw sunlight and east wind;
> Were led by instinct . . .
>
> *Excerpt from poem 'The Last Voyage of Alfred Wallis'*
> *by Cornish Bard and playwright, Donald Rawe*

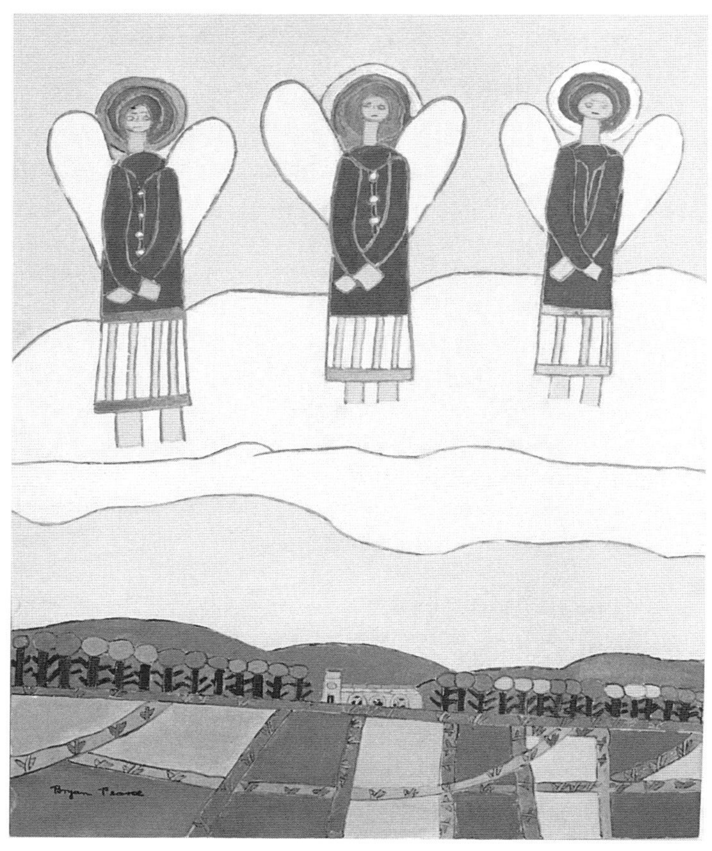

Bryan Pearce: *Angels*.

Bryan Pearce: A Sense of Order

Bryan Pearce's paintings are totally visual. Unlike Wallis, he is an onlooker, his life unruffled by direct experience. He has never known the harshness of physical labour, the rigours of life at sea. His seas are flat, blue and peaceful, on which toy-like boats do not disturb the surface but lie in harmony within safe boundaries. He also knows the hand of God, for him a gentle presence providing for his needs and his comfort. His world is bountiful.

Pearce chooses his colours carefully and mixes his paint on a palette. He paints on properly stretched canvas placed on an easel and is meticulous in his approach, cleaning his brushes and working within a strict framework. His studio is a workplace where his framed canvases line the walls. He enters this ordered space in the morning and leaves it at night. Pearce is governed by routine and confined by habit. His life is regulated and patterned, and this sense of order enables him to function.

Bryan Pearce began painting in 1953, eleven years after the death of Wallis, of whom he was totally unaware. Bryan was 24 years old, an angry and frustrated young man with nothing to occupy him except a few mundane domestic tasks. An inherited condition, developing soon after birth, had left him brain damaged, severely limiting his ability to learn. His mother Mary, in a desperate effort to find something useful for him to do and to develop his motor skills, bought a child's colouring book and paints from Woolworths. Items were outlined and colours had to be filled in. His first attempt was to paint a musical instrument. Mary, prompted by Bryan's keen interest in music, pointed out the bright yellow cornet and gently suggested he might like to paint it. 'He painted it beautifully and was so delighted. This was how it all started.'

With Bryan beginning to produce his own work, Mary asked a local artist, Isobel Heath, for her opinion. 'He's got something, you know,' she said, and after three months working with him, she advised that Bryan become a student at the St Ives School of Painting under the principal, Leonard Fuller. Bryan attended regularly for three years, working in watercolour, with Fuller taking him to several spots in the town and setting up a table and chair for him to work, letting him find his own way and interfering as little as possible. When

Mary hesitantly asked about his progress Fuller said Bryan was the most dedicated of all his students, completing his work and solving any difficulties he encountered and never giving up. Peter Lanyon, in an undated letter, wrote to Leonard Fuller, 'I think your help for young Bryan Pearce has been excellent. It is cheering to think that his life has been transformed by his Art.'

Pearce's first attempts at drawing were based on the colouring book method, but adapted to suit his tentative beginnings, firstly drawing a faint outline in pencil, on board, making much use of a rubber, going over that with a further hardly definable line, and finally with a bold yellow ochre when he is satisfied with the drawing. The colours are then filled in, meticulously and carefully, smoothing out any brush lines to a flat surface. The filling in is the enjoyable part. He also enjoys the detail in painting stones, cobbles, tiles, houses, shapes and complex patterns. Mary often despaired to see the amount of work he had created for himself saying, 'Oh Bryan, look at all those houses! How on earth are you going to paint them all?' knowing that he had given himself a task of several months. And he would say, 'I'll manage.' When questioned why he painted a picture of angels he said, 'It just came into my mind – the church in the Holy Land, with angels coming down from the sky.' This is a painting in which imagination and thought have replaced the usual carefully arranged still life, or the view that he has sketched or remembered.

One of Bryan's early paintings was *Tomato Ketchup with Condiments*. At that time he was very limited in his ability to read and yet was able to reproduce the lettering on the items on the table. Since his work is slow and careful he would have to look up many times and closely observe each letter – a difficult task but one Bryan has always tackled, never admitting defeat, or questioning his ability. In this matter he is fortunate that he cannot look deeply into his world. However, others find that this is truly a case of the work speaking for itself and communicating a sense of optimism, of peace and tranquillity. *Nescafe and Coffee Mate* was painted in 1988 and the improvement in his ability to write and confine the letters within the space is evident, and there is still the lovely shaping of the pots.

In a change of medium Bryan found oils easier to manipulate and the application of the paint more satisfying in its density, giving the flat and solid smooth surface which is always his aim. Mixing colours is something Bryan undertakes with relish using several brushes and, cleaning them as he goes, he achieves a purity and brightness, a decorative appeal that so pleased him in his first attempt at using colour. Here was something to occupy the creative side of his brain, releasing him from an impotent anger at his inability to achieve and helping him find solace and pleasure.

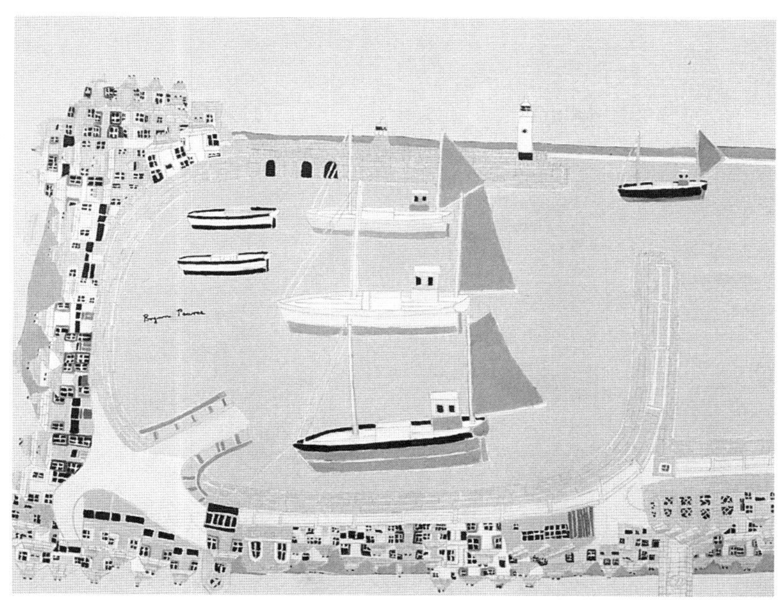

Bryan Pearce: *St Ives Harbour (all round)*, 1987.

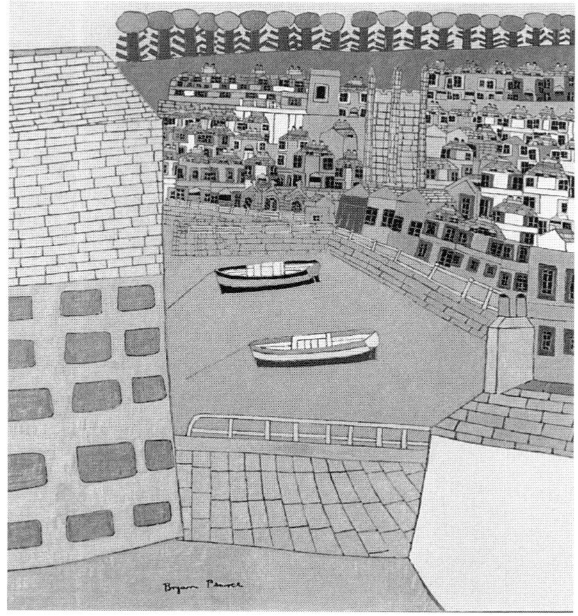

Bryan Pearce: *St Ives from Fish Street.*

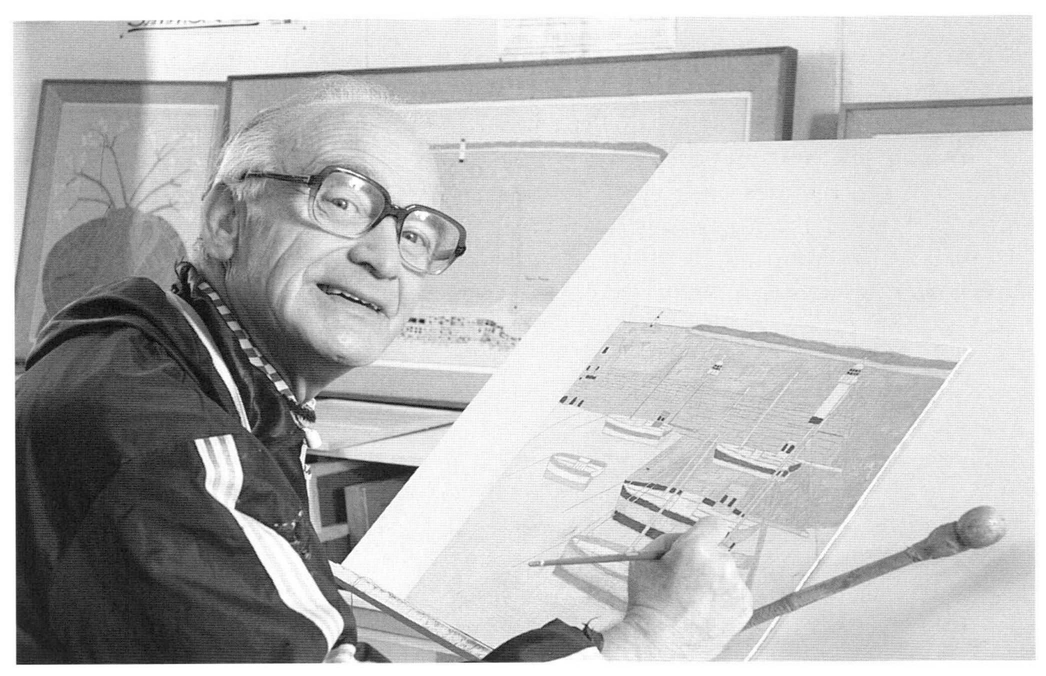

Bryan Pearce in his studio, 1985 and 1996.

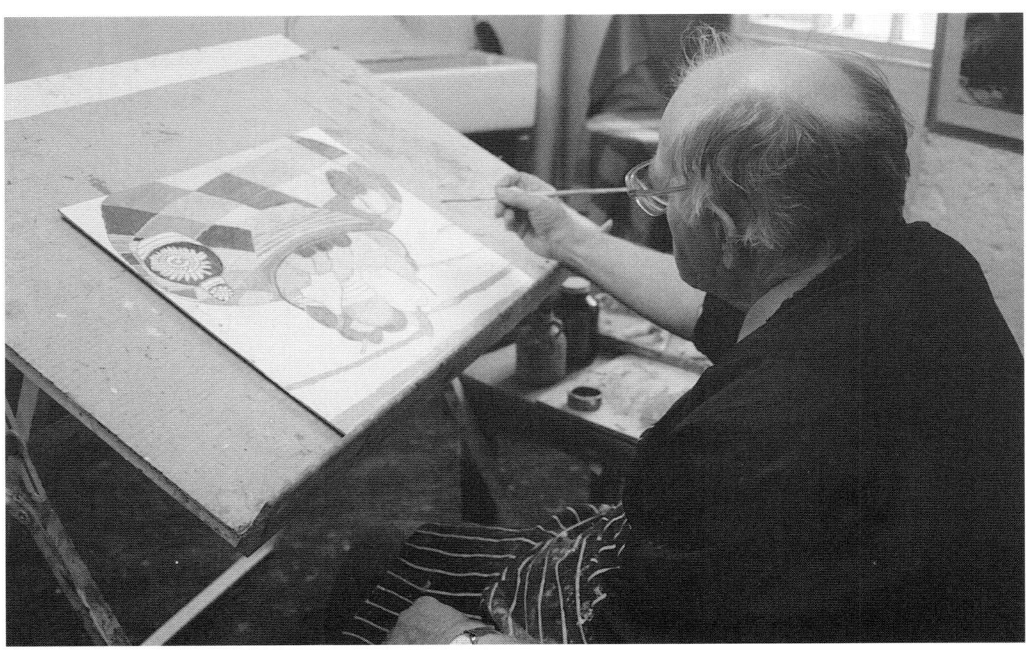

After his years of study at the School of Painting, and a growing output of work, his mother felt Bryan was ready for the professional world of painting and chose the forward-looking Penwith Society of Arts, where differing techniques and explorations of style were acceptable. Denis Mitchell, sculptor and for ten years Barbara Hepworth's chief assistant, sponsored Bryan for membership. He came to the studio and selected several paintings for the committee to consider and on his recommendation, along with the quality of the work, Bryan was accepted. Shortly after this Bryan was nominated a member of the Newlyn Society of Artists and has exhibited regularly with both societies ever since.

Bryan's first studio was in the attic above the flat he shared with his parents in Market Place. It overlooked the rooftops of St Ives, the parish church, and out to the bay. Mary Pearce had intended using it for herself but gave the studio over to Bryan, devoting herself to nurturing his career, at the expense of her own considerable artistic gifts. When the family moved into Downalong, the fishing quarter of St Ives, he acquired one of the Porthmeor Studios immediately below the St Ives School of Painting and here he succeeded notable seascape painters like Julius Olsson, who with Louis Grier had set up the first School of Painting in St Ives in 1895. Borlase Smart, Moffat Lindner, Frances Hodgkins and John Park had also occupied Porthmeor Studios and more recent tenants include Patrick Heron, who took over Ben Nicholson's studio, and Royal Academician Sandra Blow.

Only six years after he started to paint, in 1959 Bryan was offered his first one-man show at Newlyn Art Gallery. It was a major event in his life. There he succeeded the great plein air painters of vast canvases whose pictures recorded the characters and lives of the fishing village and community of Newlyn: people like Walter Langley, Norman Garstin, T C Gotch, Frank Bramley and Dame Laura Knight. Also such names as Stanhope and Elizabeth Forbes, who founded the Newlyn School of Painting in 1889, and even more significantly and recently, fellow Cornishman Peter Lanyon. After this first solo exhibition Bryan exhibited widely in mixed and one-man shows and his status as an artist was quickly established. However, he is not conscious of other artists' ways of working, is not influenced by others' comments: 'I paint as I please. It's my decision,' he says, unwittingly echoing Wallis's independent line. He looks at other works of art in exhibitions in which he is featured but his answer to the question, 'which paintings do you like the best?' is invariably: 'My own. I like my own'. This is said with absolute honesty and without guile, even without pride; it is a statement of fact.

Peter Lanyon, when asked by Bryan's mother to write a foreword for the catalogue of Bryan's show at St Martin's Gallery, London, in 1964, replied, 'I think this is a thing I can do, as a native.' Tragically, in that same year, Lanyon was killed in a gliding accident. He wrote:

> His art emerges at a time when sophistication is disintegrating St Ives paintings, and a self conscious group of artists is mourning the decline of a fictitious "St Ives School". Bryan Pearce takes a walk to Carbis Bay, returning by the cliff path to paint what has happened with a blue sea and green grass and side seen houses and around corner looks. Because his sources are not seen with a passive eye, but are truly happenings, his painting is original.
>
> These paintings may be subjects for analysis to some people but that activity is not going to make the paintings more understandable. It is necessary to accept these works as the labour of a man who has to communicate this way because there is no other. It is then possible to celebrate the facts and not the theory.

Mary considered this one of the most understanding pieces ever written about her son. Peter Lanyon invited the Pearce family to Little Parc Owles where Bryan could 'wander round the garden' and perhaps find inspiration for other paintings in that setting. Several visits must have taken place; one painting, *Little Parc Owles*, is dated 1974. At the beginning of the war the house had been occupied by Adrian Stokes and his artist wife, Margaret Mellis, who had invited Ben Nicholson and Barbara Hepworth and their triplets to join them in Cornwall. They stayed several months before finding their own house close by.

Alan Bowness became interested in Bryan's work when it was exhibited in aid of the local St Michael's Hospital. He was then a lecturer at the Courtauld Institute and later was appointed director of the Tate Gallery, London. On his retirement, when he was awarded a knighthood for his contribution to British art, he remained both friend and advisor to the Pearce family. Like his mother-in-law, Dame Barbara Hepworth, he admired the simplicity and directness of both Alfred Wallis and Bryan Pearce. In 1966 he wrote the catalogue introduction for Bryan's solo exhibition at the New Arts Centre in London. The *Illustrated London News*, *Observer* and *The Times* wrote favourable reviews and the Pearce family returned to St Ives with the satisfying feeling that Bryan could now earn his living from an activity that was his chosen occupation and helped him play a meaningful part in society.

In 1975 Bowness's text was used for a retrospective show at the Museum of Modern Art in Oxford, where 57 paintings and drawings showed Bryan's progress over 20 years. This introduction was repeated in the catalogue for an

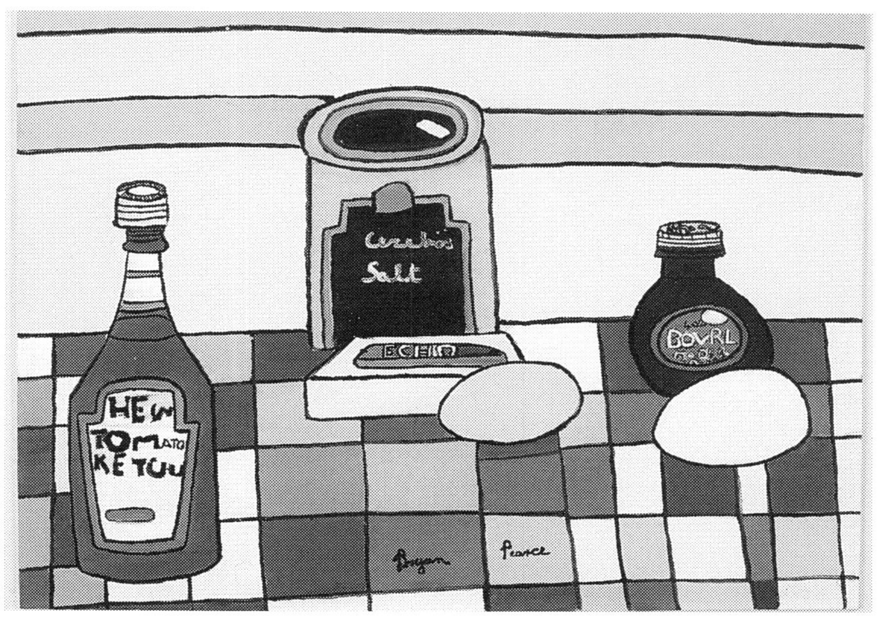

Bryan Pearce: *Tomato ketchup with condiments.*

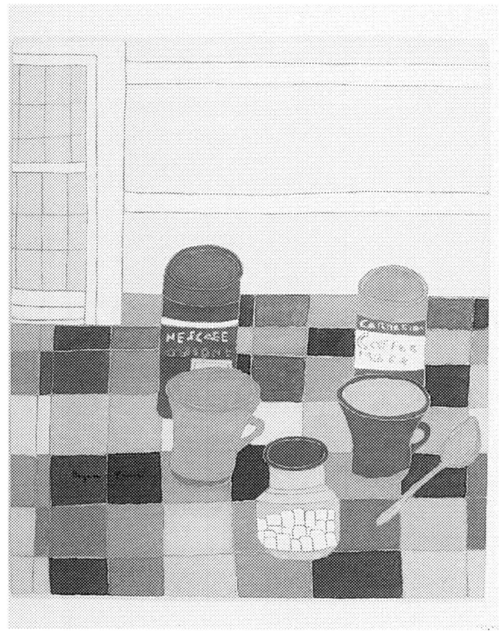

Bryan Pearce: *Nescafe and Coffee Mate*, 1988.

29

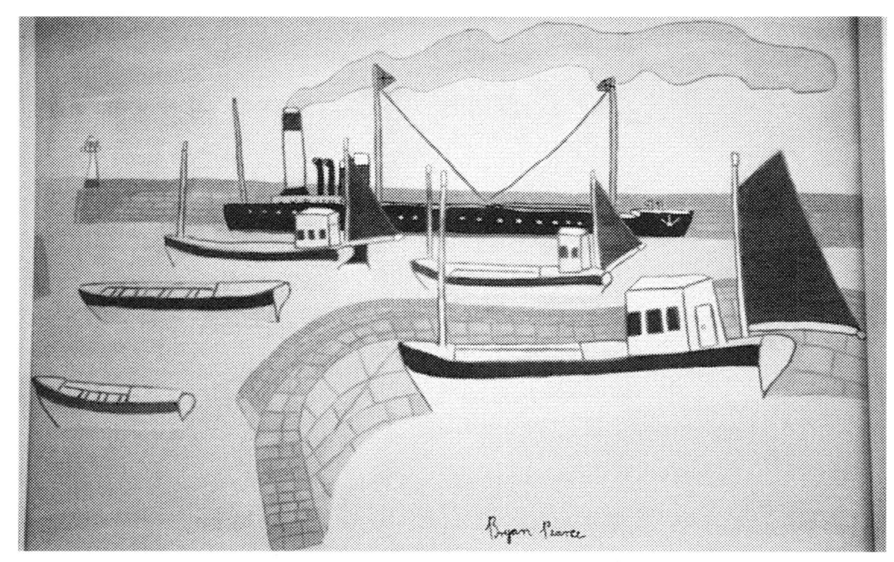

Bryan Pearce: *Newlyn Harbour*, 1958. [courtesy Jane Mitchell]

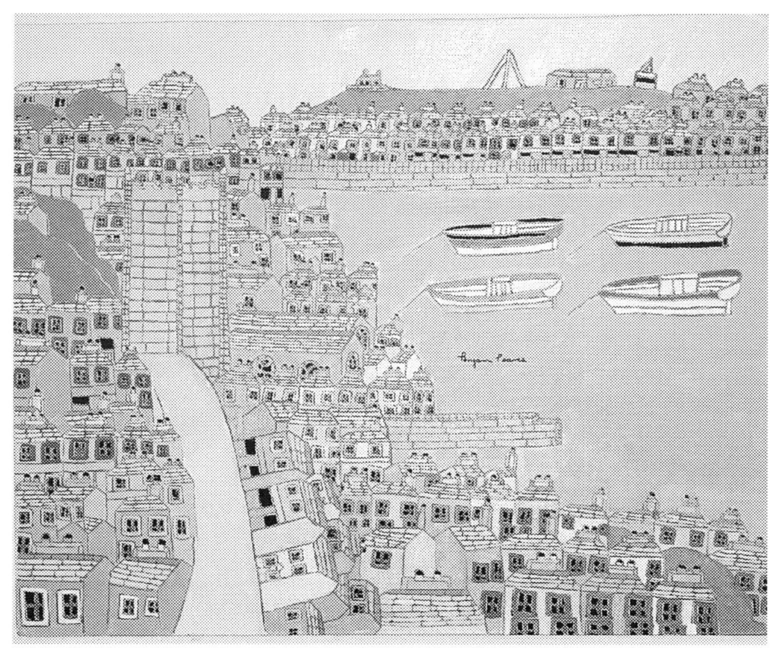

Bryan Pearce: *St Ives from Fernlea Terrace*, 1993.

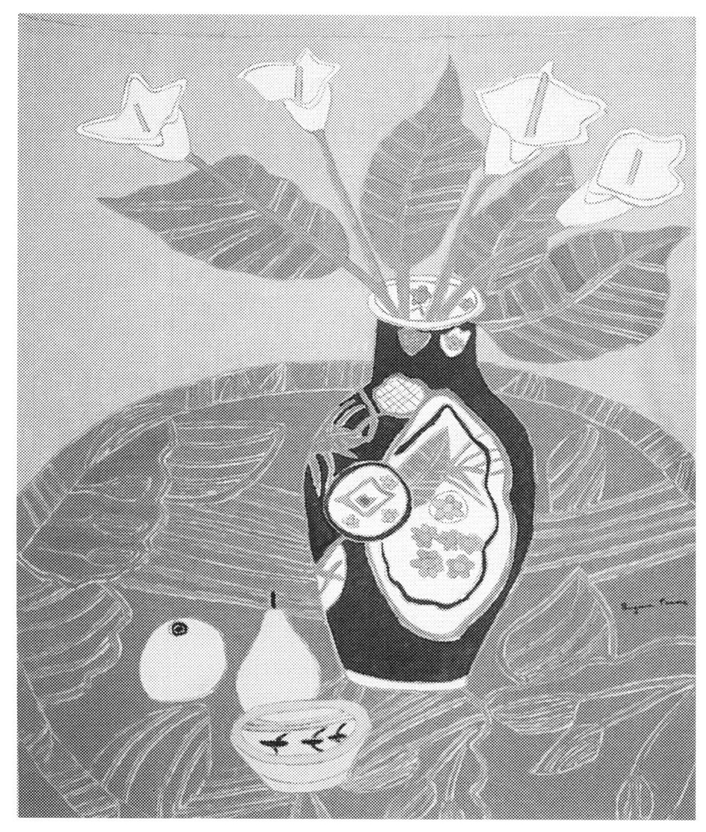

Bryan Pearce: *Lilies in Imari vase*, 1992.

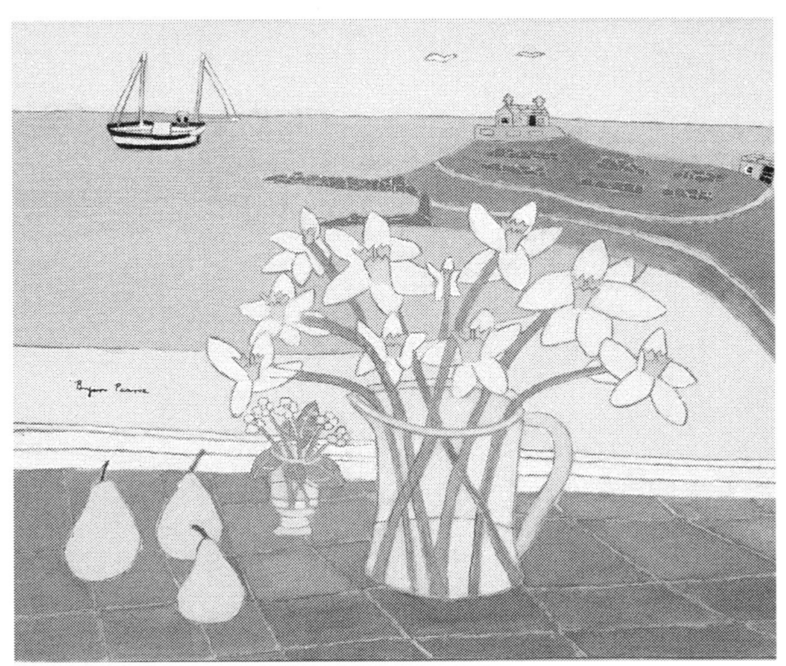

Bryan Pearce: *Lilies in the window and The Island*, 1996.

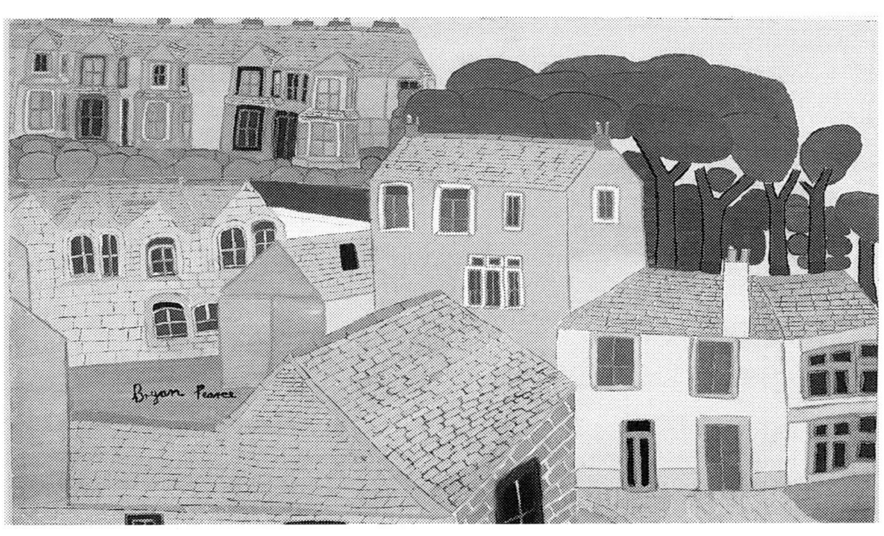

Bryan Pearce: *Rooftops*, 1958.

exhibition of pen and ink drawings and paintings at Victor Waddington's gallery in 1978:

> Bryan lives in a world a little apart from the rest of us. This has given his work a particular innocence that, in the nature of things, can't be corrupted by self-consciousness. He looks on the world with a matter-of-fact freshness that is quickly conveyed to us. We can easily respond to the vision which is in certain respects childlike yet which has some other, deeper quality that is not to be found in child art. Bryan Pearce has succeeded in offering us a new revelation of enduring insight and delight. What began as a therapy has become a profession. [excerpt from introduction]

Alan Bowness presented the Tate with Bryan's painting *The Cemetery, St Ives 1975*.

Bryan's dedication to his work, the daily purposeful application to his chosen activity – and the success he began to merit through sales – meant that he really was a professional painter, earning money to pay for paints and board, and accumulating a pleasing number of admirers and buyers. In 1963 Mary entered *Portreath Harbour* in the John Moores Open Painting Competition. From 2,500 entries Bryan's was one of 120 paintings selected for exhibition. By now Mary was fully involved in organising framing, having works photographed, and making sure that he could work undisturbed.

She remembered a blow to his confidence, when having left him one morning at the parish church to draw the window over the altar, she returned to find him upset and uncertain. A man had said he had drawn the window too high, he altered it and it still wasn't right. He was now confused and troubled. It was then she told him he mustn't listen to anyone else's advice, just do what he thought was right. She taught him to say, 'It's my decision'. Indeed, Bryan was to use this advice against her many times, and she soon learned that whatever his idiosyncratic method of approach, he was invariably right and could not be advised.

In 1982 Jim Ede wrote the foreword to the catalogue of Bryan's twentieth one-man retrospective exhibition, at Falmouth Art Gallery. 'If anyone is in need of peace, trust and joy, they will find it in the work of Bryan Pearce. He gives with his whole being, totally free of sophistication and totally altruistic; he paints as he breathes. These stones which form a pier, this blue which surrounds a ship, this island and lighthouse, this road, church, window, flowers in their

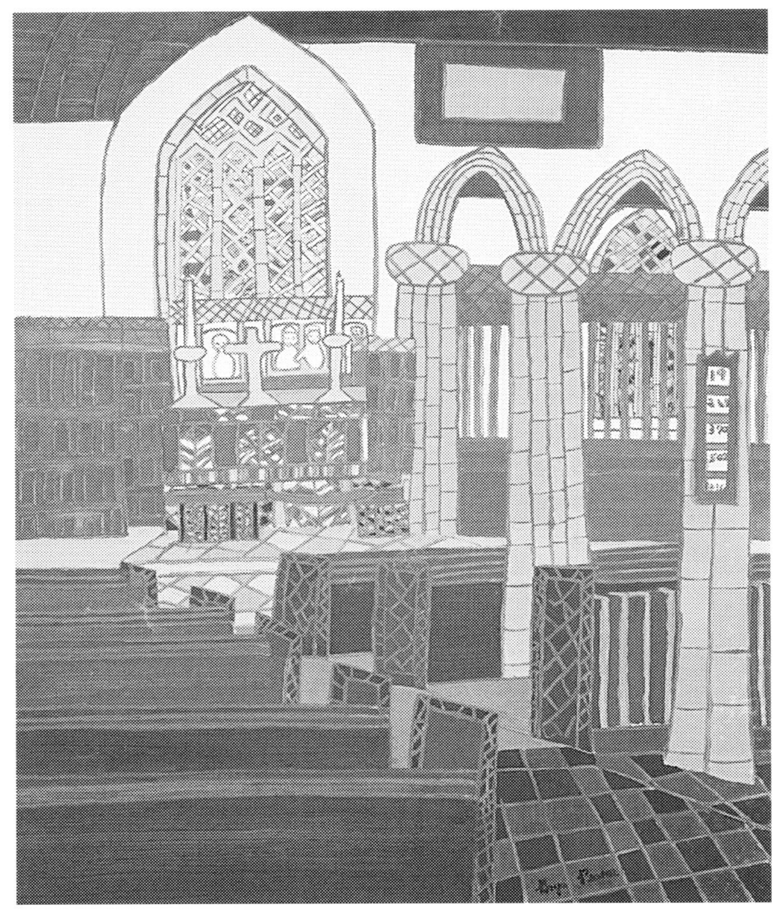

Bryan Pearce: *St Ia Church interior*, 1965.

pot, a thousand visual things, are the deep unconscious quality of his interior life and his immediate contact with his close friend God.

'I know of no artist with whom I can compare him in this direct simplicity and devotion save Fra Angelico who would place one colour against another with assurance and tenderness, and yet, so it is said, when he painted the body of Jesus, he closed his eyes in humble knowledge of his own frailty. Bryan Pearce has this inward vision, undisturbed by greed, desire of worldly achievement, concern with his own personality and much else; and such wholeness lives in his absorbed love, expressed he knows not how.'

Like Wallis before him, Bryan paints every day except Sunday, which is reserved for attending church, for morning service and again for evensong. The studio is deserted and locked, the canvas on which he is working waits on the easel, the brushes are carefully cleaned and remain in readiness for Monday morning. The parish church for Bryan becomes part of his psyche. If one is walking with him he invariably whispers reverently as he passes, 'St Ia church, St Ives church.' Jim Ede noticed in Bryan's paintings of churches 'a world of ineffable beauty which is so much part of his deepest nature'.

On Sundays he reads his books on trains, plays his cassettes of Cornish Male Voice Choirs, the St Ives Town Band, or his records of classical music. He takes his walk through the town seeming not to notice his surroundings and yet everything appears in his paintings: the minutiae of the town, the cobbles and slates, windows, bricks and stones, and the more obvious landmarks of piers and lighthouses and, of course, the parish church.

Bryan's ability as a colourist is demonstrated in any exhibition of his work, whether in still lifes, landscapes or his harbour scenes. His joy in his work, in using colour, in portraying everything he sees and loves is evident in his range of work. From his first tentative watercolours to the masterly application of paint of his middle years, his work shows the sureness of one who knows what he wants to do and does it to the best of his ability, not through habit, but through love of his chosen way of life.

When asked what he is thinking Bryan will often reply, 'Oh, I'm thinking about what I would like to paint; thinking about my subject; thinking what I shall do next.' Fortunately, St Ives, the inspiration for his painting, is all around and motivation never deserts him.

> Perhaps he sees, not this world at all,
> But something beyond we can't. I met him once
> And tried to talk; impossible to gauge
> Reactions. He only wants to paint,

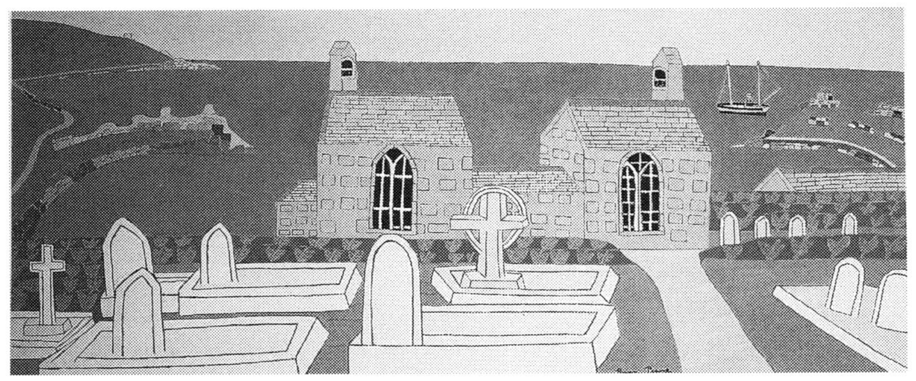

Bryan Pearce: *Barnoon Cemetery, St Ives*, 1975. [courtesy The Tate at St Ives]

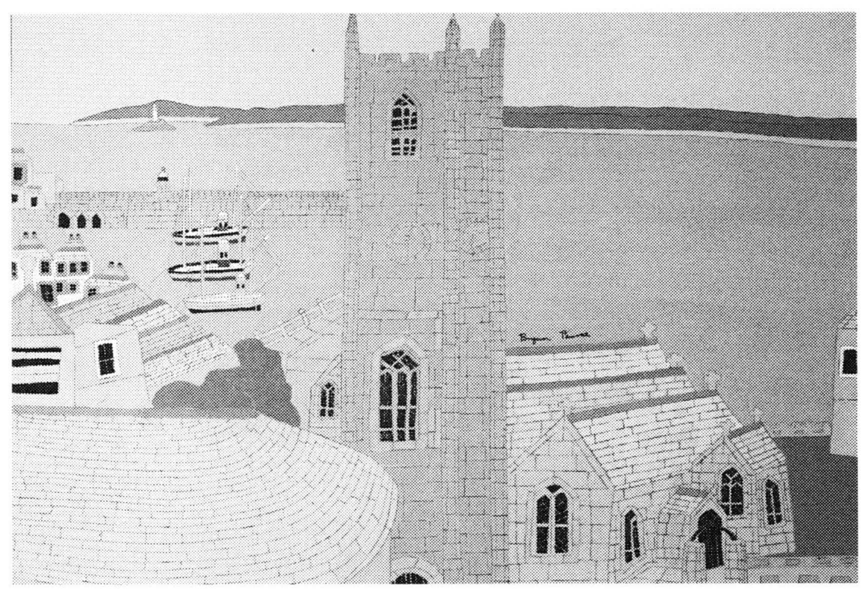

Bryan Pearce: *Parish Church and Bay*, 1980.

To use the one language he has mastered,
But on his terms, his own critique,
Pursuing his soul's vocation.

– Excerpt from poem 'St Ives Bay with Parish Church'
by Donald Rawe, 1980

Techniques, Themes and Topics

Alfred Wallis is all thick paint with scumbling effect, redolent of his feelings and experience of the subject. His seas are turbulent and dangerous. He chooses and prepares his painting surface, picking up a piece of card, tearing and shaping it to fit in the lighthouse, a boat, the chapel on the island, or the harbour. He uses the colour and texture of the board, sometimes leaving the base colour to show through. The plan is in his head, an internal logic in his use of proportion to show the relative importance of the various items in the composition. This simple scheme of things dictates that most of his vessels sail from right to left of the picture, as they would if sailing into St Ives harbour.

Sitting at his table and looking down on his subject matter, Wallis appears to paint from an aerial viewpoint so that in many pictures there is no sky and no horizon. The Wallis boats are actively engaged with the sea. They are entering or leaving harbour, or struggling against the wind and tide, roller coasting a wave, sliding down, or being lifted by the sea. His paintings are tough. There is a raw emotional content. He knows how it feels to be in that boat and part of the elements. The emphasis is on movement and experience. The texture of the paint shows the sea is black and grey with menace, or the equally dangerous white water tumbles and threatens the seamen.

In complete contrast, there is a particular gentle blue sea which is a typical Pearce colour. It is smooth, peaceful and as perfect as a colour can be painted. The emphasis is on stillness and innocence in a sea of harmony on which boats sit safely upright. Pearce's paintings promote a feeling of peace, love and joy.

It is a child-like attitude. No ripples, no brushstrokes even, disturb Pearce's sea or sky. His boats resemble the lugger carved for him by John McWilliams and lie at safe mooring within the harbour. He approaches his prepared board and works on his drawing, rubbing out and correcting, until he makes his composition fit the space. Unlike Wallis, he obliterates the surface area with colour, covering methodically, and with careful consideration.

There is no conscious disproportion in Pearce's compositions, the pier, boats, houses portrayed true to the space and size they occupy in the real world. No one item is chosen for precedence over another. Each occupies its particular

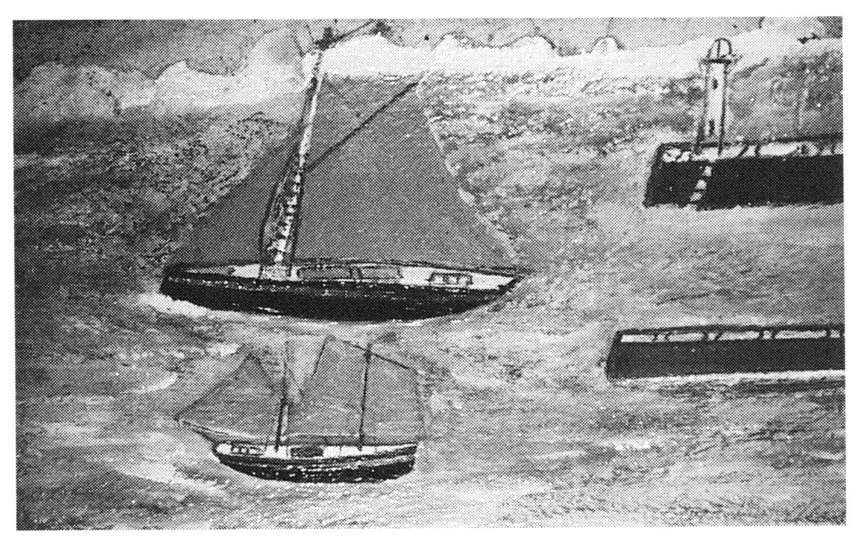

Alfred Wallis: *Two boats, two piers*. [courtesy Dr Roger Slack]

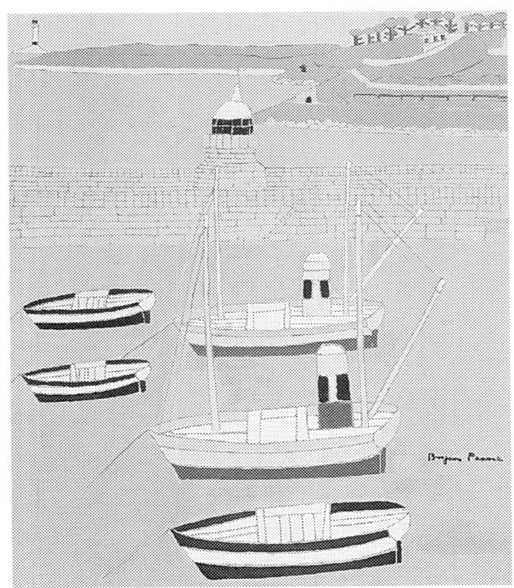

Bryan Pearce: *Smeaton's Lighthouse*, 1981.

space. Yet, if there isn't some amusing, daring, puzzling or idiosyncratic element in a painting or drawing, then it isn't a Bryan Pearce. If the flower stems are outside the vase, lines on a cloth do not meet in the middle, the rigging of the boats is wrongly placed, or the houses lying down, as in *St Ives All Round*, then this is how he sees his subject. However, the houses he is painting are always at the top of the picture. He turns the canvas to complete the rows. Painting at his easel, with just the right tilt, Pearce confronts his subject straight on so that the houses just happen to fall on their backs when the picture is finished. He knows no other way to portray the scene and is not bothered by the strangeness of the finished picture.

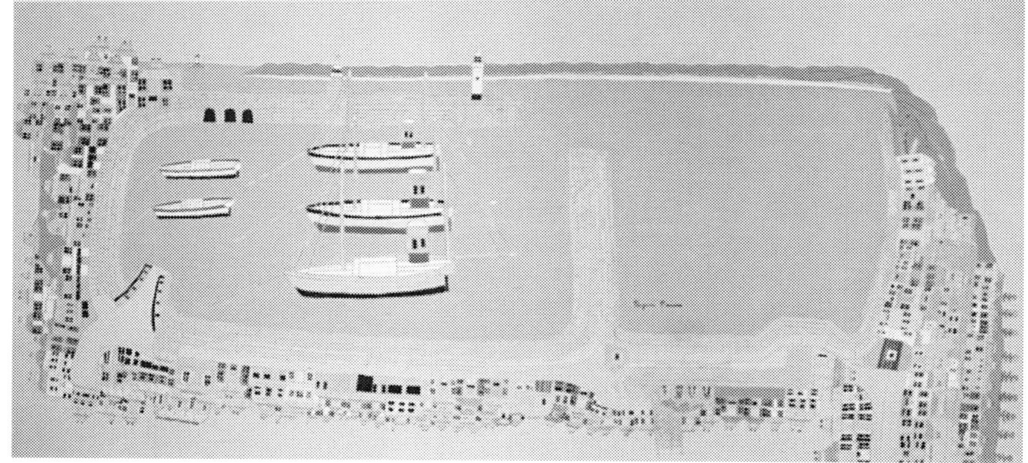

Bryan Pearce: *St Ives Harbour (all round)*.

Each painter is true to himself. Wallis limited his colour palette to the ship's paints that were available to him. But later, given a choice, these were the colours he chose to work with, brown, black, grey, white and green. He would reject blue for his seas. Holding up a glass of water to give Adrian Stokes and Margaret Mellis the benefit of his knowledge, he said, 'See this glass of water; do you see any colour? That's cause it's colourless.' And he might have added, that's what I know and those silly fools with their blues don't know. Nicholson visited Wallis in Madron poorhouse about a month before he died and on that occasion Wallis greeted him: 'I've been wanting to see you, I want black and white and green.' He firmly rejected Nicholson's suggestion that he might also like to have blue.

Although he was later given drawing paper instead of having to make use of second-hand materials, Wallis in the main was limited to painting on domestic items in use in the home, for instance, a large marmalade jar. He used the object as just another surface for his painting. In his different milieu, Bryan Pearce could chose a decorative ginger jar, a cloth from a variety of patterns and colours, fruit, and a plant to make a pleasing composition for the subject of his painting.

Pearce has his tubes of paint and clean brushes, but he still makes a choice, mixing and working at a colour, smoothing out the brush marks until it bears his very distinctive hue and shade: a Pearce colour. He puts colours together which more thoughtful painters would consider unwise or even unworkable, but in the intuitive hands of Bryan Pearce they are wonderful.

As well as their paintings being very idiosyncratic, and their colours, style, and brush strokes easily identified, their signatures also bear their hallmark. Wallis either printed his name in capitals, sometimes transposing the final 'S' or wrote in lower case, as he would also do in writing letters. Pearce writes his name carefully, painstakingly, and in full in the prescribed manner. The peculiarity is that he will often choose to place his signature in the middle of the picture, usually in the sea, or in a space of flat colour so that it can be seen. And often, if there is a boat in the picture, his signature will underline it. His mother gave up tentatively asking where he was going to write his name on the painting. His reply was always, 'I do as I please.'

The sea and harbour are the dominant themes for both painters, but their individual portrayal of the subject matter is entirely different. Although Wallis had a depth of life experience, conveyed so gallantly through his paintings, and had known the hardships of fishermen, Pearce has the wider breadth of subject matter. There are flowers in the Pearce home, beautiful cloths, pots and vases, bowls of fruit, and these become part of the language of his paintings. The view through a window overlooking Porthmeor beach is again a decorative subject to be exploited. His familiarity with the church as communicant affords other views, both interior and as an icon in the townscape.

The house, Norway Cottage, which Wallis could see from his doorway and which he painted frequently, seems to represent an ideal. He invariably painted it larger than other houses; it was clearly important to his thinking and something in its shape fascinated him, in contrast to the flat facades of other cottages.

He liked to show that he knew St Ives intimately and attempted to convey all his knowledge in one painting: the island, Porthmeor beach, the harbour, Norway Cottage and Godrevy lighthouse, the geographical elements rightly placed when

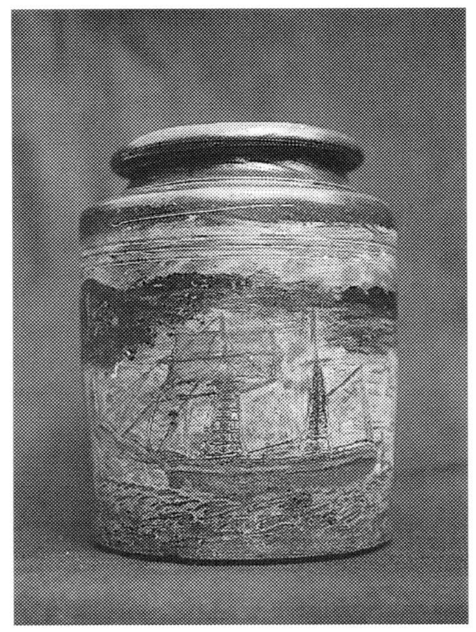

Alfred Wallis painting on jar. [courtesy Dr Roger Slack]

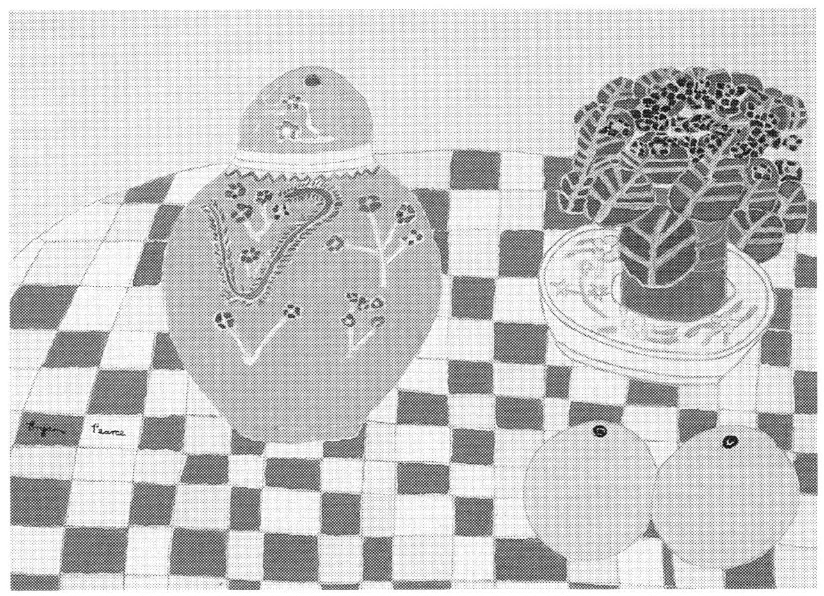

Bryan Pearce: *Ginger jar with checked cloth.*

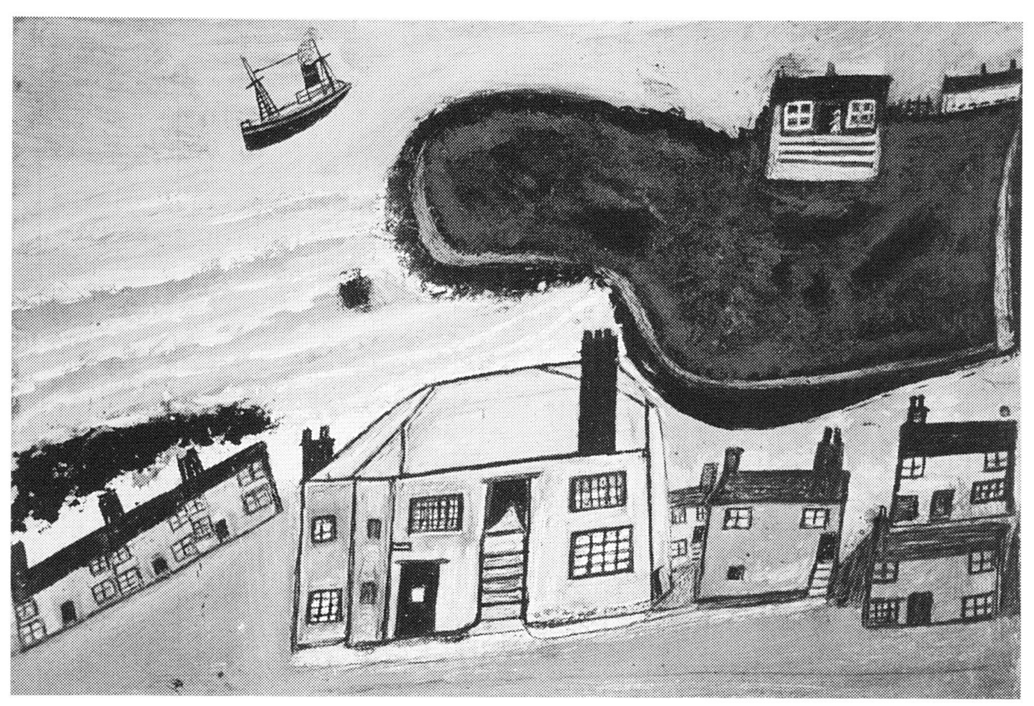

Alfred Wallis: *The Old House, Porthmeor Square and Island* [courtesy The Tate at St Ives]

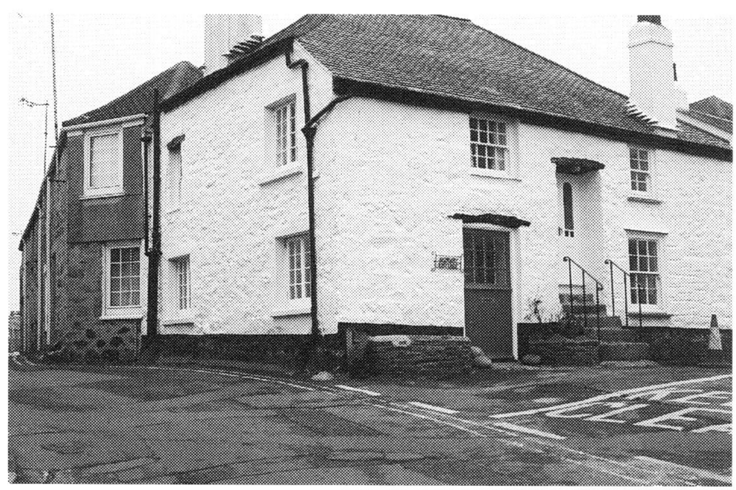

Norway Cottage, Porthmeor Square, often painted by Alfred Wallis.

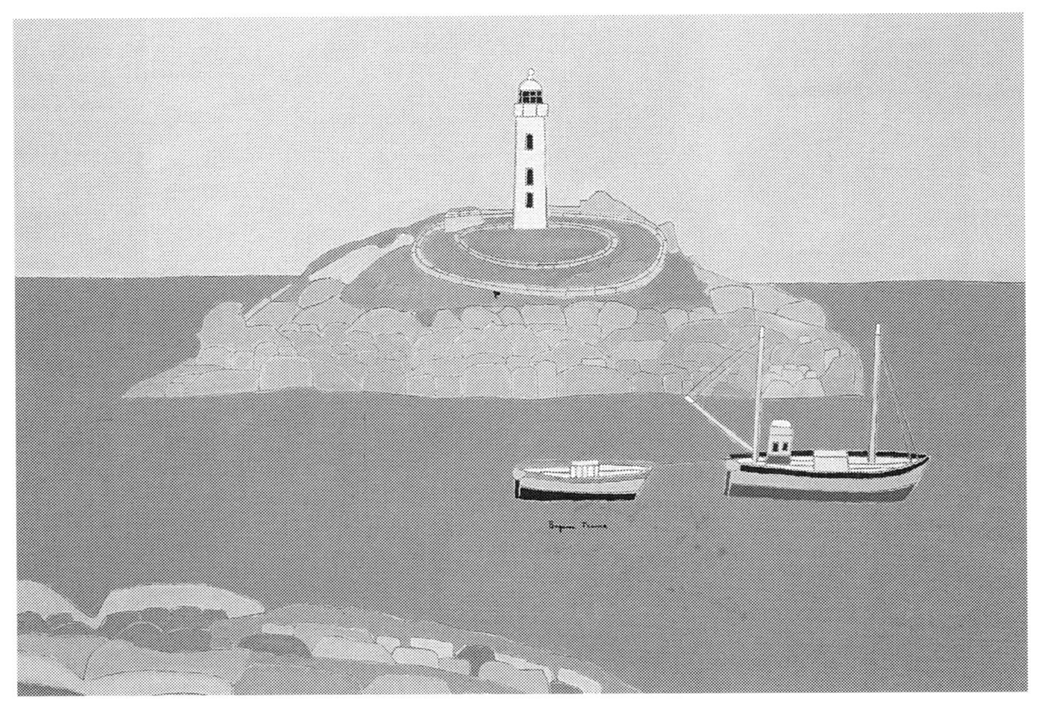

Bryan Pearce: *Godrevy Lighthouse*, 1986.

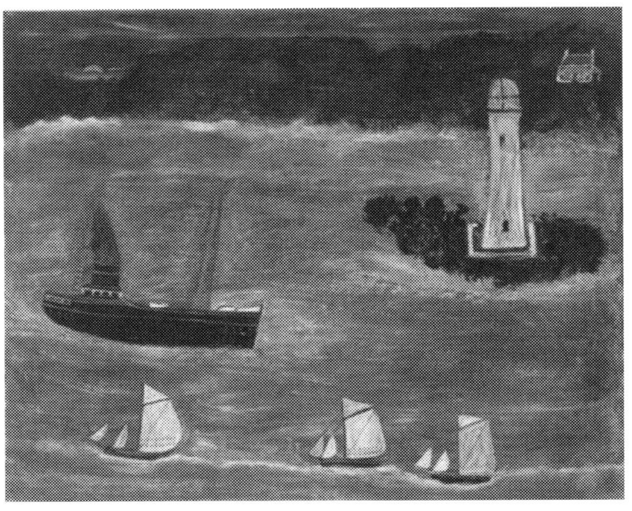

Alfred Wallis: *Seascape*. [courtesy Kettle's Yard, University
of Cambridge]

one takes an aerial view as Wallis often did. Nowhere is this better demonstrated than in his painting *The Hold House port mear square island port mear Beach*. This is one of the few titles given to a picture. The painting was bought directly from Alfred Wallis by Barbara Hepworth and perhaps she had asked for a title and Wallis had written it there and then. The title was uncovered in 1969 when the picture was temporarily removed from its backboard, also revealing that the painting was executed on a printed advertisement for an exhibition of the St Ives Society of Artists. Wallis describes the features in the painting starting with the most important element, the old house in Porthmeor Square. Above is the Island with the chapel on top, and Porthmeor beach between a row of houses in Back Road West (one of which may be his own cottage) and a dark layer of stones, which often appear on the beach in tidal movements, even today, and then are covered up again with deep layers of sand. A boat comes into view, rounding the island on its way to the fishing grounds.

In *A Way of Life: Kettle's Yard*, Jim Ede writes of his collection of Wallis paintings, 'So, with Wallis design comes, with its subtly variant lines and spaces, not through experience in the art of drawing or painting but from closeness, almost identification with the thing he is drawing.'

When Wallis or Pearce took a walk along the harbour the two lighthouses on Smeaton's Pier would be familiar landmarks, and out in the bay would be Godrevy lighthouse. These lighthouses are used constantly in their paintings, sometimes as dominant objects and at other times dwarfed by other subject matter. For Pearce they are part of the scenery of his childhood and manhood, offering no threat to man or boat but there simply because that is where they are. He knows their shapes and their differences. On Godrevy lighthouse Pearce has seen a building and a series of protective walls surrounding a garden, but he doesn't see them as fulfilling a function; he just chooses to include them in the picture. He could as easily have left them out. The rocks on the small island are smooth blue and grey jewels set in an idle sea.

In contrast, Wallis's lighthouses are always threatened by the sea, and at the same time warning of its perils. They are there as a protective element, with boats bowing or dipping in respect as they leave or enter the harbour. Godrevy lighthouse is the big one, the dominant force. He stands magisterially on his throne of black rocks and in some paintings the reef, known as 'the stones', bead their way through a turbulent and heavy sea, where a boat sheers away from certain disaster. The vessel in *Seascape* is large and black, sailing close to the rocks and under threat, while the small boats with white sails are scudding along at a safe distance.

Wallis would sometimes include large fish swimming beneath a boat at sea, explaining to his great-nephew, Albert Rowe, that these fish, large in proportion to the boat and therefore signifying importance, were all the fish that have ever swum – 'all the fish that God ever put in the sea,' he said, 'That's why they're so big and powerful.'

When Pearce tackles a picture of the St Ives School of Painting, it seems *that* only is the subject matter. He has totally ignored the door to his studio and left out the window, which is situated below the sign of the school. This seems extraordinary, but the reason according to Bryan is 'because that's how I did it, see.'

However, Jim Ede offered another reason in a letter to Mary in 1983. 'I wonder if I have hit on his reason for not putting in his studio window apart from his proper feeling that it would upset the balance of the white board. I think I see his reason in the fact that for him his studio is LIGHT and he cannot reconcile this with a totally black interior although he has made other rooms seem black.'

The windows in the Pearce houses are painted black. He paints them as though seen from a distance when windows appear to be black; so he is painting what he sees, while Wallis paints what he knows. The windows in Wallis's houses are painted a light colour. He knows they are glass and uses a light reflecting tone to show their transparent quality.

As with many naive painters Pearce makes much use of patterning – bricks, tiles, window shapes, anything that can be regulated and ordered and satisfactorily dealt with. He positively enjoys the meticulous covering of a surface with pattern, the careful outline and filling in of a mosaic of colour, whereas Wallis – although he knows that some house elevations are slate hung, the roofs tiled – ignores these details and features the blocklike shape, and important items like windows and doors. The images are simple and uncluttered.

The portrayal of trees in the hands of each artist is very different. Wallis uses a freehand scattering of daubs of green, a lively splashing of colour as though celebrating trees. As he looks up to the head of leafy green, the trunk graduates like a ship's mast. Pearce trees are in serried rows of lollipop heads of a uniform size on stick-like trunks. They are a decorative item in the painting, a repeated motif. They represent trees. He appears to be saying 'I am not interested in trees.'

The two paintings, *Gateway* and *St Ives from Barnoon*, illustrate their different approach in each painting. Pearce shows his mosaic-like patterning of houses, blacked out windows and the stylised trees. Wallis houses are block-like, windows clear glass and his mast-like tree trunks reach almost out of the picture frame.

It is surprising that Wallis does not attempt to portray birds in flight; something with which he would be familiar, both at sea and in St Ives. This may be something he felt uncomfortable with in drawing, or he discounted birds as insignificant in his life, or in his overall design. At some point Bryan Pearce was

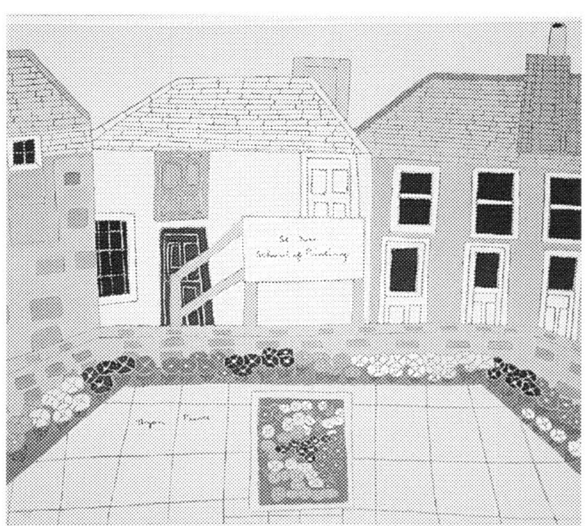

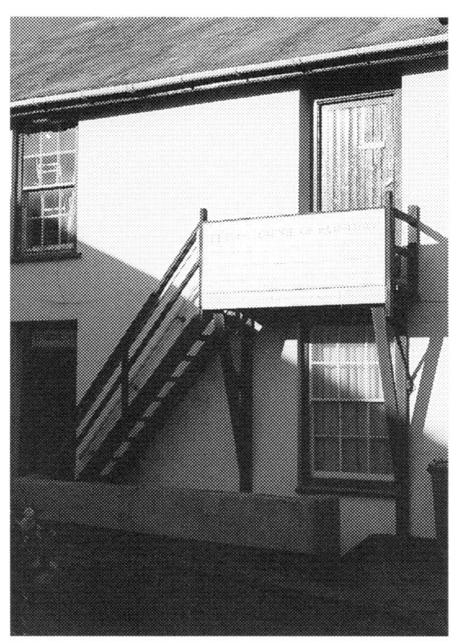

Above – Bryan Pearce: *School of Painting.*

Right – St Ives School of Painting, 1996.

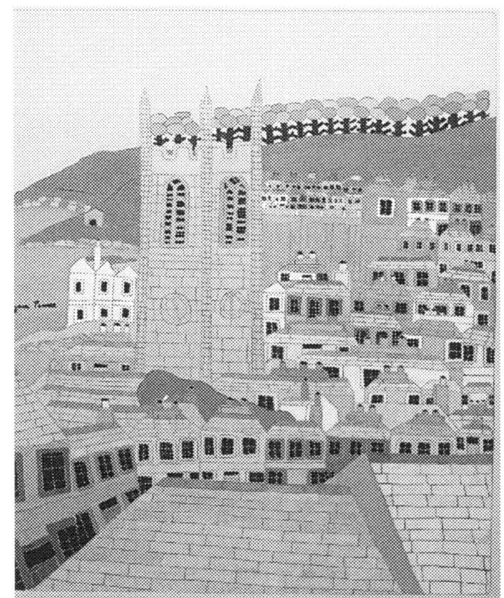

Above – Bryan Pearce: *St Ives from Barnoon*, 1979.

Right – Alfred Wallis: *Gateway.* [courtesy Kettle's Yard, University of Cambridge]

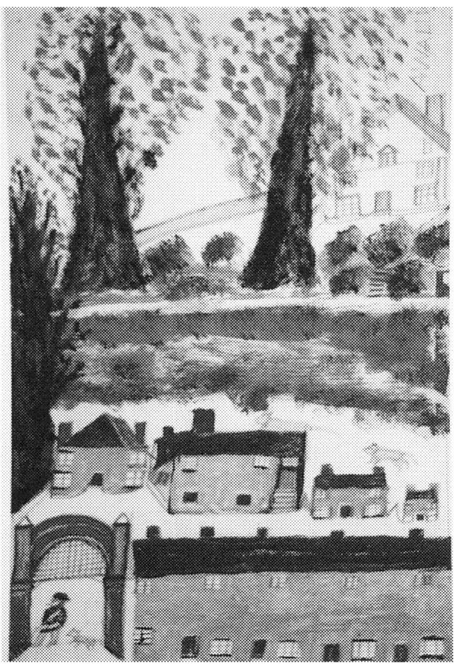

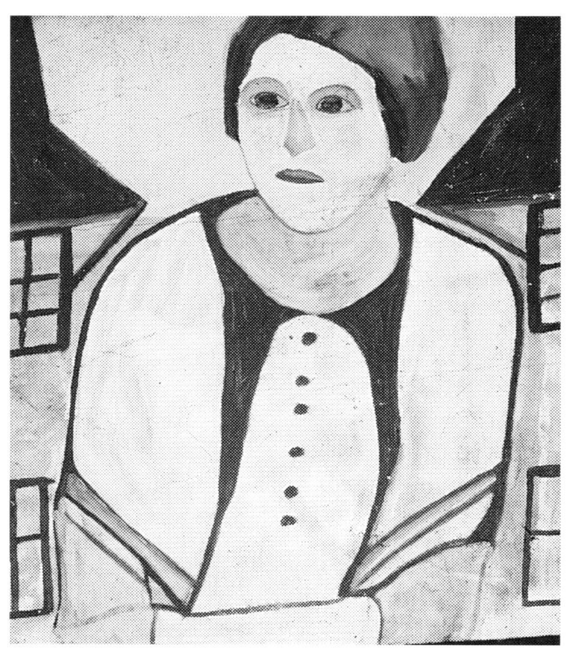

Alfred Wallis: *Portrait of a woman.*

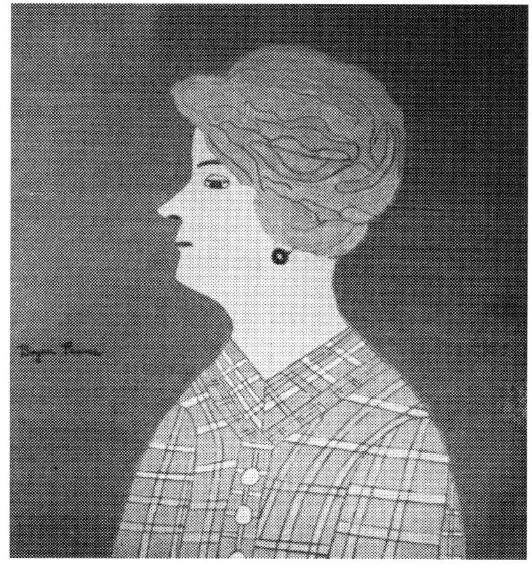

Bryan Pearce's painting of his mother.

taught to draw stylised birds in flight and 'it took ages.' This would seem a simple idea to a normal person, but to Bryan it was a complication beyond his understanding and an intrusion into his way of seeing, a trial for him to assimilate. Birds in flight do not appear often in his work, but the seagulls he paints standing on the beach are charming and entirely his own.

Neither artist is keen to reproduce people. Pearce never allows figures on his boats. They would not fit with such an inanimate structure. They are not working boats, but part of the decorative feature of the harbour. His boats have no relationship with people, fish or water, but sit solidly upon a blue colour. Wallis sees figures from a distance, their outline is part of the shape and structure of a boat, merely part of the workings. They are black shadows with caps, all facing towards the prow. One of Wallis's rare attempts at painting a portrait of an unknown woman was said by Michael Canney, in a letter to Dr Roger Slack in 1975, to have been a portrait abandoned by the artist Alethea Garstin which Wallis reworked to suit himself.

Albert Rowe as a child took meals to Uncle Alfred, and one day he was lured upstairs in the cottage at Back Road West to see a life-size painting of Susan Wallis daubed in black upon the door of a wardrobe, and to be told, 'She's inside and her likeness is outside.' The child fled the cottage, later to destroy some thirty or forty paintings that Alfred had given him after Wallis had accused the family of trying to poison him. This is the only sighting of this portrait and since the account was broadcast and written as a story, this may have been added to give greater dramatic effect, although Margaret Mellis recorded in her notebook of 1939 that 'Adrian and I found Wallis in the middle of painting over an old calendar. He painted over what was there, enlarging the areas and going freely over the edges without changing the subject. He said he was improving it. We also saw him painting a portrait, another improvement, on top of an academic face.'

Pearce's people are those largely known to him through attendance at his mother's bowling club. He shows the team in action, each figure bending, standing, facing different directions, the feet as incapable of fluid action as the feet of mediaeval paintings. He also painted a picture of his mother which is one of his best attempts at portraiture. Other portraits were of the artist, Misome Peile, unidentified Irene and a pen and ink sketch of Leonard Fuller.

An artist at the Newlyn Gallery once explained to Mary that he was a lonely man and portrayed large numbers of people in his pictures for company. Bryan, he thought, was not lonely and therefore did not need to paint people. Mary gained some comfort from this. She would often worry that Bryan might be unhappy because he had no friends but Bryan's reassurance to her was simply stated: 'I am never lonely and I am never bored.'

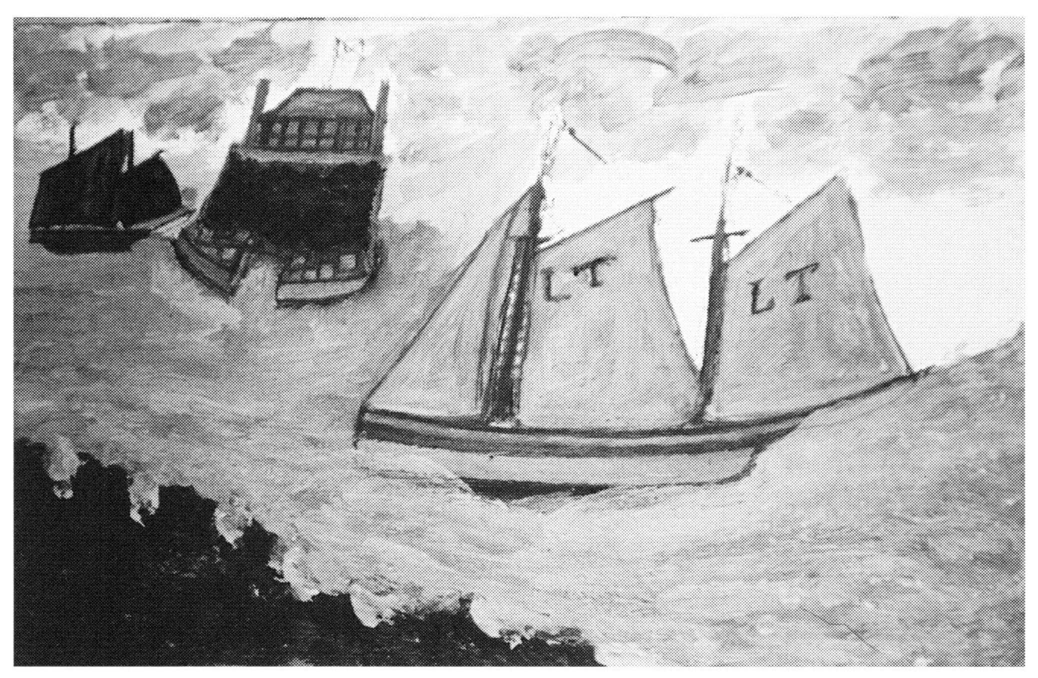

Alfred Wallis: *St Michael's Mount*. [courtesy Dr Roger Slack]

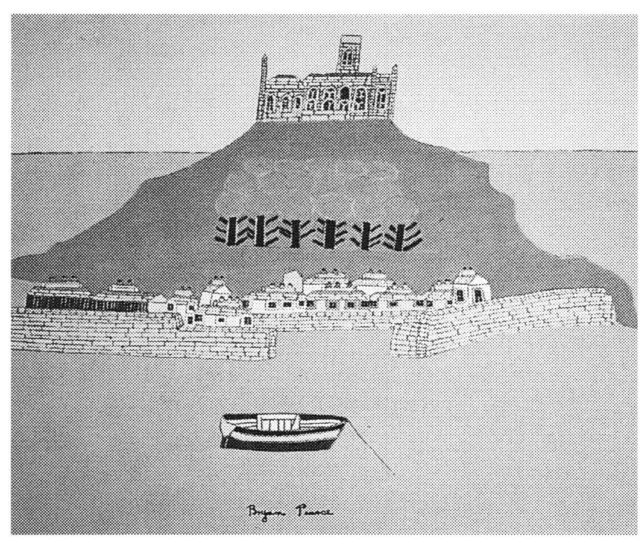

Bryan Pearce: *St Michael's Mount*, 1972.

In truth both men are uncomfortable with the idea of painting people. The childlike portrayal is apparent to themselves and the unequal challenge best avoided. They are stuck in medieval times. Pearce seldom paints the objects of his great love, trains, though he has produced a number of drawings. He dislikes other artists' attempts to paint them and will accept only realist photographic posters on his studio walls.

They are on safer ground with the mastery each shows with the subjects they repeat over and over again: boats, streets, houses and the familiarity of their local neighbourhood, or landmarks, as in St Michael's Mount. It is unlikely that Wallis ever visited the island and he portrays a fortress-like structure of the mount with a small entrance to the harbour. A black boat sails perilously close but another boat, all white sails and hull with the LT of Lowestoft clearly displayed, tacks safely at full and tumbling tide between the mount and land mass. Characteristically, Pearce paints the chapel, which he has visited and knows is at the top of the island. It is surrounded by greenery and trees. Houses crouch and crowd the quay and the walls provide a welcoming entrance and safe haven on an unthreatening blue sea.

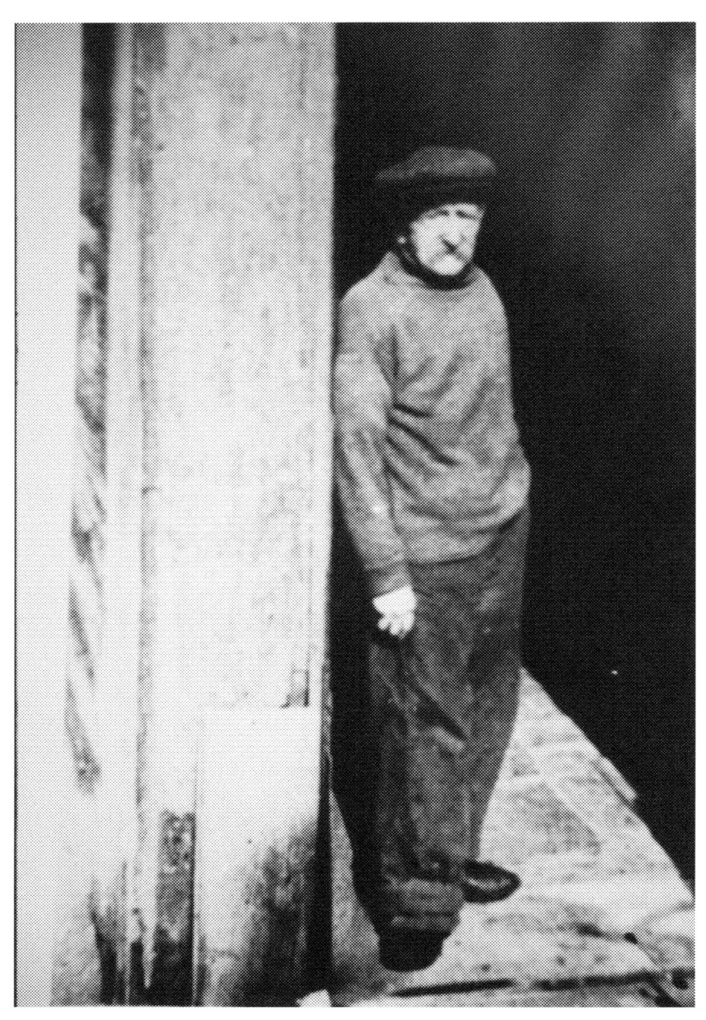

Alfred Wallis
1855–1942

He always struck me as being extraordinarily integrated and single minded in his personality – Barbara Hepworth

Alfred Wallis was born in Devonport on 8 August 1855 to Jane and Charles Wallis. According to the latest research both parents were born in Cornwall, at Sennen and Penzance respectively. Jane died when Alfred was barely ten years old and is buried in Devonport cemetery. Plymouth, the neighbouring seaport, was the home of naval and merchant seamen and it is natural that the boy Alfred went to sea, especially after the death of his mother when there would be nobody at home to care for him. So as a young lad he was crossing the Bay of Biscay in a wind-blown schooner, serving as a cabin boy, then cook, and later as an ordinary seaman fishing off the deep-sea coast of Labrador.

There has been some controversy as to whether Wallis did actually go to sea. According to some locals, he went just once 'and was so scared that he never went again.' Nancy Ward, for one, has no doubts, remembering Wallis talking in her mother's house. She recalled those conversations for the Roger Slack interviews. 'He did go to sea and he'd been in my mother's house and telling my grandfather all about his experiences. He was a little cabin boy in one of the big boats. In them days it was the three-mast ships and he told him he wasn't more than between nine and ten when he was in the Bay of Biscay. So what do you call that? That isn't dry land is it? Been most interesting to hear him talk about the sharks and that. No boasting and bragging nothing like that. He was what you call plain and innocent.'

When Alfred moved to Penzance and fished with the fleet, he lived with his younger brother Charles who had set up in business as a marine merchant. Alfred and Charles both married in the same year, 1876. Alfred married the widow Susan Ward, 22 years his senior and with eight children from her previous marriage. Although it has been generally believed that Mrs Ward had 17 children from her first marriage, Peter Barnes in his recent research, *Alfred Wallis and his Family, Fact and Fiction*, revealed that she had only seven, possibly eight. 'Jacob and his wife were only married for little more than fifteen years: there was no evidence of any illegitimate children and only seven baptisms were found. They were spaced at about two year intervals with a gap between 1861 and 1865, which suggested that there might have been another child born about 1863. For Susan to have had seventeen children it would have been necessary for her to have given birth every eleven months or so for all fifteen years of her marriage. Dr Roger Slack has pointed out that if Susan did have nineteen children in total, they suffered a mortality rate of seventy per cent which was very high, even in those times.' According to Barnes' record, the younger brother Charles and wife Jane had fourteen children. Six of these died in infancy and this seems to be where the mistake has occurred.

Alfred and Susan lived at 15 New Street, Penzance. They had two children, a boy and a girl, who both died in infancy.

In the 1880s Alfred gave up deep-sea fishing and joined the local fleet, out of Penzance and Newlyn. They then moved to St Ives where Alfred again worked with the fishing fleet. *Two Sisters*, *Faithful*, *Alpha*, *Dolphin*, *Omega* and the *Flying Scud*, are named by Sven Berlin as boats on which he served as crew but according to Peter Barnes' research, 'the name Wallis did not appear on the surviving crew list of any Cornish boat registered during the period 1871–1891.' However, since then, further research has revealed that Alfred's occupation was described as sailor on the wedding certificate in April 1876. Furthermore, Wallis was registered among the crew of a topsail schooner, the *Belle Adventure*, registered in Brixham. He seems to have left the ship at Teignmouth in November 1876, suggesting that indeed Alfred Wallis was a true seaman, as most believe and as his paintings so plainly reveal.

By 1887 Alfred and Susan had set up as marine merchants, running scrap metal and rag and bones stores. They seem to have traded in premises in Bethesda Hill, on the Wharf, and Back Road West. The business was usually housed in the basement and they lived above. Thomas Lander remembered that '[one] marine store was in a kind of cellar. He used to buy any kinds of metals and as boys we used to go on the beaches and collect rags and bones.' Joe Burrell reported, 'He had a little pony by the head and he wouldn't ride the pony. He was walking the same steps as the pony.'

At some point Wallis turned to making ice cream. George Farrell recalled that 'somebody trading to Italy on a ship brought the recipe home and he used to make it. He had an ice cream barrow. Push it sometimes to Penzance to sell ice cream. Market days. Quite a long way to push a barrow I should think.'

The Wallises moved to Bethesda Hill just off the harbour – from where a photograph was taken of Susan Wallis and her daughter Emily standing on the

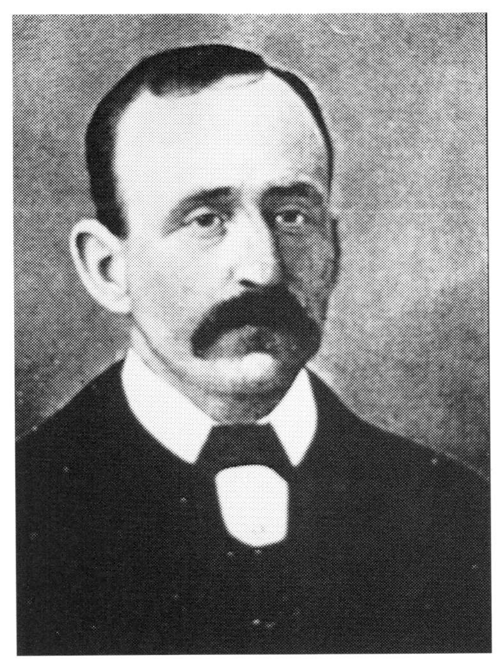

Alfred Wallis.

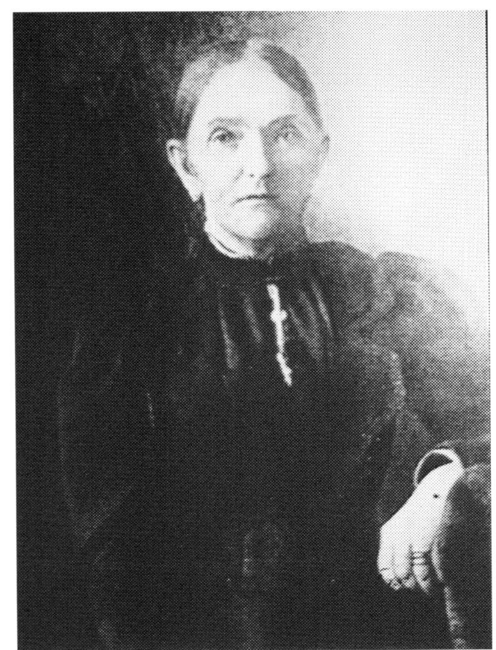

Susan Wallis.

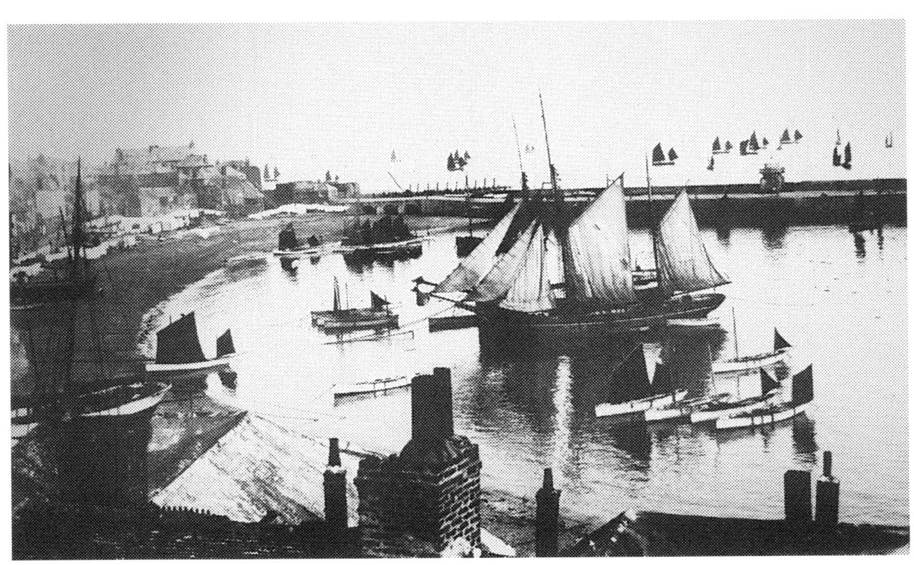

St Ives Harbour c.1890.

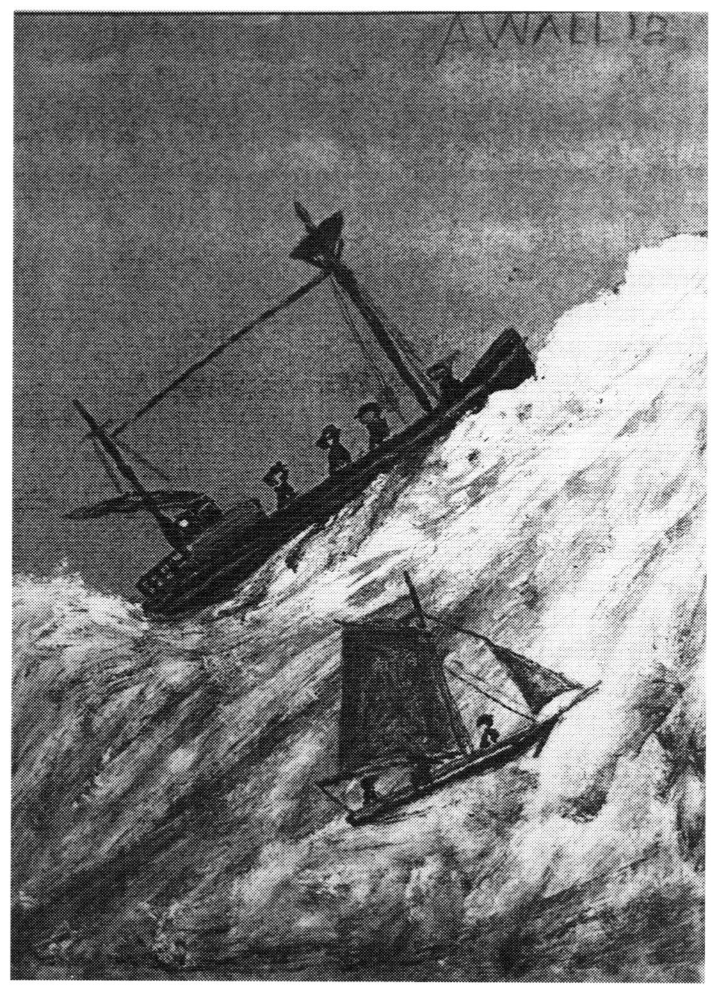

Alfred Wallis: *Two boats sailing and huge wave*, c.1930.

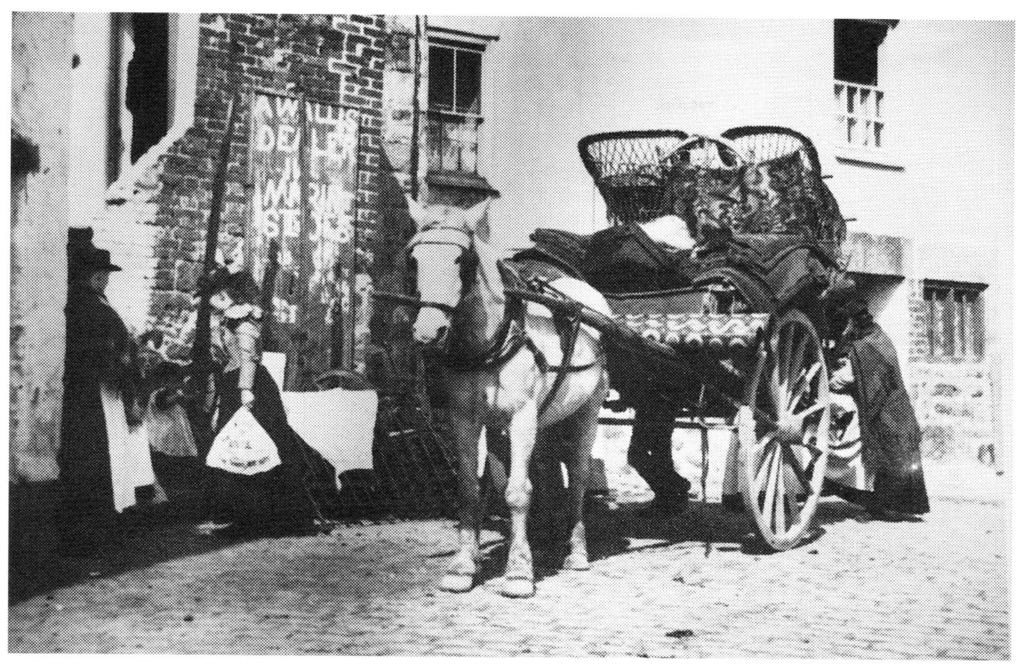

Alfred Wallis with horse and cart,
The Wharf. [courtesy Andrew
Lanyon]

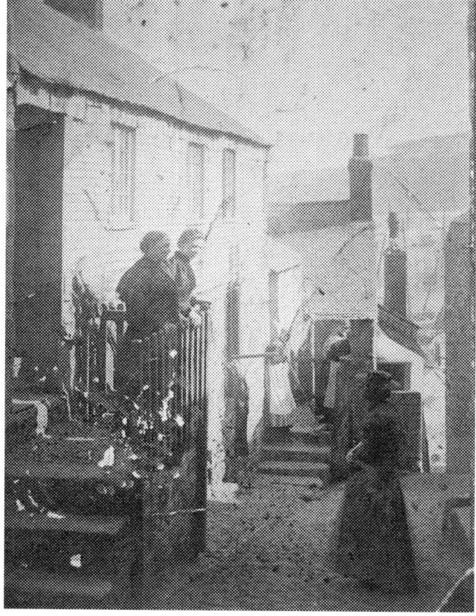

Susan Wallis with daughter Emily.
[courtesy Dr Roger Slack]

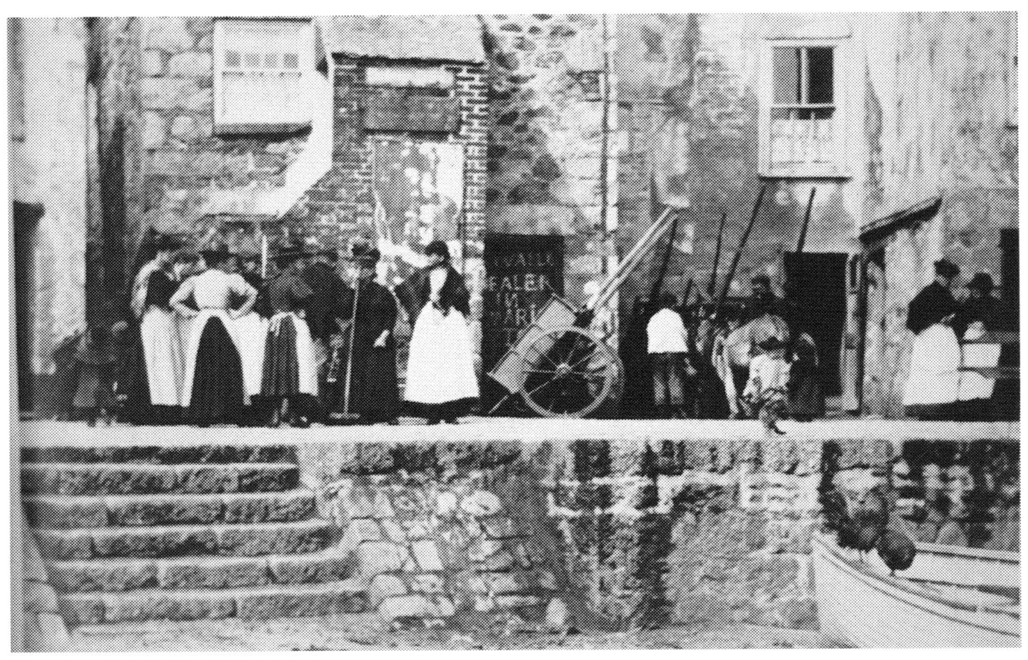

Alfred Wallis: store on The Wharf. [courtesy Andrew Lanyon] *Below* Alfred Wallis in bowler hat at a Salvation Army gathering c.1910.

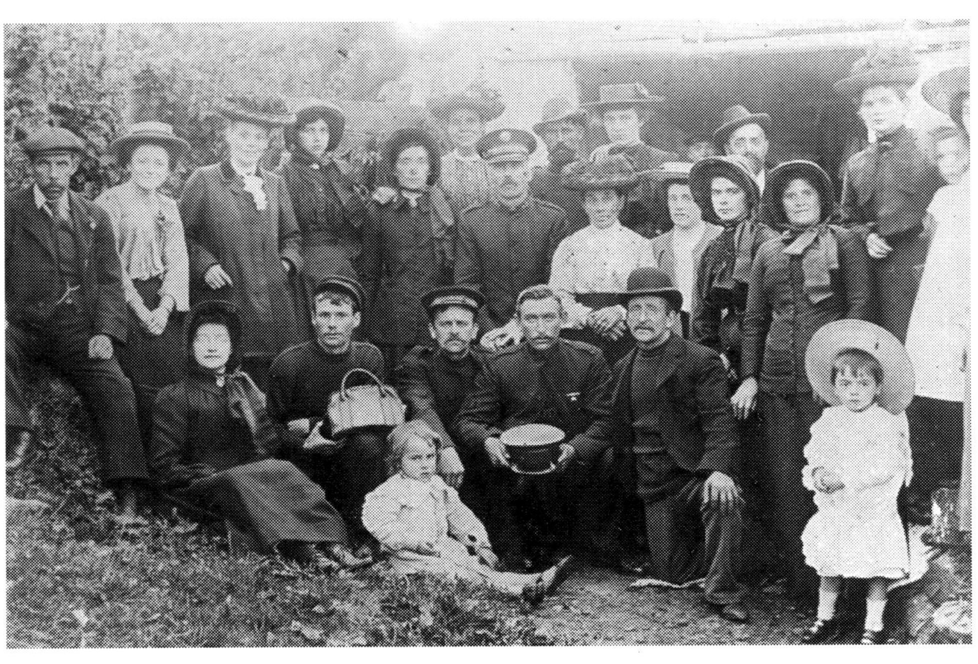

steps of a cottage – and then in 1908 bought a cottage, for £93, at 3 Back Road West, where Susan died in 1922 at the age of eighty eight.

In *Unknown Colour*, Winifred Nicholson described her impression of Wallis living in that cottage. 'He lives in one room. He is suspicious of all the neighbours who do not understand him. He reads out of a great bible aloud to himself. He has a kind of mouth organ wrapped up in a purple-spotted handkerchief. He plays out of his head strange melodies which he improvises by the hour. He used to be a rag-and-bone man. He once had a shop and made money. It was all stolen. He distrusts people. He loves ships with passion.'

Jessie Farrell, a step-grand-daughter, who also took up painting at a late stage in life and sometimes signed her work Jessie Wallis, remembered that 'he had a family bible, I don't know what became of that. See you'd know everything in the family bible wouldn't ee.' Barbara Hepworth, too, remembered that bible. 'Mind you read your bible every day and mind you see what company you keep,' he admonished her on one of her visits with Ben.

Another relative, Nancy Ward, said 'He had a little harmonium and he would sit down and try to sing and grandma would say to him, "for goodness sakes Alfred put it down, you can go up to the army to sing, don't sing here".' Both Susan and Alfred were staunch Salvationists. Alfred signed his allegiance to the faith in 1904 in a document now held in the St Ives Museum, along with his little cottage harmonium.

Some critics have suggested that the artists who so admired his work could have done more to help Wallis in his declining years, but even if they could have afforded to do so, he was by then incapable of looking after himself and suffering from senile dementia. In the last year of his life in the poorhouse he was freed from domesticity and could carry on with his painting without the 'demons' upstairs in his cottage bothering him or the local children making fun. Barbara Hepworth sympathised with Wallis's predicament, suggesting that some of his torments were real. She had visited the old man with Herbert Read and recorded their conversation in a broadcast for the The BBC Third Programme in 1968. 'He spoke of all his life, his friends, his troubles, his cousins, the bible, the course one must take in life.' She wrote to Roger Slack in 1964: 'Is it paranoia when you really are being persecuted? I do feel that his path was difficult and the teasing he had to bear, very real.' Roger agreed: 'I think it uncharitable to call this [behaviour] paranoia.' Wallis believed that at some time he had been robbed of some of his savings and his behaviour to his family after that was understandable. Emily Woolcock told Roger Slack 'I think they were worth a few pounds but some of our own family even delved into their money, borrowed money from them. Then you see I could mention one in particular, and when they really wanted something they turned their back on them.'

When in June, 1941 the authorities committed Wallis to the poorhouse at Madron, near Penzance, he took no personal belongings with him. He wasn't allowed to take the family bible which had been the source of comfort to his afflicted mind. He often advised people that it was their duty to read the bible, saying of himself that he was a bible keeper and he read the bible three hundred and sixty times a year. After his removal to the poorhouse, the artists did not desert him. They visited, took paints to ensure that he could continue to work, and minded that he was properly treated, entrusting the kindly matron with his welfare. Indeed he became something of a celebrity among the inmates during his fourteen months' stay.

Years earlier, Christopher Wood had written to Winifred Nicholson from St Ives: 'When someone dies here, they burn the mattress, the clothes and even the bedstead of the defunct on the beach. The male folk, these darkly dressed men, carry it all down on their shoulders and make a huge fire among the rocks and stand round with paraffin cans in hand, musing on the life of the dead person. It is rather impressive with the huge green waves like horses bounding and pounding in on to the sand.' This is what was happening when Adrian Stokes came upon the authorities in the act of clearing Wallis's cottage and taking paintings to be burnt on the beach.

Many years before Wallis's deterioration into poverty and neglect, someone had listed the items in his cottage. *Front room*: A cupboard with glass doors, containing china. A bellows with ships painted on it. A brass fender with fire irons. A round wooden table on which Alfred had painted boats. A glass dome of stuffed birds stood on a mahogany table with china vases. A leather armchair, window seat and a framed picture of Susan. *On the landing*: a large oak wooden chest where Mrs Wallis kept all her linen. *In the front bedroom* was a brass bedstead, dressing table and chest of drawers with several china figurines. *The second bedroom* held a brass bedstead and a seaman's trunk, in which Wallis was reputed to have stored several gold sovereigns. He thought these had been stolen by Susan's relations when they tended her in the last days before she died. As a neighbour reported, 'He was a quiet and industrious man. He was never poor, never poor.'

The photograph of Alfred in a bowler hat was obviously taken when he was a younger man and still in business. The bowler hat could indicate that he was a man of property and wealth, or simply that he was wearing his Sunday best.

In 1965 Dr Roger Slack began his documentary record of the memories of people who knew or were related to Alfred Wallis. The following tales relate to his gradual mental and physical deterioration after the death of his wife and are excerpts from the many recorded.

Sarah Langford: 'After she died Alfred Wallis never went upstairs any more. He said the devil was upstairs. He made up a little bed, behind the table, because he was a very small man, you know.'

Emily Woolcock describes the pictures in the cottage: 'I can see grandpa Wallis now on top of the stairs. Lord Baden-Powell on the wall there. Queen Victoria somewhere else. And over here was Peter, walking over the sea. And they did have marvellous china, marvellous. Well you see, after my grannie died, he did go a little bit eccentric and he kept people away from him.'

Carrie Lander: 'He used to chase us as kids, you know, if we was round the house or anything, but mind you, he was quiet. I mean, he didn't interfere in any way. Nobody didn't have much to do with him, did they really? Just went there for business. Of course he wasn't like a St Ives man, where everybody knew each other. He didn't mix, like a St Ives man would, you know. You couldn't carry on any conversation with him. He wouldn't be friendly enough for that.'

Nancy Ward: 'I used to say, grandad, why don't you come up and live with me, you've got the little bedroom – that'll be your room. No, he said, I'm going to stop here while I can. Well, then he got off his head, you see. Went awful queer.'

Dr Roger Slack: 'I think he was only a very isolated figure as an old man when his wife died and after he'd rejected his own family. I wouldn't have thought that when he was younger, he was isolated at all.'

In 1977, with the debate continuing among family and friends and into the medical profession, Roger Slack wrote to a consultant psychiatrist: 'I think senile dementia is a better name for his condition. I do not believe that Wallis's paintings originated from a disturbed mind, however disturbed he may have become in his dotage. It is perhaps significant that the gradual deterioration in his normality appeared to have little effect on his style, or quality and quantity of his output.'

Alfred Wallis died in the Madron poorhouse in 1942. Adrian Stokes was appointed executor of Wallis's effects and he was responsible for the funeral arrangements. This must have been at the request of Wallis, who still had relations in the town. Perhaps he was thinking about the safety of his paintings locked up in his cottage for who, among his relations, would have any use for poor old uncle Alfred's daubs? He could entrust them only to one of his sponsors.

Stokes paid the Salvation Army an extra amount of money so that Wallis would not be buried in a pauper's grave, ever the great fear of most working-class folk at the time. In his position Stokes was able to prevent many of Wallis's

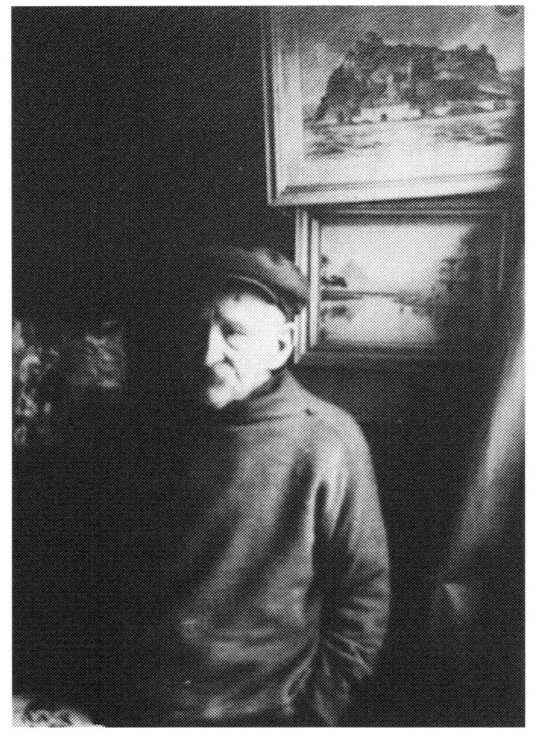

Alfred Wallis in his Back Road West cottage.

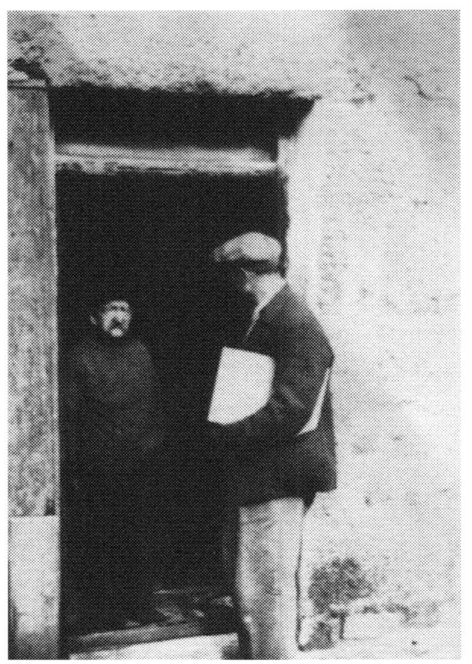

Ben Nicholson with Alfred Wallis.

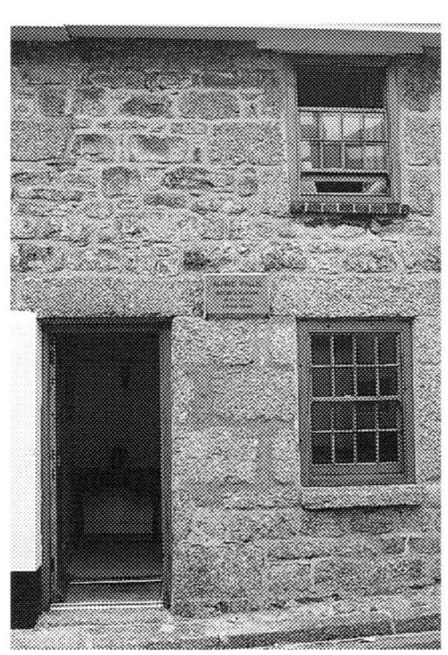

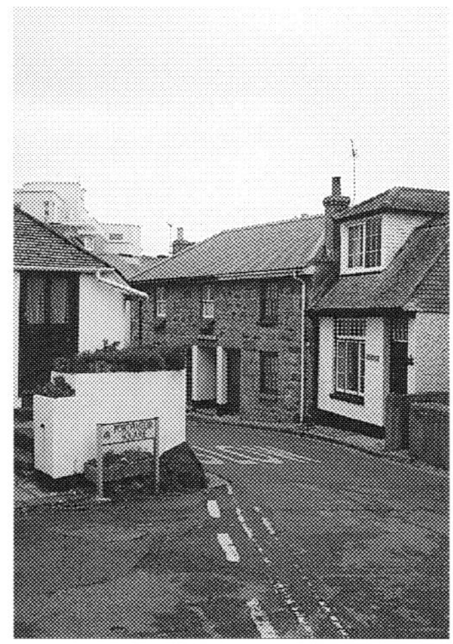

Alfred Wallis's cottage at 3 Back Road West, 1997, and Porthmeor Square looking towards the cottage. The Tate St Ives is in the background.

paintings being burnt on Porthmeor beach, along with other articles from his cottage. He carried the paintings home in his car, so once again, luck played a part in preserving Wallis's work for posterity.

At the time, Margaret Mellis recorded her version of the visit to Wallis's cottage with Ben Nicholson and Adrian Stokes after he had been taken to the poor house. 'In Wallis's cottage we saw all his paintings face down piled on a long table stretching from door to opposite wall. We went in and started to turn them over to see them. After a bit I felt nip, nip on my ankles, I went on looking and said "something is biting me." The other two said, "don't be silly it's imagination." The paintings were so fascinating I went on but at last I looked at my navy trousers. They had turned to reddish brown from the fleas swarming up to my knees! By then the others had got bitten, so we bundled the paintings into the car and drove home. On the way Ben got out and walked up to his neck in the sea with his natty blue shorts, white shoes and cap. He stayed in the sea until the fleas were dead. We put all our clothes in a cold bath with weights to keep them down. But the fleas crawled out and we were bitten for six months!'

Mellis also told how they distributed the paintings in the cottage, 'Ben chose the paintings he liked best, then Adrian chose and then I did. Luckily Ben didn't like the ones with orange, so I got some. We asked everyone who might be interested to come and take some. Hardly anyone came. This explains why we didn't put Wallis in a private nursing home. But he was better off at Madron, where he could be seen. Ben explained to the master how important a painter he was and people went on giving him materials and paints. Everyone there respected him and he went on painting and drawing until he died.'

Stokes gave a kitchen table from the Wallis cottage to Sven Berlin, who had helped him with the funeral arrangements. The table wasn't accepted for its useful function but for the paintings of ships and lighthouses that decorated every part of it. Berlin's intention was to leave the painted table to the Tate Gallery but at the end of the war, to alleviate his financial burdens, he was forced to sell it, and with some sorrow, watched its new owner, Eardley Knollys, saw the legs off so that it would fit into the boot of a car.

Sven Berlin, in *The Coat of Many Colours*, wrote that he 'started a collection for Wallis's gravestone. I wanted to carve it myself, but could not, Barbara Hepworth refused and in the end Bernard Leach produced the tall pottery lighthouse in large golden tiles with the inscription "Into Thy Hands O Lord". Adrian Stokes bought the grave to save him from the paupers' corner – one with a sea view, as Barbara succinctly put it. I helped to arrange the funeral when Wallis's body was already on the train from Penzance to Little Park Owles, Adrian Stokes being the executor of the estate.'

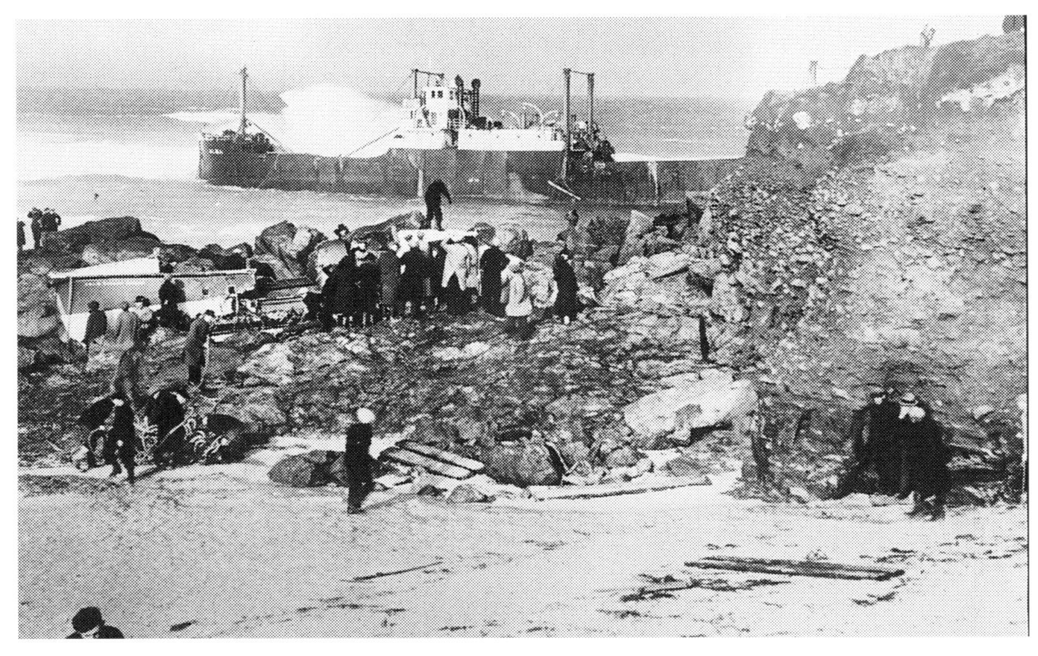

The wreck of *The Alba*, 1938 and, *below*, Wallis's painting of the subject.

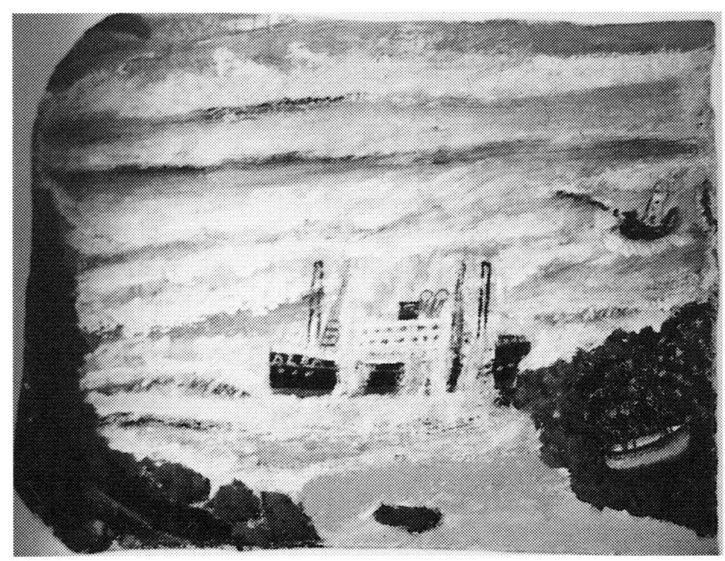

Berlin had intended carving a granite man on the high point of Rosewall Hill to be seen by fishermen as they returned to harbour and as a final tribute to Alfred Wallis, but Barbara Hepworth, with her greater experience, pointed out that it would take many years to carve and weigh several tons and Berlin abandoned the idea. Leach in designing Wallis's unique gravestone took into account that his paintings often featured Godrevy lighthouse with a cross. 'That is why I did this tile set for his tomb. I put one of his towers, a great tall one with a cross on the top, and a door at the bottom and a little man climbing into the dark to climb into the light.'

Attending Wallis's funeral were the artists who had bought and admired his work, Adrian Stokes and his wife Margaret Mellis, whose floral tribute bore the words, 'A tribute to an extraordinary artist'. From Ben Nicholson and Barbara Hepworth, 'To a great artist'. Naum Gabo and his wife Miriam wrote, 'In homage to the artist on whom nature has bestowed the rarest of gifts, not to know that he is one'. The writer George Manning-Sanders, along with Bernard Leach, also attended. They had never met Wallis, but were representing Sven Berlin, who was in London trying to find a publisher for his book on Alfred Wallis. Sven's tribute was 'To a great painter from Helga and Sven'.

Alfred Wallis – The Legacy

It is known that Alfred started painting after the death of Susan in 1922. Just how soon after is not certain. After Wallis' death, Ben Nicholson's often quoted article was published in *Horizon* 1943, and recalled his visit to Wallis in 1928. 'When I returned to London I showed his work to many friends, and he soon had a large number of admirers like H S Ede, Herbert Read, Adrian Stokes, Geoffrey Grigson, C S Reddihough, John Aldridge, Helen Sutherland, Margaret Gardiner, John Summerson (Hepworth's brother-in-law), Barbara Hepworth, Winifred Dacre (Nicholson) and many others. Ede in particular took a great deal of trouble about him and his work, and several Wallises were usually to be seen hanging in his office at the Tate Gallery. He used to post us parcels of paintings done up in many sheets of old brown paper, criss-crossed and knotted with a thousand pieces of string, and it was always exciting opening these parcels to see what good ones might be inside.'

Ben Nicholson wrote to Wallis in 1929 after receiving a parcel of paintings. 'Dear Mr Wallis, Many thanks for the new paintings. There are some lovely ones among them, and we like them very much. Mr Wood and Mrs Nicholson both liked one of them as much as any you have done – one with the land like clouds behind a ship with white sails, blue sky, yellow sun.'

That issue of *Horizon* also carried an article by Sven Berlin, then serving in the army and struggling to find time to write his book on Wallis. He commented, 'In the work of these famous artists we read clearly the debt they owe him: I refer to the Cornish landscapes of Nicholson and the Breton and Cornish seascapes of Wood. Several artists have benefited pictorially by Wallis's achievement. The admiration extended by this circle, headed by Nicholson and Wood, was an encouragement to Wallis, because they were the only people who believed in his work, though it had little effect in ameliorating his circumstances.'

Patrick Hayman, visionary painter and poet, was first struck by the Wallis pictures in *Horizon*, and later admired Peter Lanyon's collection. Hayman identified with the elemental purity of the old fisherman's work, Philip Vann commenting: 'Wallis's primitive directness combined with an unconscious formal, almost post-Cubist sense of composition, appealed to him greatly.' Hayman paid homage in 1970 with his painting *The Spirit of Alfred Wallis Descending near Porthmeor Beach*, showing Wallis landing by parachute among tree-like shapes.

Certainly Christopher Wood acknowledged his debt to Wallis. He wrote to Winifred Nicholson, 'More and more influence de Wallis, not a bad master though: he and Picasso both mix their colours on box-lids! I see him each day for a second. He is bright and cheery. He's working hard. I'm not surprised that no one likes Wallis's paintings; no one liked Van Gogh's for a long time, did they?' At some point Wood had photographs of his own paintings showing the influence of Wallis. When these were shown to the old man he responded by painting pictures on the backs and returning them, probably to show he could do equally well, not realising the tribute being paid to him.

Ede, although he never met Wallis, corresponded with him over the years. In *A Way of Life: Kettle's Yard*, many years later, he wrote: 'I think it was in 1926 [almost certainly an incorrect date] I first began to get paintings by Alfred Wallis. They would come by post. Perhaps sixty at a time, and the price fixed at one shilling, two shillings or three shillings, according to size, but usually I could not afford so many. On looking back it is odd to think how few people even wanted one as a gift. I was grateful for the unsophisticated beauty of his work.' A typical letter from Wallis reads: 'Dear Mr Ede, I have about 30 or 40 paintins They must go By Train somone fetch Them if Their was any coming from your place They Could Call and Take Them away I want Them Cleard out i do not know how soon i shall have To moove The house want a great Repairs I think They are so good i think They are Two many for to send By Post.'

In the late 1930s, Alethea Garstin met Jim Ede in Morocco, and Ede asked if she could get some of Wallis's paintings for him. Ede by then had already acquired a sizeable holding. On her return to Cornwall Alethea introduced herself to Wallis, and as a result became a regular visitor. She recalls him vividly, sitting at his table with his work in front of him. She bought from him *Three-master at Anchor* for herself and perhaps purchased work for Jim Ede. She was helpful to Wallis in assisting with wrapping and posting parcels of paintings.

She told writer Frank Ruhrmund that 'Alfred Wallis was aloof, very dignified, but very nice. He sat there with one finger on the bible, a bit like an old prophet. I paid him ten shillings for the painting, and when I paid him the money on the dot he said to me, "That's all right, my dear, they that don't pay me are robbing the children." I didn't know what he meant at the time, but it turned out that the old fellow used to send money to the seamen's orphans in Plymouth. Quite wonderful.' He liked Miss Garstin because 'she was a lady'.

Winifred Nicholson, at her home at Bankshead, Cumbria, owned forty to fifty paintings by Wallis which she had bought direct from him. She also had letters in which Wallis supposed that she painted what she saw while he painted from memory. In 1940 she took Margaret Gardiner to visit Wallis, who as well as offering the gift of a painting advised Margaret to pay more attention to the Bible. This painting, among others which she bought from Wallis, helped form part of her collection at The Pier Gallery, Stromness, Orkney, a group of eighteenth-century buildings standing on the pier, converted to an arts centre and given to the people of Orkney. The larger part of her collection comes from the many painters and sculptors closely associated with St Ives. Like many astute collectors Margaret Gardiner began acquiring works by young unknown artists, in which she showed an unerring instinct for lasting works of art.

Some critics, looking for a new angle, suggest that Wallis was exploited by the artists. The reality is that they paid (albeit shillings and pence) for paintings which Wallis would gladly have given them, while countless friends and neighbours thoughtlessly destroyed their gifts. 'My family burnt a fortune,' 'We burnt a king's ransom,' are cries still heard from St Ives folk. There is little evidence to substantiate the exploitation claim, especially when one considers that many of the paintings Nicholson and Hepworth bought from Wallis were donated to the Tate collection, the Museum of Modern Art, New York, or passed on to friends.

Wallis gave hundreds of paintings to neighbours, family and friends, for any little kindness shown him and was surprised when Ben Nicholson – 'a real artist', the genuine thing – offered to pay for a painting. The money he received for paintings meant that his work was taken seriously, a great source of pleasure and pride.

Margaret Mellis recalls that 'Wallis didn't mind what people gave him; he was more interested in seeing that the pictures were wrapped in newspaper. I bought a long narrow painting with four boats sailing before the wind, probably an early one, painted on a wooden board.' Margaret tried to improve his prices but he was incapable of specifying a price and told people to put their money down, wrap up their painting in newspaper and take it away. Generally people did not give much.

Wilhelmina Barns-Graham first came across Wallis paintings at Little Parc Owles, the home of her friend Margaret Mellis. She later had a studio at Porthmeor and used to see him. 'I got to know some of his relatives and friends. Some of them thought him a little mad. I took people to his house once or twice to see his work but I thought it wrong to buy it. He charged so little. But some time later Ben Nicholson very generously gave me a painting.'

The artists painting their traditional seascapes in the nearby studios took little heed of a social inferior's childish daubs. Their art was destined for the Royal Academy. And yet, on Open Studios Day, Alfred would open his cottage door and display his works alongside these prestigious artists, explaining the pictures in fine detail to anyone who showed an interest. Denis Mitchell recalled passing the cottage many times and seeing unframed works propped up on the kerb outside. Though he didn't appreciate them at the time, he later acquired three Wallis paintings for his home.

In 1929, Wallis's paintings were, unknown to him, being shown in the Seven & Five Society exhibition at Tooth's Gallery in London. Nicholson had also given a painting to the Museum of Modern Art in New York, and an article on contemporary art in England in *Cahiers d'Art* in 1938 included a reproduction of a painting by Wallis and an appreciation by Herbert Read. In his *Horizon* article in 1943, Nicholson recalled that, shown that reproduction, Wallis, not understanding and unimpressed, pushed it aside, saying, 'I've got one like that at home.'

Denis Mitchell included Wallis in an exhibition which he organised at Heal's Mansard Gallery, in London in 1951 called *15 Artists and Craftsmen from around St Ives*. There were further London exhibitions in 1962 and 1965, when 60 paintings by Wallis were exhibited. Seventeen of his works were shown alongside 14 each by Nicholson and Wood at the Crane Kalman Gallery in 1966. All this interest would surely have been beyond Wallis's belief.

By now Alfred Wallis's reputation and the future of his work were assured. In 1974 traffic in St Ives was held up for half an hour while Patrick Heron unveiled a plaque to Wallis on the wall of his former cottage at 3 Back Road West. The plaque – made by David Leach at his Lowerdown Pottery in Devon – was suitably covered in a dark brown mizzen sail from the ss *Bluebell*, while Patrick

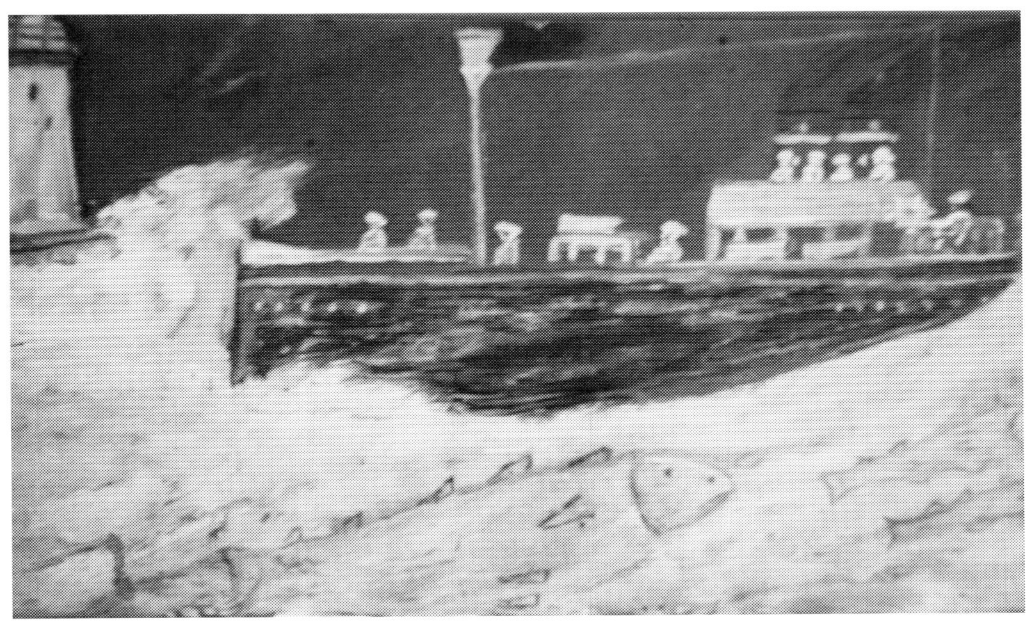

Alfred Wallis: *Coming into harbour.*

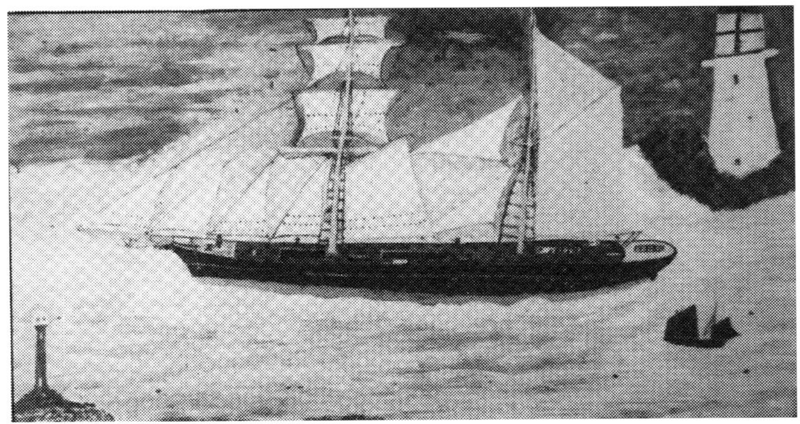

Alfred Wallis table painting.

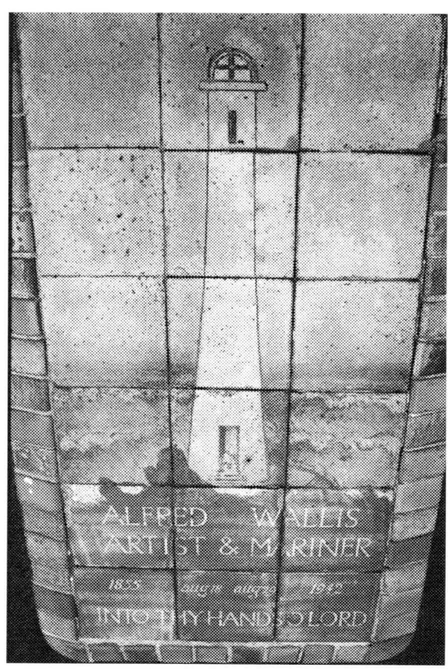

Left – Bernard Leach tiles on Wallis gravestone and, *below*, Patrick Heron unveiling the Wallis house plaque, 1974.

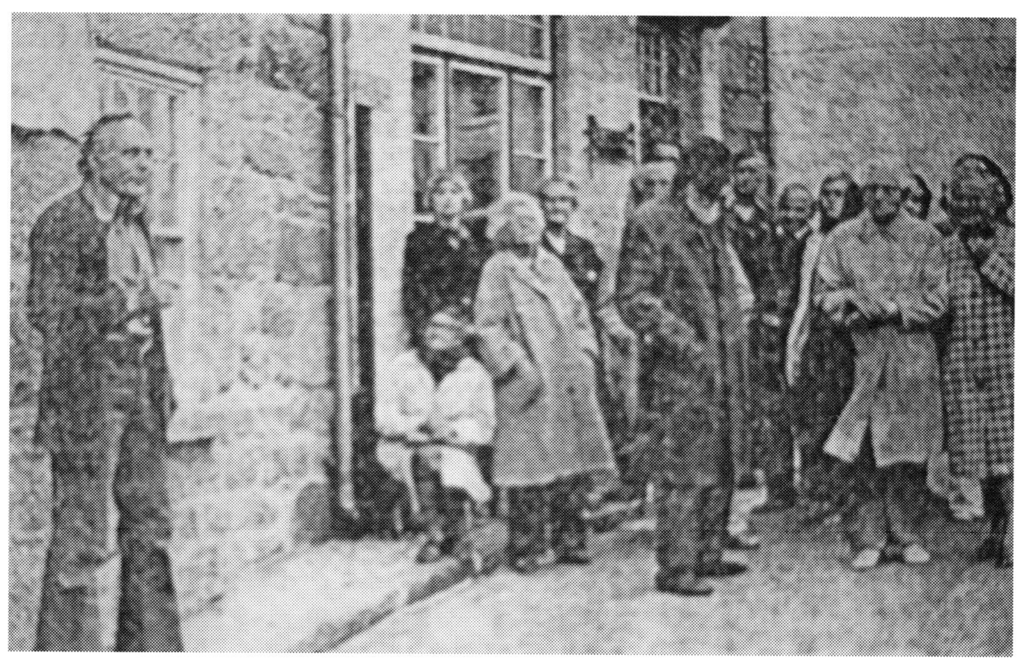

extolled the merits of the now famous St Ives fisherman/painter to a large audience. The company then walked to the nearby Penwith Gallery where Roger Slack gave a talk, with slides and tape recordings. Funds for the erection of the plaque had been raised by the Old Cornwall Society. At last Cornwall was recognising its own, but it wasn't sufficient to save a mural which Wallis had painted on the walls of a reception area at Madron poorhouse. This was discovered and debated over during alterations to the Grade 2 listed building. Margo Maeckelberghe and her husband remember the mural in the mid-sixties: 'Wallis asked Alethea Garstin to bring him gardening catalogues of plants and flowers. These were used for illustrating his mural.' At the time there was no strong feeling that the mural was worth the expense of saving it. Margo said, 'The overall effect was rather strange and different, but I think we would look at it with a different eye in the nineties.'

In 1995 the Tate Friends of St Ives bought *The Wreck of the Alba* for the Tate Collection from Brett Guthrie of St Ives. Wallis did several studies of the wreck and it is likely he witnessed the event. One stormy night in 1938 the *Alba* ran aground on rocks off the Island. Hundreds of people from the town were on Porthmeor beach that night dragging men from the sea. In effecting a rescue, the St Ives lifeboat overturned and five crew from the *Alba* were drowned.

Brett said he bought the painting direct from Wallis. 'It was May 1940. I was passing along Back Road and there was Wallis sitting outside his door with two paintings on the ground beside him. I paid four shillings for the two. The other was a four-masted barque with a great fish in the sea. I tried to sell the painting of the *Alba* some time later to a gallery in Piccadilly. The owner was very snooty. He looked down his nose and said nobody was interested in buying paintings on old bits of board.' Now hanging in the Tate, the painting still shows the holes where Wallis had nailed it to his wall.

Local man George Farrell recalled his memories of Wallis in the late sixties for Roger Slack, 'Just before the war, when the *Alba* went ashore, I remember him painting a picture of the *Alba* and the lifeboat. But he brought the lighthouse in as well, but it was impossible to see the lighthouse from there. He used to have a passion for painting mackerel luggers, used to make a frieze of them all the way around the wainscoting. Mind, if you looked closely at what he painted, the boat itself, the detail in it was true. He used to have luggers painted all round the table and on the wall.'

Sven Berlin was serving in the armed forces and writing his ground-breaking book on Wallis when time allowed. He regretted never having met the unique character of his biography and when he did finally knock on his door, Wallis had been taken to the poorhouse the day before. He looked through the window

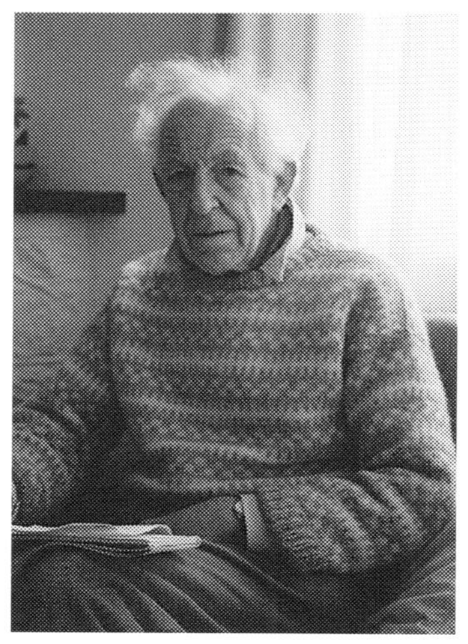 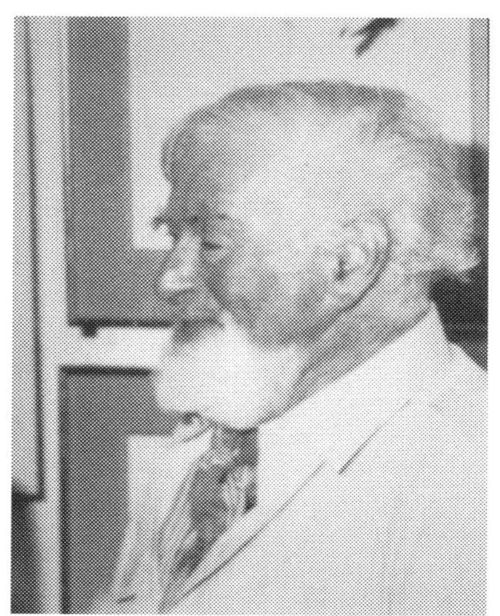

Dr Roger Slack photographed
by Marion Whybrow, 1997.

Sven Berlin, Wallis's biographer.
[courtesy Dr Roger Slack]

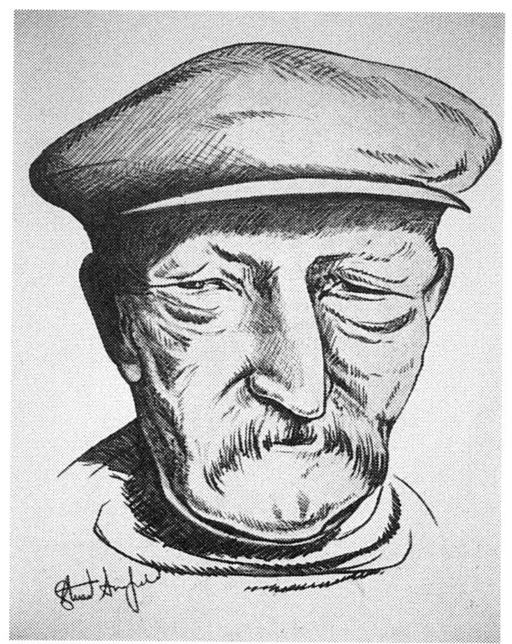

Stuart Armfield's drawing of Alfred Wallis.

and saw the place just as it was left with the remains of a meal on the table and a scattering of paintings.

Bernard Leach read Berlin's first draft, which was later abandoned and rewritten. Berlin was at that time working on the land and also helping at the Leach Pottery and researching among the Cornish folk who had known Wallis, sitting by their firesides and gleaning their memories. Some of the old man's life and difficulties were revealed, and also the stories which seem to have built up around him. He was out of kilter with his community of fishermen and hard working local folk, whose standard of behaviour was not to aspire beyond their station. Perhaps this was one of the criticisms levelled at Wallis, that he aimed at something his neighbours clearly thought he wasn't, a painter. This led Berlin to write in close sympathy with Wallis, having himself suffered hardship and been buffeted by misfortune and misunderstanding.

Sven Berlin visited Ben Nicholson and Barbara Hepworth to see their Wallis paintings. 'Barbara got out a large portfolio, opened it and passed it to me, one after the other, on irregular bits of cardboard, paintings by this old seaman,' he recalled in *The Coat of Many Colours*. 'The impact was tremendous, in a world changed to an abstract utopia under which the powerful seas and turbulent history of this wild old mariner surged. I was profoundly moved.'

Alfred Wallis Primitive was published in 1949, ten years after Sven Berlin had started his research. The delay was caused by paper shortages and production restrictions still in operation after the war. It was republished by Redcliffe Press in 1992 with new illustrations and a new introduction by Sven Berlin.

In 1967 Edwin Mullins wrote *Alfred Wallis, Cornish Primitive Painter*. He calculated that he had seen over a thousand pictures and drawings in the course of two and a half years of research. He concentrated on Wallis's work, but in 1994 when a shorter version of the book was published as *Alfred Wallis, Cornish Primitive*, he made use of the many interviews conducted among Wallis's neighbours and relations, by Dr Roger Slack, who was familiar with and respected by the local population. They were prepared to talk freely to their trusted local G.P. The tapes of conversations were obtained over a period of about five years, 1965–1970; used in a BBC radio programme in 1968, these oral testimonies have been available to many researchers looking for the true Alfred Wallis.

Two plays have been written and performed in Cornwall, *Back Road West*, a monologue written by Marion Whybrow and performed by Gerry Phillips, an artist in his own right, at the St Ives Arts Club in 1992 for the 50th anniversary of Wallis's death. In 1994 a full-length play written by Cornishman Donald Rawe, was performed at Falmouth Arts Centre by a few professionals and a large company of people drawn from the local community.

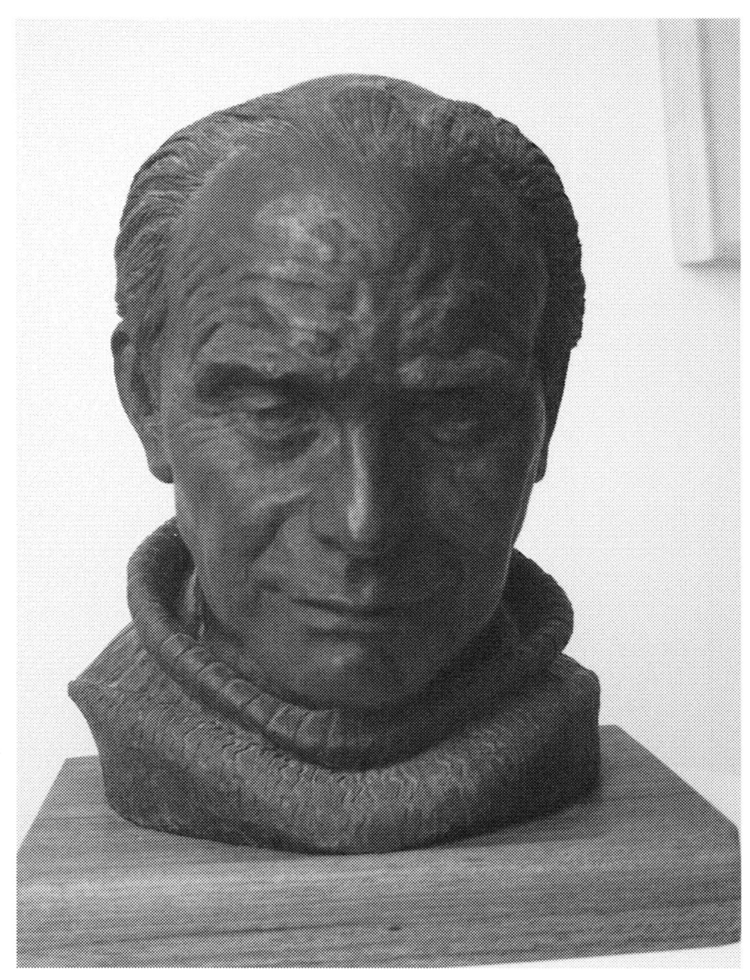

Bust of Bryan Pearce by Barbara Tribe.

Bryan Pearce
1929–

Bryan's achievement proves that the human spirit is beyond mundane things and that it can transcend everything – Peter Lanyon

Bryan Pearce was born in St Ives on 1 July 1929 to Cornish parents Mary and Walter Pearce. Mary's parents, the Warmingtons, lived in Carbis Bay. Walter, one of eight brothers, inherited the St Ives family business which he managed until his retirement in 1963. Bryan was born an apparently healthy baby and would have developed into a healthy adult but for a faulty metabolism caused by two similar genes from both parents, which allowed the condition P.K.U., phenylketonuria, to retard natural progression. All infants are now tested at birth for the condition, but its discovery in 1959 came too late to save Bryan and his sister Margaretta, born in 1941, from the deterioration which would spoil their lives.

Bryan was a bright, blue eyed, fair haired child whose sister showed the same attractive features – their portraits were painted in 1950 by Margery Mostyn – but both children were slow to develop physically and mentally. They were provided with all kinds of activity to stimulate them – horse riding, dancing and music lessons – and expert help was sought. Specialists of every kind, faith healers, osteopaths and physiotherapists, were called in, but there was no possibility of restoring the damaged brain. Margaretta died at the age of 20.

One of the specialists who treated Bryan was Dr Brian Kirman, a consultant psychiatrist at Queen Mary's Children's Hospital, Carshalton. He had a special interest in genetic disorders and was familiar with Bryan's paintings when he said of him, 'He has a natural talent set against a background of genetic hardship and he uses this talent in a natural unsophisticated and appealing way.' He upheld the contention that we underestimate the potential of people of supposed limited ability and that such potential should be cultivated. Doctor Woodard, a medical doctor who also believed in divine healing, had helped the family by the laying-on-of-hands and became a good friend. Mary felt with

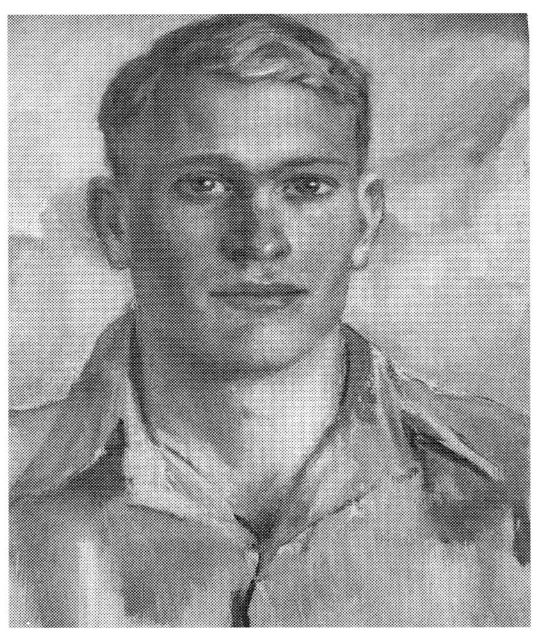

Marjorie Mostyn's painting of the young Bryan Pearce, 1950.

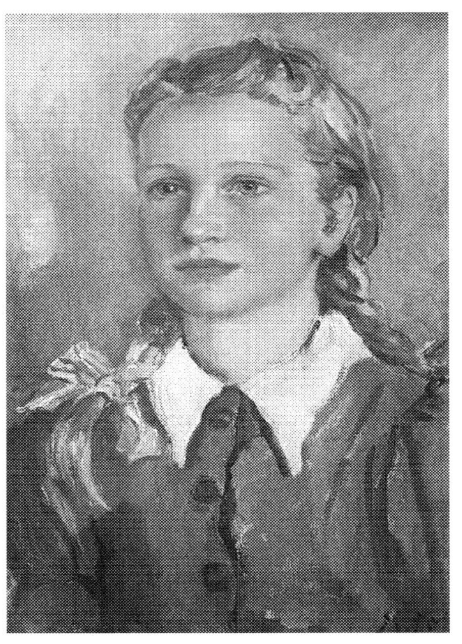

The same artist's painting of Bryan's sister, Margaretta, also in 1950.

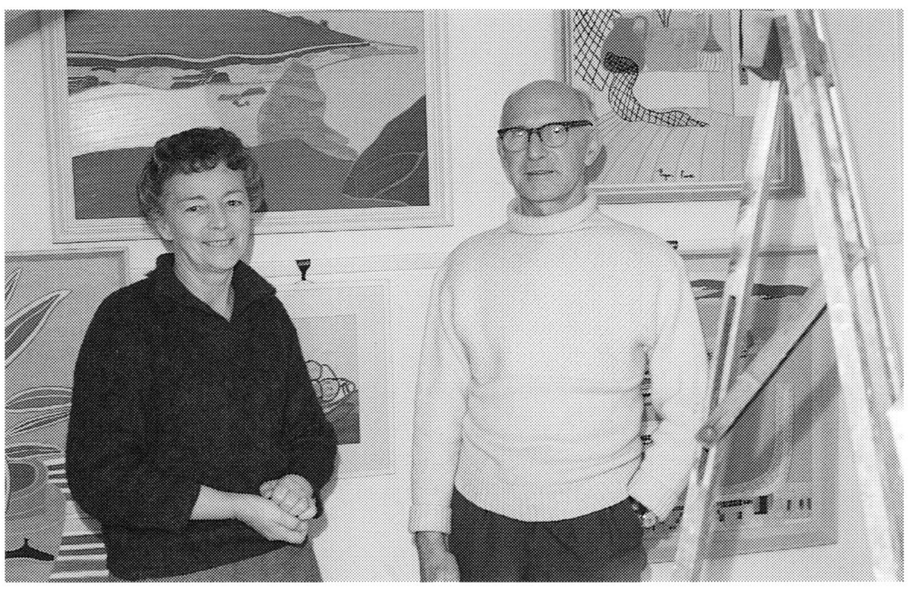

Mum and Dad: Mary and Walter Pearce in 1962.

certainty that Bryan had gained a 'fundamental source of strength' from this spiritual contact.

Bryan took to painting as though a lifeline had been thrown to him. At the age of 24 it became the important factor that governed his life from then on. The careful drawing of his subject in a hardly discernible line, the going over to make it visible, and then the strong yellow ochre, and now sometimes other coloured outlines, to clearly define the shape of the composition, all helped control his erratic behaviour and calm his frustrated need to satisfy the creative seam that remained untouched in his shattered intelligence. Choosing and mixing colours, and filling in these shapes is something which he enjoys above all other activities. He also enjoys choosing flowers, a jug or bowl for his subject, or a cloth for the background on which to place the key item, each piece of the composition playing a role in the picture.

Music has always been a great love. Mary's mother, who had spent hours trying to teach Bryan to play the piano, admitted defeat and realised that his inability to learn to read music restricted him to listening and to not playing an instrument. Bryan's innate affinity with music was demonstrated when he talked to the author about a concert he had attended at the parish church. 'A choir needs an organ. A piano is not as deep as an organ, it sounds a bit empty.' I was lost in admiration while he continued to explain. 'A piano is all right for a solo singer, but a choir needs an organ because it has a deeper tone.' 'Did somebody tell you that Bryan?' No, he just knew it, full of confidence in his knowledge. 'I would have been a musician if learning hadn't been so difficult.'

One summer morning the author accompanied Bryan to Sunday service. They were late and the church was full. The organ was playing the last few bars before the arrival of the priest. Suddenly Bryan stopped abruptly in the centre aisle and asked if they had a new organist. 'I don't know, Bryan,' I replied, taking his arm to hurry him. He stood still, listening, while the eyes of the congregation seemed focussed on us. I turned the question to him, 'Have they got a new organist Bryan?' Yes, they had, he replied with conviction. 'How do you know?' 'I can tell by the touch,' he said simply.

Although Bryan can understand music, keep time and follow intricate patterns in his head, this does not extend to a rhythmic understanding of movement. He cannot sway to music and his dancing is ponderous and without feeling. It is a mere plod of timekeeping, whereas Margaretta, his sister with the same condition, could dance and sing in a very carefree fashion. However, Bryan said he enjoyed the Arts Club dances where he would be whirled around and directed by one person or another in a country dance. Apart from his membership of the Penwith and Newlyn Societies, the Arts Club was the only place where he could join in social activities and meet people who understood him and who were prepared to talk to him and not mind his questions. 'What is the play about?' 'Are we going to have tea?' 'What's on at the tea talk?' 'Will there be slides?' 'Will it be interesting?' But Bryan also joined a music group at the Arts Club and learnt to play tunes by heart on the glockenspiel, keeping perfect time, and in some small way helping to achieve his ambition to play an instrument.

Walter Pearce retired in 1963, with nearly 50 years of service in the butcher's shop inherited from his father. This meant that the family were now free to take the car and travel about the countryside, visiting villages and churches and finding different locations and scenery for Bryan to draw. Walter and Mary would occupy themselves leaving Bryan to tackle his new subject in whatever way appealed to him. They also moved to the Piazza flats overlooking Porthmeor beach and Bryan was able to obtain a Porthmeor studio, directly beneath the St Ives School of Painting, where he had spent three years under the kindly eye of the proprietor and painter, Leonard Fuller.

Walter died in 1979 and Mary carried on the task, which had always rested on her shoulders, of fostering Bryan's career and hoping that the death of his father would not interfere with Bryan's ability to paint. She grieved alone, not allowing her emotion to affect Bryan's daily routine. She saw that this helped him remain stable and probably planned this way for Bryan to cope after her own eventual death.

In Bryan's bedsit, as he refers to his room where the sea sometimes reaches the balcony, Mary placed a printed text 'Expect a Miracle'. And the sort of life Bryan has led in this room is miraculous. This is where he works on his conte drawings and sets up his still life subjects of flowers, fruits, vases and cloths, with finely sharpened colours laid out on his table. This is where he houses his collection of books on steam trains, listens to classical music, writes his simple daily diary, receives lessons in reading from Win Cothey, a St Ives woman and retired teacher (who took over from the author when she began working on a book). However, the miracle doesn't extend to progress beyond a reading age of about eight to nine, but merely carries on the activity so that he doesn't lose the ability to read.

His Porthmeor studio is where his own collection of paintings is stored, from his earliest beginnings. These are the works that Mary put aside for retrospective exhibitions, such as that held at the Penwith Gallery in 1992. One hundred paintings, pastels and prints were shown together, including one of his first paintings, a brown-sailed blue boat. Walter questioned Mary's decision to keep these early works, and wanted to sell them, but Mary had judged well. People would be interested in a painter's development, from the pale watercolour still lifes, the progression to oils and the gradual accomplished use of the medium in

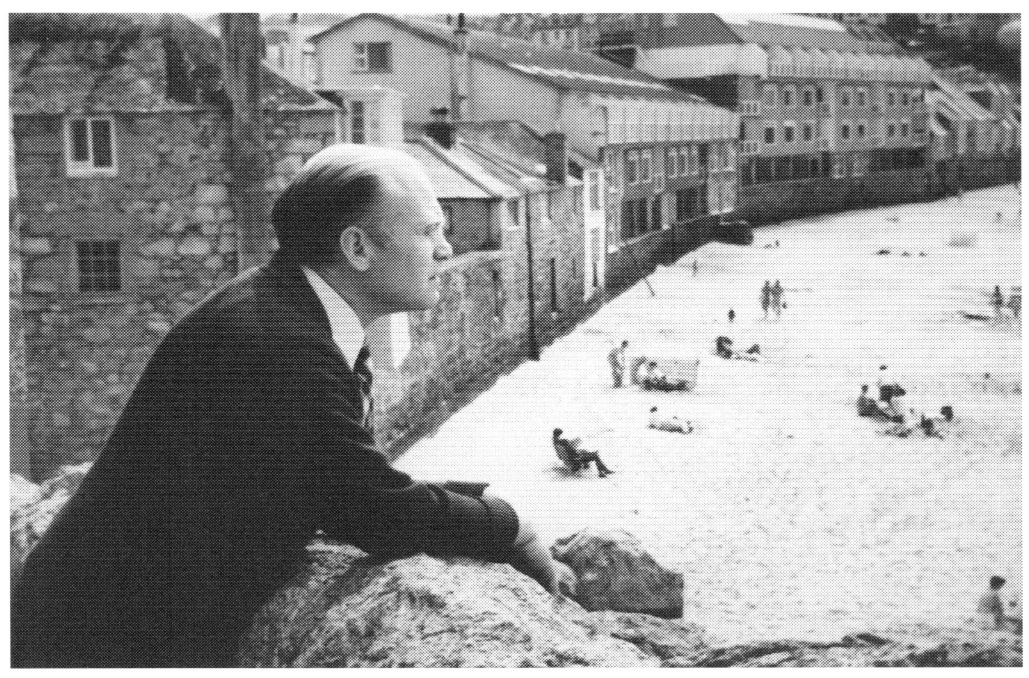

Bryan Pearce looking out over Porthmeor Beach, 1968 and, *below*, in his studio, 1970.

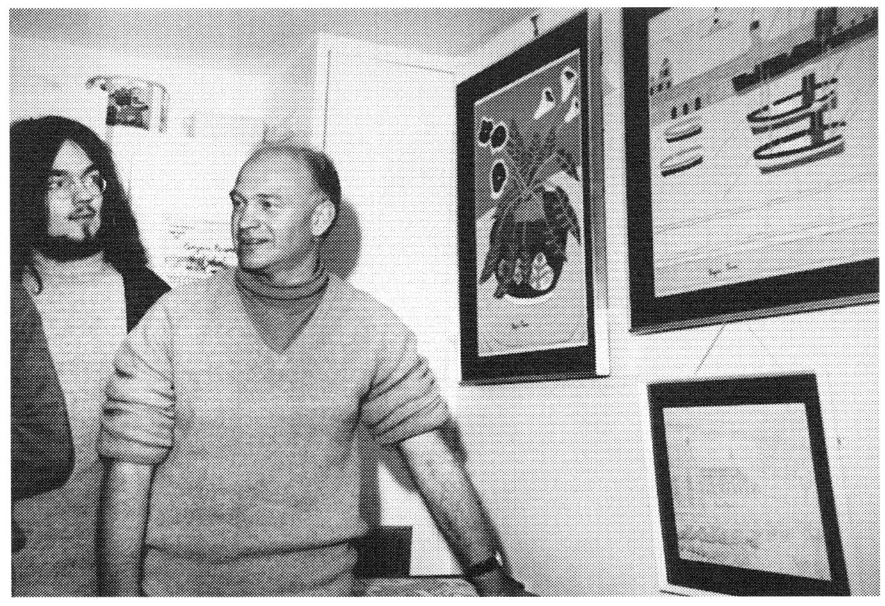

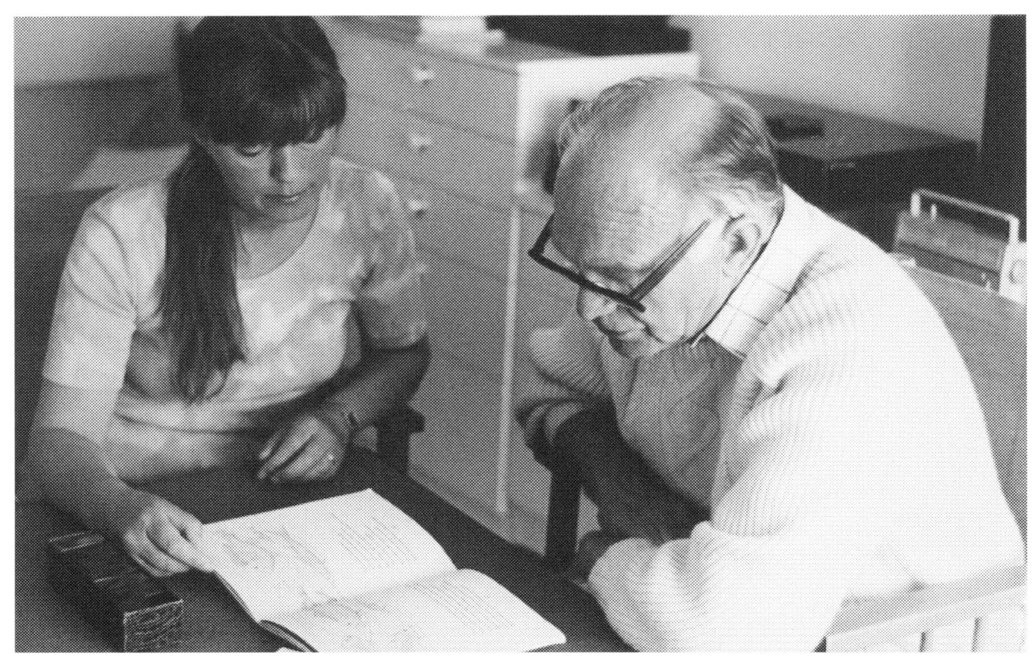

Bryan Pearce reading with the author, Marion Whybrow.

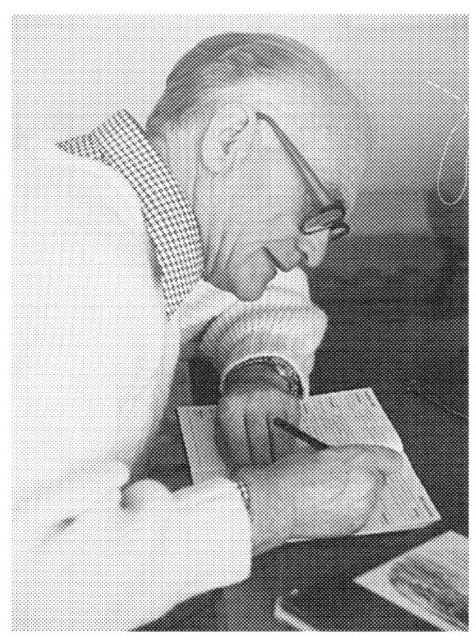

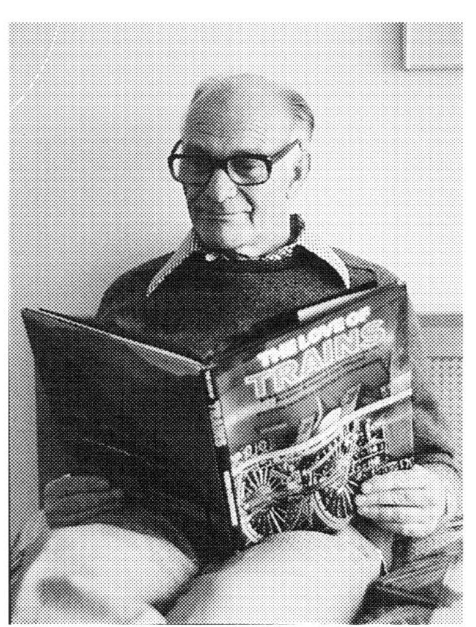

Bryan Pearce writing . . .   . . . and reading.

his middle years, to the inclusion of conté drawings – the unbroken output of work to the present day. Bryan's ability to work with disciplined and concentrated effort continues, whether he is working in his Porthmeor studio or in his bed-sit. In the Porthmeor studio there is a bronze head and plaster cast of Bryan commissioned by Mary and made by the Newlyn sculptor, Barbara Tribe.

There were always visitors to the Pearce home – people who had bought Bryan's work, a student writing a thesis, another writing an article, someone who wanted to see the studio, or to meet Bryan. All were generously welcomed by Mary, who introduced Bryan proudly. Bryan would usually behave in a very polite manner as befitted his mother's expectations of him, answer questions and explain in a limited and matter-of-fact manner whatever he was working on at the time. During Open Studios Day – a once-a-year tradition in St Ives, which started when the early painters would show the work they planned to submit to the Royal Academy exhibition – Bryan and Mary, and friends willing to help, would open the door and allow the public in to see a working studio and to meet Bryan.

Bryan's working day starts at 7 am. He used to take a cup of tea to his mother, cook his breakfast, make his bed and be out walking in the town by 8.30 am. Now his nurses, who have come to live in the Pearce flat since his mother's death, are the recipients of the early morning tea. The pattern of his life must continue. After his walk he opens up his Porthmeor studio and continues working on his latest painting. He stops for mid-morning coffee, which he makes in the studio, and at 12.30 he locks up and goes home for lunch. After a rest, he works on conté drawings in his room or spends another hour walking through the town, around the harbour, past the church, seemingly uninterested in his surroundings but all those areas of his walks appear at some time as a painting or conté drawing.

Mary was always thankful for the talent that Bryan had developed, and mindful of what his life would have been like without this special gift, she was generous in donating many of Bryan's paintings and prints for those in less fortunate circumstances than her son. Letters of appreciation and pleasure have poured in from hospitals, homes, and special schools.

Father Leah of St Ives Parish Church wrote to Mary after visiting the Tate Gallery exhibition in London in 1985. 'Almost the last painting I looked at before I dragged myself away was Bryan's *St Ia Church, St Ives*, April 1971. It is familiar because of the prints so generously given for the restoration fund. Like all of his paintings it is done with loving care. It was a revelation to see the actual colours. And there was something I had not noticed before: you look through the screens of the Lady Chapel and your eye is led to the Resurrection Window. Yes, an Easter message from the Tate Gallery! Bryan has painted it largely in reds. Red is one of the traditional colours of Easter. Bryan's pictures have something of the quality of icons; light comes through from the Other Side. It really is remarkable. Visionary.'

Bryan has always been very pleased to sell a painting. His invariable response, when she was alive, was to ask his mother if she was proud of him. This mattered very much. He next asked whether the money was enough to pay all his bills. His mother invariably said it was, at which he would suggest he might now buy a new record or book to add to his already large collections. The sale of a painting, for Bryan, was an exchange of money to supply his passion for music and steam trains.

When Pearce first started to sell his work, it was Mary who was modest and surprised that people should take such an interest. She recalled how, early on, a man called at their house in Market Place asking to see some of Bryan's work. She took him to the studio and to her astonishment he bought two oils and three watercolours, but explained that he didn't have any money or carry a cheque book with him. Could he send it on? Mary decided to take a chance. She hadn't realised until the money arrived that the purchaser was Jim Ede, former assistant curator at the Tate Gallery in London. They became firm friends and in 1966 Ede arranged for an exhibition of Bryan's work in a Cambridge gallery. Ede's assessment was that Bryan was undisturbed by greed or wordly achievement, his only desire to recreate his inward vision.

Mary Pearce had slides taken of every painting, kept details of sales, arranged interviews, organised works for exhibition and attended to Bryan's every need. She would order his day so that he painted in the morning, rested after lunch, walked in the afternoon and afterwards perhaps set up a still life for a conté drawing. His work has been exhibited widely and he has taken part in solo and mixed shows every year since he started painting in 1953.

In this time, Bryan has notched up around 30 one-man exhibitions and taken part in numerous shows with St Ives artists in the West Country, London and throughout Britain and abroad. His work has often appeared in exhibitions where entry is by open competition, as in John Moores, the Bath Festival and the International Drawing Biennale, and has also been chosen to appear by invitation at special shows. He has seen success in his lifetime and yet, although his work is in public collections, this means little to him. It is beyond his comprehension, as it would have been for Wallis.

Bryan's contemporaries are well aware of his achievement and appreciate his skill and dedication, although he may be more successful in exhibiting and selling than many of them. Indeed, the St Ives artists have been supportive, creating prints, sharpening his pencils, wrapping and transporting work for

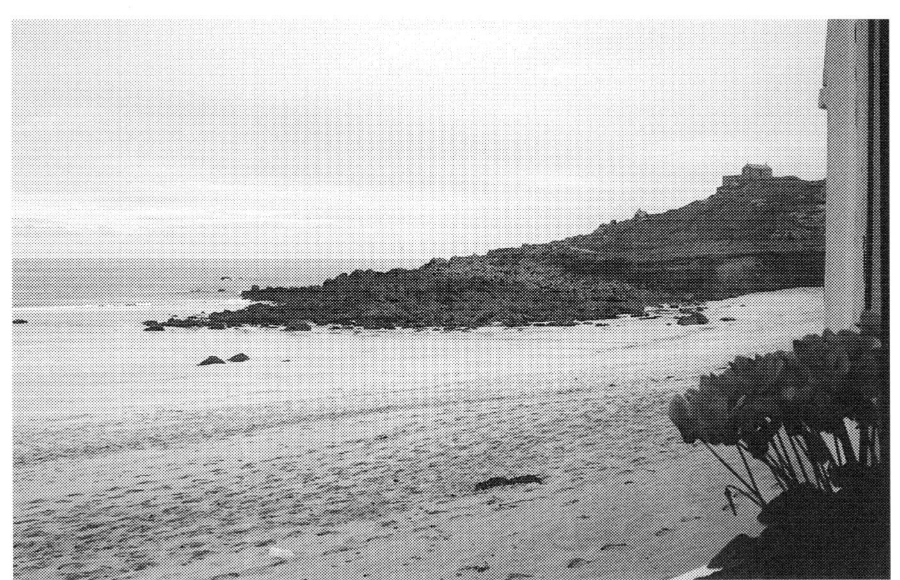

The Island, Porthmeor Beach, from Mary Pearce's window in the Piazza Flats.

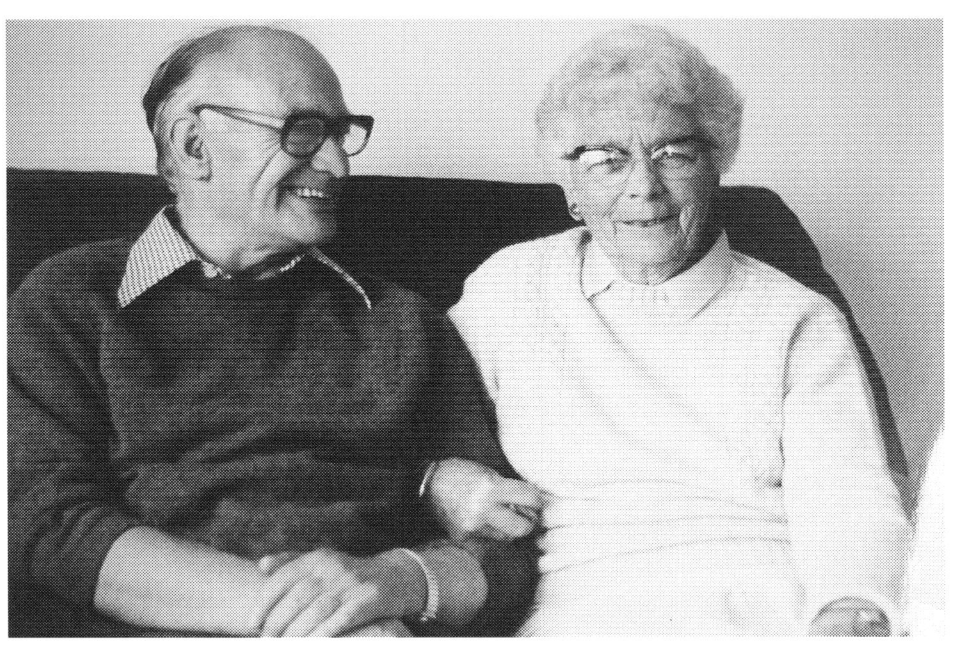

Bryan and Mary Pearce, 1985. [courtesy Marion Whybrow]

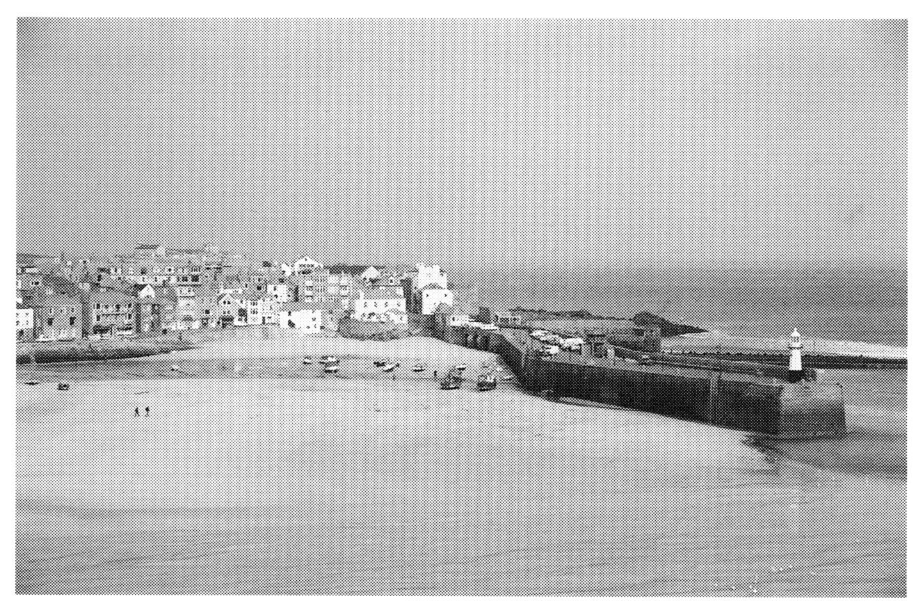

St Ives Harbour. [courtesy Marion Whybrow]

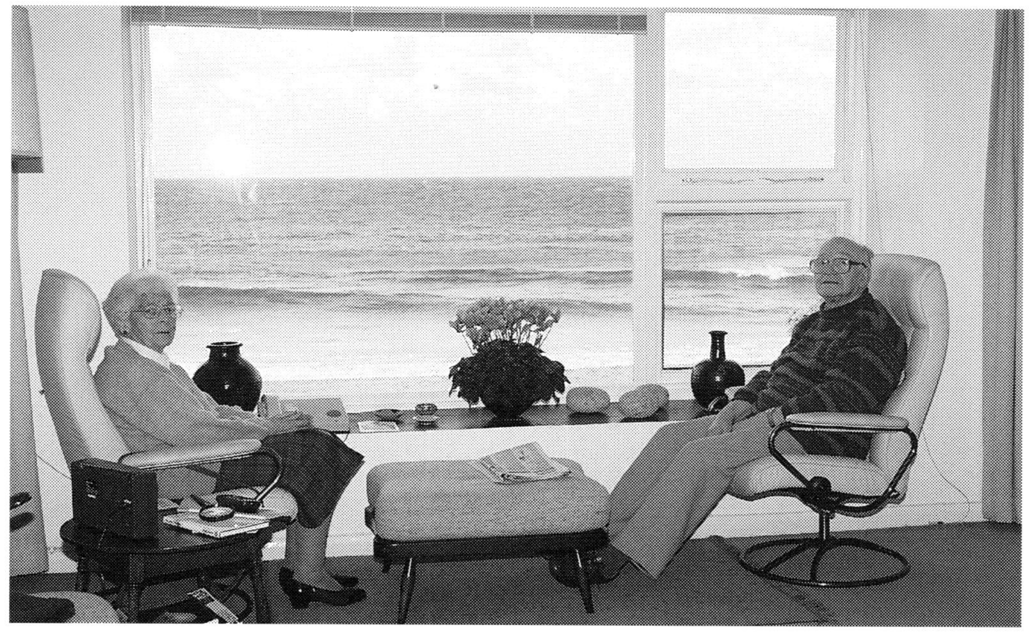

Mary and Bryan in the Piazza Flats, 1996.

exhibition, and helping out with whatever is required, although Mary would always be more than generous in payment for services. Kathy Watkins, curator at the Penwith, would always inform Mary of forthcoming exhibitions at the gallery or outside the county. Lieke Ritman, framer and artist in her own right, made beautiful and distinctive frames for Bryan's oil paintings, which now have plainer surrounds.

It was the Wills Lane Gallery owner, H C Gilbert (Gillie), who suggested to Mary in the early 1990s that Bryan might like to try the medium of conté oil pencil on tinted paper, working on smaller pictures which could be completed in a shorter time, thereby cutting Bryan's work-load, reducing the price of an original work and appealing to a wider public. Bryan took to this idea immediately.

Mary Pearce died on Sunday 23 March 1997 at the age of 91. In a tribute, Sir Alan Bowness observed that she transferred her own never-realised ambitions as a painter to Bryan. Friends wondered how Bryan would cope after the withdrawal of this lifelong support. Would he ever paint again? Mary had predicted that as long as Bryan's routine was strictly followed and no change disturbed the habits of a lifetime, he should be as little affected as possible. Peter Dexter, the family friend and solicitor, took charge of affairs and two nurses arrived to fit themselves into this prescribed mould. Bryan continued his working life, cared for twenty four hours a day and now the centre of attention.

Valerie Dodds, who had worked for Mrs Pearce for eleven years and increased her work-load to help Mary during the last few weeks of her life, helped Bryan in talking with him about how he intended setting up his still lifes, what cloth he would choose, what flowers he would like. Valerie recalls asking Bryan if he would like to draw the anemones which were in his mother's room. 'Yes please,' he said. Valerie removed one flower with damaged leaves. She presented him with all his cloths and several pots for him to choose. She placed the cloth he had chosen and left him to work. Returning later, she found the damaged flower put back and another pot chosen for the flowers. 'It's my choice,' he told her, 'I changed my mind.' After this experience they felt happy that Bryan's lifelong discipline would carry him through. Another time, Lady Sarah Bowness brought in some hydrangeas and asked Bryan if he would like to use them for a conté drawing. 'I'll think about it,' he said. The flowers were kept watered for a few days while he made up his mind. When he was questioned again, he finally said, 'No thank you.'

Mrs English accompanies Bryan to concerts in the town and Del Castagli, another family friend, who travels with Bryan to his private views out of the county, continues this valuable service. Win Cothey pays her weekly visits to help Bryan retain his reading ability and to encourage him to write his daily diary. David Bennett, musician, organist and lifelong friend of the Pearce family, who played at Mary's funeral, takes Bryan to music recitals, while Sir Alan Bowness advises on Bryan's exhibitions. Bryan has found himself, not deserted, but surrounded by loving and affectionate friends. His 68th birthday was celebrated with the usual coterie of friends at the Mermaid, in Fish Street, with a birthday cake made by Sheila Bennett and so, as Mary predicted, Bryan continues to live a happy and fruitful life.

Bryan Pearce: The Public View

As well as the interest and understanding shown by neighbouring painters Bryan Pearce had become well known, both as a recognised painter and as a person who needed sympathetic understanding of his disability. Since Bryan had been introduced to the world of exhibitions and paintings, and was greatly satisfied and confident in his chosen profession, his frustrations had been mitigated and his behaviour towards other people was less brusque. People were admiring and appreciative and he was able to respond in a socially acceptable way to the many questions about his work. Charles Causley, poet of the West Country, wrote, 'Bryan is writing his name securely into the history of art, and the history of Cornwall.'

Jim Ede had been assiduous in accumulating over one hundred paintings by Alfred Wallis, to display first on the wall of his office at the Tate Gallery, and then on retirement at his home-cum-arts centre at Kettle's Yard, Cambridge. He later turned his attention to Bryan Pearce, becoming a good friend of the family. He was to bequeath Kettle's Yard and the collection of paintings and sculpture – many by St Ives artists – to the University of Cambridge in 1966. Mary Pearce, over many years, sent Jim Ede the latest screen prints of Bryan's work and treasured the occasion when she, her husband Walter, and Bryan spent a marvellous two weeks at Kettle's Yard surrounded by beautiful works of art. It was an experience she never forgot, and on that visit Bryan painted a number of works, two of which, featuring the King's College Chapel and the Round Church, are part of the collection.

In writing of Bryan Pearce in the *Cornishman* in October 1985, Frank Ruhrmund observed a sense of serenity, 'a quiet power in a Pearce painting that defies description. He uses simple shapes and bright clear colour to portray the world as he sees and remembers it. In many ways an enviable world, where the sun always shines, where no storms ruffle the surface of his seas, no people

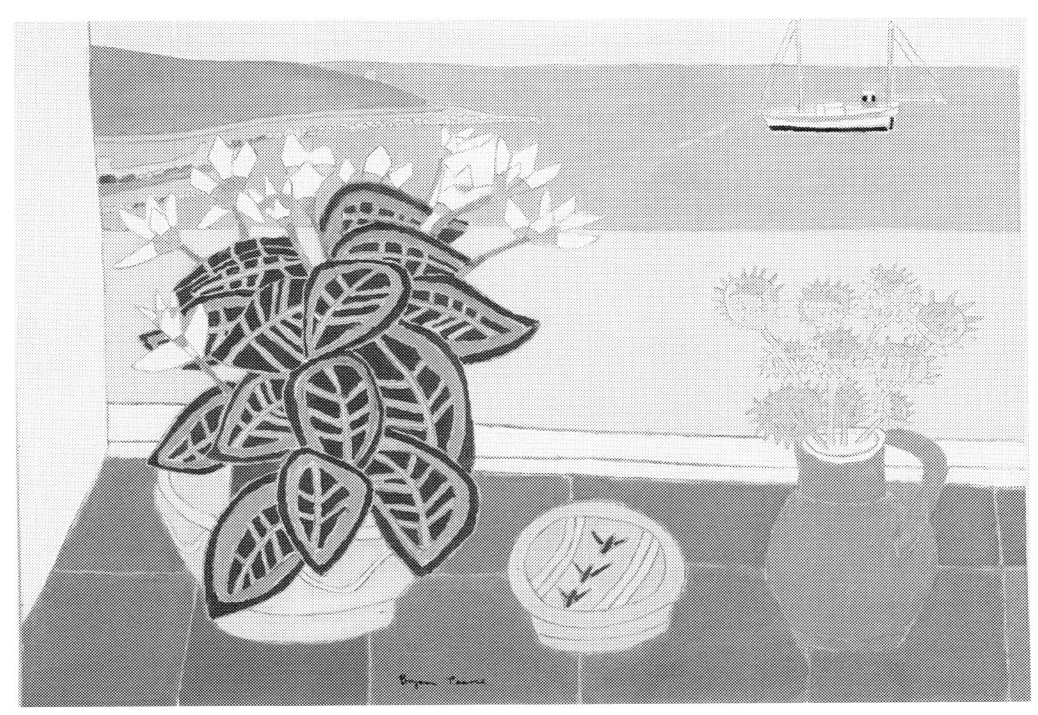

Bryan Pearce: *Cyclamen in the window*, 1991.

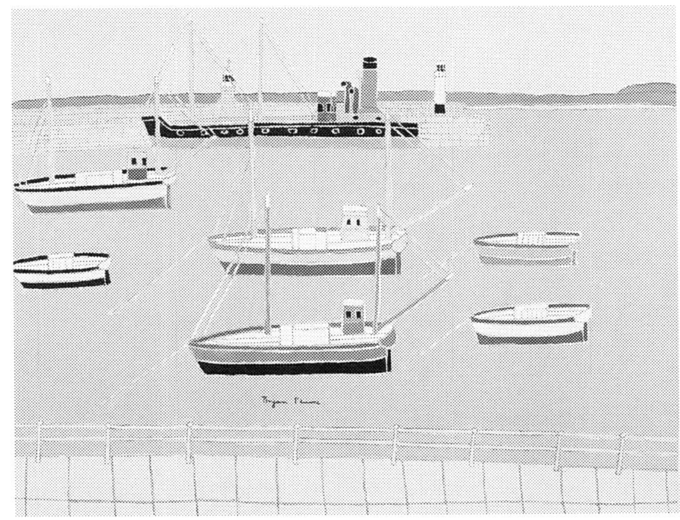

Bryan Pearce: *A visiting boat, St Ives.*

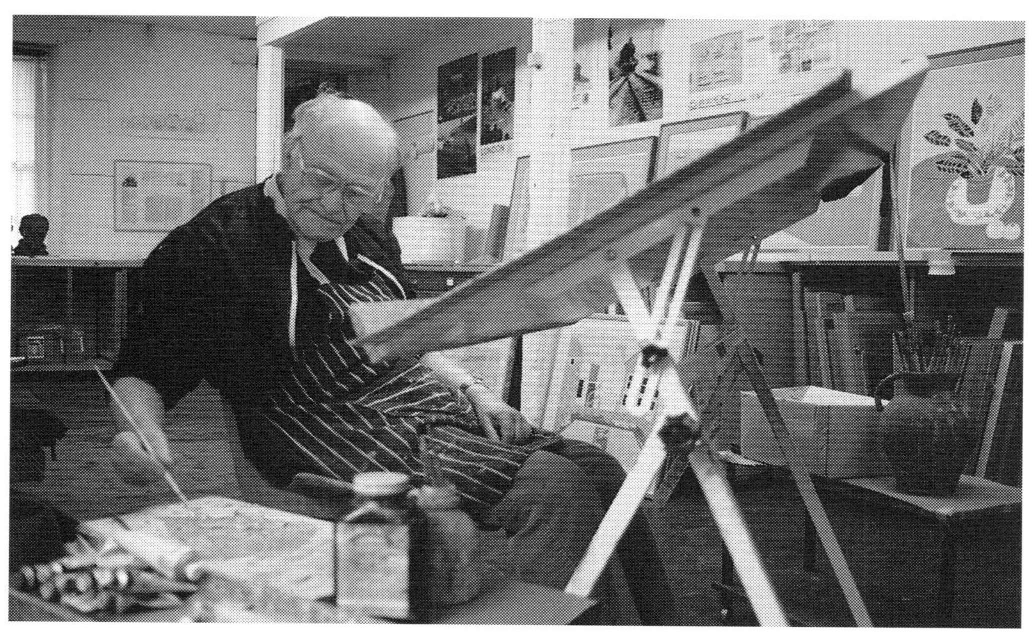

Bryan Pearce, October 1996. [courtesy Marion Whybrow]

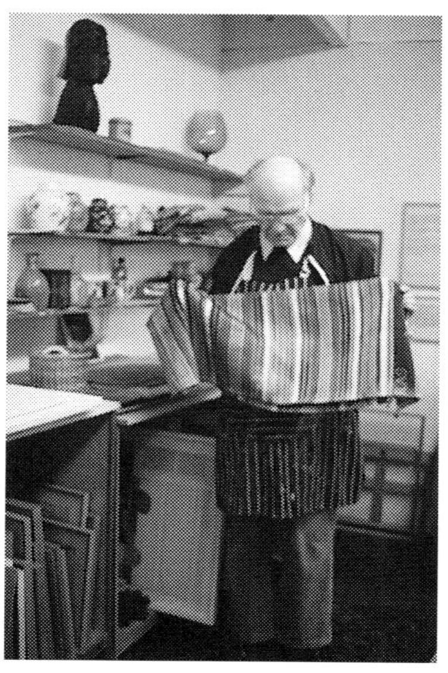

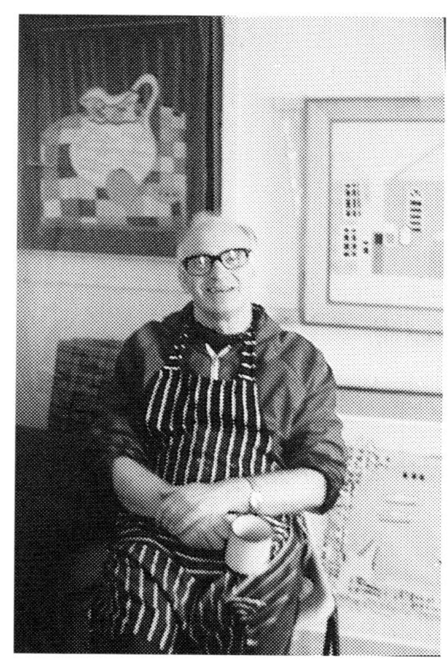

Bryan Pearce choosing a cloth . . .   . . . and at coffee time in his
                                                     studio, 1985.

enter his cottages or walk upon his piers, a semi-detached world where contentment reigns and peace is king.' He also observed that Bryan was a natural and wouldn't know a gimmick, a short cut, or a clever way out of a painting problem if it rose up and bit him.

A small book, written by George T Noszlopy, describes Pearce as 'a primitive painter in the sense that hardly any external cultural influence determined his art. Though he lives in a 20th-century culture and is encouraged by many members of the St Ives artists colony, Bryan Pearce is an outsider.' However, he is no outsider to exhibitions and has, without fail, been represented in every recent exhibition held to celebrate Cornish artists, both within and outside the county and abroad.

Michael Holloway, who was later to open the New Millennium Gallery in St Ives with David Falconer, wrote to Bryan about his retrospective at Penwith Gallery in 1992. 'It was wonderful to see so many paintings assembled in one place. I think that all creative talent is a divine gift, and I feel that is especially true of your paintings. I visited the show on several occasions, and each time was conscious of the great aura of spiritual light and clarity in the room. I regularly visit art exhibitions, but I don't think I have ever been quite so moved and excited by a particular show. I saw you in the distance at the Private View. Shyness prevented me from coming up to you and shaking you by the hand. Yours is a real gift, communicating the spirit of St Ives and Cornwall following quite naturally from Alfred Wallis and the artists who have been before, but bringing with it something which is uniquely and unmistakably yours.'

Although Pearce might follow on from Wallis he was unaware of him or his paintings. As Charles Causley said in his broadcast for the BBC in 1962, 'There is little in common between Wallis's intensely subjective, tormented inward-looking vision and Pearce's lyrical world of colour and sweetness and light.' Mary Pearce, busy with her own intense problems with her son, was also totally unaware of Wallis, either as a painter, or as a member of the St Ives community. Their social paths did not cross. Bryan, as a child, would not have noticed the old man, or later known or heard of his work, entirely wrapped up as he was in his own private world of painting in his very instinctual way: unaware, uninfluenced, and unconcerned with the lives or paintings of any single being except himself.

In 1985 the Tate Gallery in London held the celebrated exhibition 'St Ives 1939–64 Twenty Five Years of Painting, Sculpture and Pottery'. As well as work by Alfred Wallis, Barbara Hepworth, Ben Nicholson, Patrick Heron, Terry Frost, Peter Lanyon, Wilhelmina Barns-Graham, John Wells, and other well established artists, two of Bryan's paintings were exhibited, *St Ives Parish Church* and *Portreath Harbour*. Mary and Bryan attended the private view;

when asked whether the two selected paintings were his favourites, Bryan said no, he liked them all the same.

After the death of his mother, and largely because of his age and a growing inability to control a shaky hand, Bryan's paintings took on another quality. The smooth application of oil paint was no longer possible and the pictures showed a much freer hand movement to their finish. This could be considered by some to be a deterioration and by others a pleasing increase of paint texture. The conté drawings also became a little uncertain and yet at the same time, he enjoyed a kind of flowering, working on larger drawings of still lifes and *St Ives harbour all round*. This subject has been studied and produced many times over the years in both drawings and in paint.

The first book to be published on Bryan Pearce was by Ruth Jones, friend and admirer of Bryan's work. *The Path of the Son*, published in 1976, updated and re-issued in 1994, charts the tragedy and the triumphs, and deals honestly and sympathetically with the parents of two children born as normal healthy babies, whose brains are virtually destroyed because of a defective gene recurring in both parents. Margaretta, a beautiful girl, died just 20 years old, while Bryan went on to achieve fame and recognition well beyond all prognostications.

The second book, by Marion Whybrow – *Bryan Pearce A Private View* – charts his development as an artist and gives an insight to the world of Bryan as seen through the close proximity of one who has helped him with reading over a period of seven years. This was published in 1985 and launched at Wills Lane Gallery, St Ives.

In 1988 Bryan featured in *Very Special Arts*, a magazine that explores the talents and artistic abilities of people whose lives are dominated by mental and physical challenges. Jean Kennedy Smith, sister of the late President Kennedy and founder chairman of the Magazine and Arts Festivals, based at the John F Kennedy Centre in Washington, USA, travelled to Cornwall to interview Bryan. Bryan (with Marion Whybrow's help in the way of questions) made a tape recording thanking her for her visit. He outlined the fine detail of his day, spoke of his interest in steam trains and named his favourite engines and at least seven of his favourite classical musicians, the contents of his bookcase and also, at great length, the St Ives views which were the subjects of his paintings.

There have also been many catalogues and articles, studies and dissertations, and several films for television.

Other Artists, Other Visions

Whether Wallis or Pearce were aware of their heritage is doubtful. In the 1880s large numbers of artists had arrived in St Ives and set up the artists' colony that survives in many different forms to this day. Until the late 1930s the traditional seascape and landscape artists held sway in St Ives: largely artists of means, choosing painting as a career but not relying on their work to provide a living. They coveted the prize of having their work accepted and hung in the Royal Academy and Paris Salon. They built large houses, converted fishermen's lofts to studios, and employed local families as models, cooks, maids, nannies, housekeepers and gardeners. To an extent they refloated the economy when the fishing industry was in decline.

The 'modernist' artists, who began arriving in St Ives at the beginning of the second world war were also middle-class, and did not have to rely on selling their paintings and sculpture to provide a living. They brought with them the influences of London, Europe and America and introduced a changing climate in art, philosophy and thinking, outside the purely academic. Their growing reputations over the years led to their works being acquired by the Tate Gallery, which staged the major exhibition in London in 1985, 'St Ives 1939–64 Twenty Five Years of Painting, Sculpture and Pottery'. In 1993 the Tate Gallery, St Ives, was built as a permanent showcase for this collection and has attracted increasing numbers of visitors ever since.

'Every truly naive painter has his own vision of the world which, in some mysterious way, is uniquely different from that of any other,' wrote Anatole Jakovsky in *Naive Painting*, 1979, adding that any attempt to imitate would be spurious. The work of such painters as L S Lowry was disqualified from the term 'naive' by reference to his earlier work, which was sophisticated, competent and art school-taught. He developed the apparently naive style for which he is known – of crowds of matchstick figures against an industrial backdrop – at a later date.

With naive and primitive painters, there is no room for development to a more sophisticated style of painting; in this, it is unlike child art, which is a temporary state of being leading to maturity. What differentiates naive from folk art is that the latter follows a tradition, usually passed down through generations, relying on story telling, magical symbols or legends, or the belief and culture of a people. And the roving peasant painters who produced pictures of cattle, horses and sheep with an exaggerated girth, to show off the prize animals of up-and-coming farmers and yeomen, disappeared with the coming of the industrial revolution.

There are no firm guidelines to distinguish between naive and primitive paintings and the terms are widely interchangeable. The cult of the naive or primitive artist is now fostered and their work collected. Among recent or contemporary artists working, living in and inspired by Cornwall, the Cornish-born Mary Jewels is especially interesting. She leads this otherwise alphabetical collection of profiles of artists to whom the terms intuitive, original or natural might just as easily be applied.

Mary Jewels
1886–1977

Mary Jewels is a very underestimated painter – David Brown

Mary Jewels was born, barely a hundred yards from the harbour, in Newlyn, one of the largest fishing villages in the South West. Her family, with the Cornish name of Tregurtha, had lived in Newlyn for many generations. Mary's husband, a carpenter, died during the first world war shortly after their marriage, and appears as A O Jewels on the war memorial in Newlyn.

Mr and Mrs Tregurtha's home was Vine Cottage, The Combe, which the family had owned since 1812. It was once used as the vicarage, where babies were baptised before St Peter's Church was built in Newlyn in 1866. The children – Weymouth, Mary, Cordelia and youngest brother, John – were born in the cottage, where they lived with their parents into adulthood.

Their mother, Jane Downing, was from County Waterford in Ireland. She died at the age of 97. According to a nephew, her family came to Newlyn in 1755 and set up a brewery and fishing business. The 1851 census records several Downings as shipwrights and shipbuilders and another as part-owner of a boat. They were all born in the parish of Paul which at that time encompassed Newlyn.

According to Cordelia's account in a taped interview with Geoffrey Wollaston, 'my mother's father helped to build St Peter's church with John Paul Vibert. He would attend church at Paul practically every day. He said: "let's see if LeGrice will let us have a bit of land to build a church."' The foundation stone was laid in 1864, the day her mother Jane was born, and the first service was held in 1866. 'The vicar apprenticed his son to grandfather to learn the wine and spirits trade.'

Their father was Cornishman Thomas Tregurtha, who came from a long line of blacksmiths from Wherrytown, Penzance. The 1851 census records another Thomas Tregurtha, with the note: 'grandfather, wine merchant's son.' The Tregurthas were tenants from 1703 to 1759 of Treropy land which belonged to the Robartes of Lanhydrock. There was also a Tregurtha Farm. The cottages in Newlyn which belonged to the family – Vine Cottage and its neighbour, Newlyn Cottage – seem to adjoin the Treropy farm land which was split up around 1818.

Thomas emigrated to Africa to seek his fortune, followed later by his elder son, Weymouth, but in 1915 in some money trouble Thomas shot himself. The family never spoke about this source of shame. It was a well kept secret for many years, and even close friends were unaware of the tragedy. Weymouth stayed in South Africa, where relatives still live. John remained in Britain and his son Peter was nephew to Mary and Cordelia.

A one time guest at Vine Cottage was the artist, Cedric Morris, who was to have a profound influence on the life of Mary Jewels. The other big artistic influence on the family was artist and sculptor Frank Dobson, who studied under Stanhope Forbes in Newlyn for a short unsatisfactory period; Dobson found Forbes' methods of teaching too entrenched in the past. Dobson had a studio behind Vine Cottage, a second house belonging to the Tregurthas, which they eventually sold. Dobson became a friend of the family and would later marry Cordelia. He drew a pencil portrait of Cordelia in 1912, and the following year painted *The Fortune Teller* in which he portrayed Mary Jewels as a gypsy.

Dobson later took to sculpture and was taught stone carving by a monumental stone mason at Newlyn. W H Snell & Son, Sculptors, Carvers and Granite Merchants, counted among their friends the artists Stanhope Forbes, the Harveys, the Garniers, and the Gotches for whom they produced memorials in Sancreed churchyard, as well as war memorials at Newlyn, Mousehole, Penzance and several other Cornish towns. It was probably the son William Arnold Snell from whom Dobson learnt some of his skills and he completed some of his first attempts at sculpture in Newlyn before the first world war. One of his earliest pieces to survive was made in 1915, *Seated Female Nude*, carved from a piece of oak from the local carpenter's shop. He sculpted a bronze head of Mary's classic beauty in 1920. Peter Tregurtha, Mary's nephew, remembers a granite head of Dobson's standing in the garden of Vine Cottage when he was a youngster, and that Elizabeth Muntz, sculptor and one time assistant in Dobson's London studio, gave him a hammer with his name, Peter, carved on the haft to try his hand in shaping stone.

Mary and Cordelia were well known in local artistic circles, getting to know the racy painter of horses Alfred Munnings, who established a studio and stables in neighbouring Lamorna Valley, where S.J. 'Lamorna' Birch held sway. Munnings was unpopular among the Methodist populace for his riotous parties. In 1913 Augustus John, whose reputation as a philanderer went ahead of him,

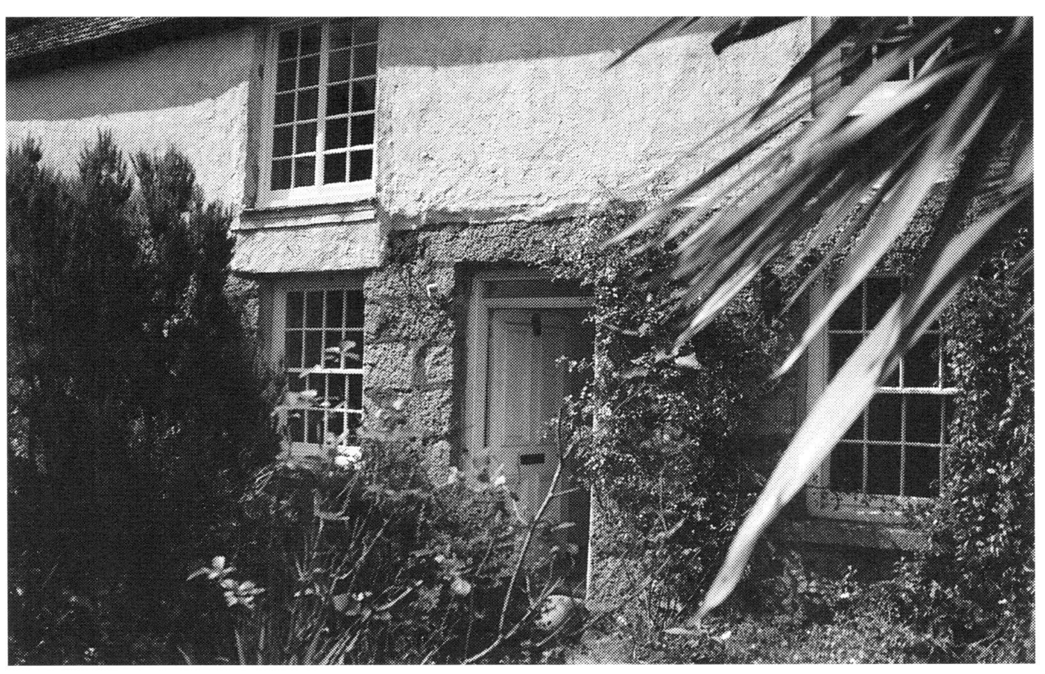

Vine Cottage, Newlyn in 1997, and sculptor Elizabeth Muntz (left) with Mary Jewels. [courtesy Dorset County Museum]

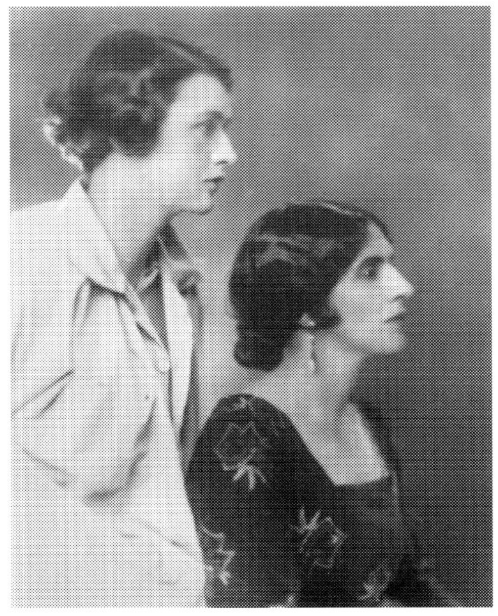

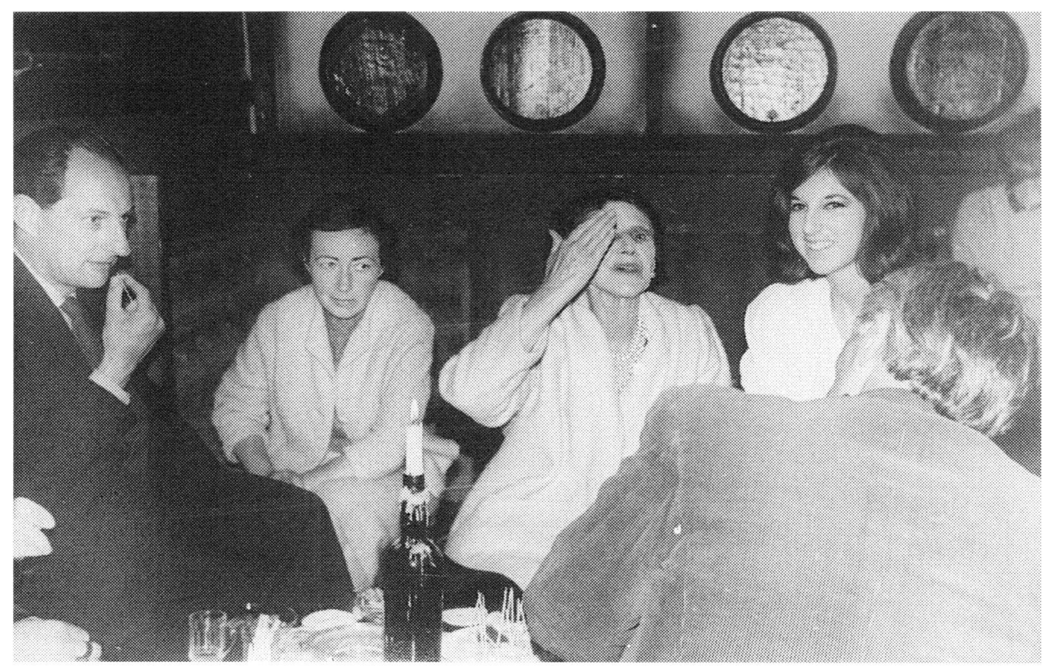

Mid-1960s: Michael Canney, Gwen Wood, Mary Jewels, Penny Sagar-Fenton and, back to camera, Arthur Caddick.

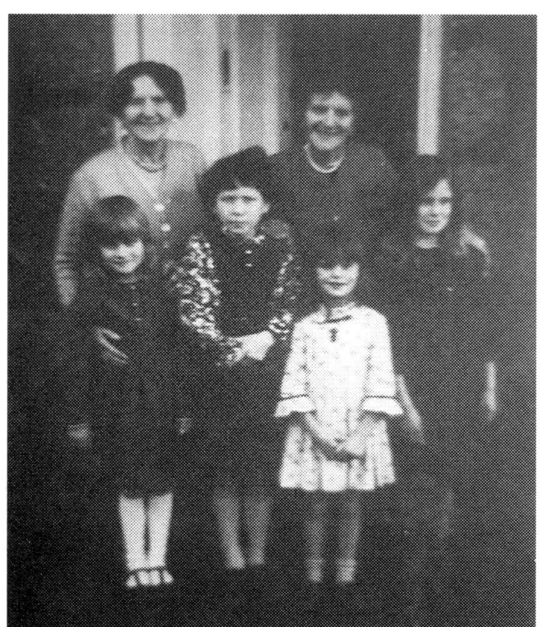

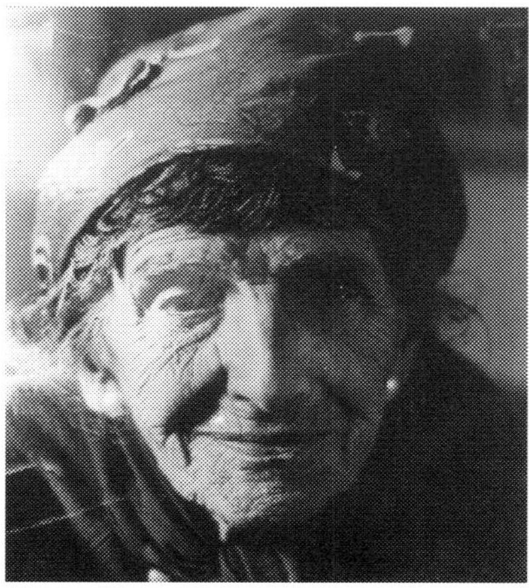

Mary Jewels in old age.

Mary and Cordelia with young friends, Newlyn 1966: second from left, Adrian Ryan's daughter, Vivien, among Polly Walker's daughters, from left to right, Anna, Holly and Sarah.

caused a stir locally when with his wife, Dorelia and family, he arrived to take up residence in Lamorna. They naturally met the Tregurtha sisters; John admired Mary's 'dark Romany beauty' and his fascination for the gypsy in her led to frequent trips over to Newlyn. Many artists took an idealised interest in folk life, gypsies, fair-ground and circus people, with Laura Knight, Munnings and Augustus John in particular endeavouring to capture the essence of their colourful, free spirit in their paintings. Indeed, John was always an active supporter and defender of the gypsy way of life.

Mary received great encouragement from Augustus John, who admired and collected her paintings. In 1928 he persuaded her to exhibit at the Warren Gallery in London and in an article on 'The Woman Artist' in *Vogue* magazine that year wrote that 'Mary Jewels' Cornish landscapes are remarkable for their intensity and earth-feeling. They blaze in the sight and are almost menacing in their hint of place magic. The colour and design carry something of the wonder of primitive vision and the luxuriance of barbaric nature. If Mrs Jewels avoids sophistication, her paintings will be of a refreshing interest.' Mary would not have been happy to see her work described as 'primitive' and 'barbaric'. She was simply painting the life and times of the fishing village of Newlyn as she saw them, with no thought of the menace which Augustus John read into her work. However, he genuinely thought a great deal of her paintings and was anxious to obtain some for his own collection. He sent a postcard (since lost) telling her to get out of the kitchen and paint. According to Sven Berlin, the sisters in turn 'thought the world of Augustus John'.

In 1929 John wrote from Chelsea:

Dear Mary,

I would greatly like to see your recent work. Are you coming up to London with it or sending it? I will do my best to get you a show arranged somewhere. I shall want some of your things myself, I am sure. Let me know when I shall be able to see them.

In 1932 he was writing from Salisbury:

Dear Mary,

Here's the cheque. I am delighted with the additions to my collection. The Village, Paul, The Mill, all excellent. [he names two other paintings which are indecipherable] 'I think I could have one of your things for a drop-curtain for the [indecipherable theatre] if you like it. Dodo [Dorelia] hopes to go over to see you, and the Pitmans would like to accompany her. I told them you probably would not object. I much enjoyed seeing you and Delia again and meeting your excellent mother. I look forward to another visit. Remember my parting words. Hope they will be fully justified. A J

Those parting words were doubtless encouraging, perhaps suggesting that her reputation would grow. The letters he wrote showed respect, and a careful choice of words. It is likely that their 'excellent mother' was a careful chaperone and ever alive to the possibility of unseemly advances from the notorious John. Mrs Tregurtha used to 'preside over things' and could be quite overawing.

Mary began painting in her mid-thirties after being given a canvas, a brush, and four tubes of paint by Cedric Morris in 1919 and told to complete a painting by the end of the day. Morris came to Cornwall from London in 1916 and lived in Zennor, from where he paid frequent visits to St Ives and the studio of New Zealand artist, Frances Hodgkins, whose portrait he painted. In 1919 he was in Newlyn and painted *Landscape at Newlyn*. He also assisted Dobson with the casting of some of his sculptures and modelled for him. Morris was a guest of Mrs Tregurtha for a short time but moved to a house overlooking Newlyn Harbour, named the Bowgie, with his lifelong friend the artist, Lett Haines. Mary began helping Cedric 'decorate lamp shades with seagulls', perhaps for his house. Morris was impressed with her work and declared her 'a natural artist'. He left Cornwall in 1920 but made frequent return trips.

From the moment she completed the first painting for Cedric Morris, Mary became entranced with the idea of being an artist. She began to paint the life of her native Cornwall, its fishing fleet of seine netters and trawlers, harbours, landscapes, and the tumbling cottages of the inhabitants. She also painted biblical and literary scenes like *Resurrection* and *Leder and the Swan*. In their dream-like quality and innocence, these have some likeness to the work of Chagall, although Mary's figures have also a seductive appeal. *Leder and the Swan*, also titled *The Lady of Shallot*, was exhibited at the Newlyn Gallery in 1976. Her paintings of trees have a lyricism and charm unique to her and quite beyond the capabilities of either Alfred Wallis or Bryan Pearce.

She was entirely self taught, rather like William J George, who lived in the neighbouring fishing village of Mousehole. He was a fisherman, who took to painting when he retired from the sea. Mary would have felt some affinity with George, not only because he was Cornish, but because he was well read. She knew of Alfred Wallis, whose paintings she did not admire, and was quick to tell people that she began painting some few years before he did. Sven Berlin recalls her saying that she met Wallis, but they did not get on – Wallis was 'very

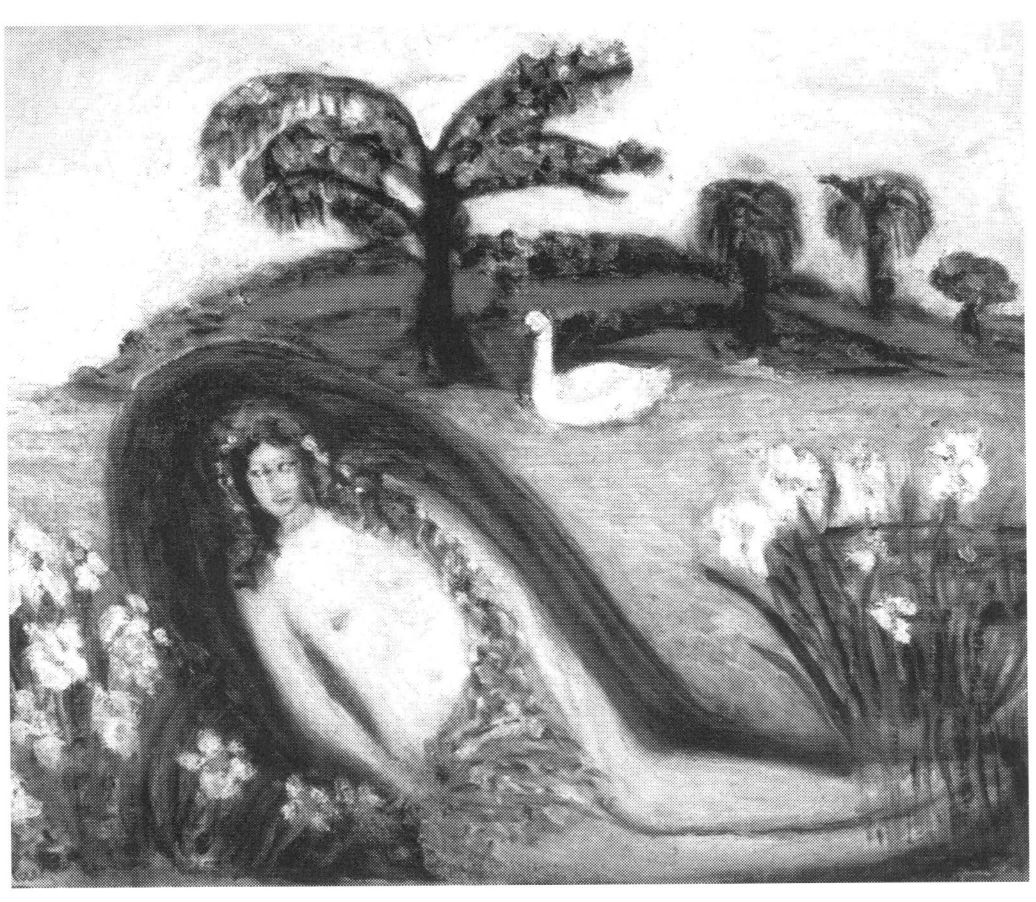

Mary Jewels: *Leda and the Swan*, oil on canvas. [courtesy Austin/Desmond Fine Art]

difficult' – or like each other's work. Unlike Wallis, of course, she was well educated, having attended private schools, and according to Michael Canney's notebooks was 'touched by a certain metropolitan sophistication'. Cordelia always said that it was her sister Mary – a native Cornish woman – rather than Wallis, whose paintings represented the authentic Cornish voice.

In the presentation of her work Frank Ruhrmund thought her 'as unchanging as a slab of Cornish granite'. Certainly Jewels remained true to herself, untouched by any influence other than her subject matter. But was this unpolished slab of Cornish granite, who had had no art training, used by Cedric Morris as an experiment? Did he give her paints and canvas to see what would happen? He was interested in primitive art (as shown in his painting *Landscape at Newlyn* 1919), as were Frank Dobson and Ben Nicholson, who knew each other at this time. Primitive and naive art were fashionable among the younger, more progressive artists and many were themselves exploring the genre. Whatever Morris's motive, they had found a natural painter in Mary Jewels.

Writing about 'The Newlyn School of Painters' in the Winter, 1974 issue of *Cornish Review*, Lorraine Craig states that 'another famous visitor in those days was Augustus John. It was he who gave Mary Jewels, the only living artist left of the Newlyn School, the few art lessons she ever had. Finding her confined to the house after hurting her leg, he caught her dabbling with pencil and paint to pass the time. Looking at her work he exclaimed, "Why, you're an artist" and was so impressed by her picture that he sat down there and then to teach her.'

Nearly forty years after she had begun to paint, Alan Bowness wrote of Mary Jewels in an article 'Mary Jewels and Naive Painting' in the autumn, 1958 issue of *Painter and Sculptor*, 'Her paintings have a certain grace and air of distinction that is hard to explain. It perhaps results from the fact that she is not the popular conception of a naive painter – an illiterate peasant working in a vacuum of ignorance – but the very opposite – a woman, by no means out of touch with artistic circles, whose great natural gifts for art have gone untrained and remain intact and unspoiled.'

At the outbreak of the first world war, Frank Dobson joined the forces, but was invalided out and sent to recuperate at the Great Central Hotel, Marylebone, London, which had been acquired by the war office as a convalescent home for soldiers. Cordelia travelled up from Cornwall and they were married at Christ Church, Marylebone in April, 1918. They found accommodation in Chelsea, at 14 Trafalgar Studios, Manresa Road, where they met and were befriended by many people whose portraits were sculpted by Frank Dobson. The summer of 1919 saw Frank and Cordelia in Newlyn where he began carving *Concertina Man* from Portland stone and his career as a sculptor was well underway with a variety of commissions.

Mary Jewels was a frequent guest at the Dobson's Chelsea home. The young Canadian sculptor, Elizabeth Muntz noted in her diary that sometimes, when Cordelia could no longer tolerate the noise of chiselling stone, she would go out with her sister Mary or the wives of writer Leo Myers and the painter Edward Wadsworth. Elizabeth Muntz enjoyed working with Dobson and from Cordelia she learned about the fishing industry and life in Newlyn as they sat by the studio fire drinking tea.

Friends of the Dobsons included the Russian ballerina Lydia Lopokova, who trained at the Imperial Ballet School and afterwards left Russia to join Diaghilev's company. Dobson carved a bust of Lydia in 1923 and caught the grace and balletic nature of the dance in a study of her hands. It was while sitting for her portrait that Lydia became a particular friend of Cordelia. Other friends were the three Sitwells, who lived close by in the King's Road, Chelsea. Dobson made a polished bronze head of Osbert Sitwell, later owned by another friend, T E Lawrence, and presented to the Tate in 1950. He had also designed and painted a huge curtain for Edith Sitwell for the celebrated performance of *Facade*, in which she recited her poems, which had been set to music by William Walton, through a megaphone behind the closed curtain.

In these early years Ben Nicholson was a frequent visitor to the Dobsons at Chelsea. Cordelia recalled one incident. "Ben was considered at that particular stage rather a dandy. On one occasion when he was invited to tea, he took hold of the tablecloth and pulled it off the table with all the china, because he didn't like the cloth. The next day he sent a tea service from Heals with a note of apology."

In later years Nicholson saw Mary Jewels' work in Newlyn, although no comment is made of any influence she may have had on him. Cordelia and Frank Dobson often stayed with Ben's father, Sir William Nicholson, and his second wife Edith at Rottingdean, near Brighton, probably at the time Dobson was forming the cast for a bronze of their small daughter Elizabeth (Penny) which was completed when the child was two or three years old.

Cordelia and Frank Dobson parted company early in 1924. Lydia Lopokova remarked in a letter to her husband, Maynard Keynes, 'Delia [the name by which Cordelia was known generally] is a changed woman.' She had taken up weaving which was 'uplifting to her', and tried to be independent on separating from Dobson. 'Her work is great contentment for her, so that she does not concentrate as much as she used to on Dobby [Dobson] . . . Her heart is not of Dobby's stone, Poor Delia! We were true friends to each other.'

Cordelia's attempt to earn a living was short lived. Unable to support herself, she returned to Newlyn, where she had a nervous breakdown and lived a fairly reclusive life, hiding behind her mother and Mary. This lasted for some years, but she later reasserted herself and became a dominant figure for Mary, their lives so inextricably entwined that one cannot write about Mary without regard for Delia. The sisters lived for the rest of their lives at Vine Cottage. In 1926 Cordelia had known Dobson for 15 years and been married to him for eight, although they did not divorce until 1929. This association had been fruitful for both sisters. They had moved in artistic and social circles quite outside any such possibilities in the small fishing village of Newlyn, where, it was true, many famous artists visited but few remained. Neither remarried; Mary, after being widowed in the war, nor Cordelia, after her divorce.

Of herself as a painter, Mary Jewels repeated her often quoted words in an interview with fellow Cornishman, Frank Ruhrmund, the year before she died, 'I am influenced by nobody and entirely self-taught. A true Celt, loving my Cornwall, with its lovely stone hedges, the beautiful blue sea, puff-ball clouds, little fishing coves and corn in stooks. What more could one wish for?' She always disliked the 'primitive' label, saying it made her sound 'like some sort of savage'. Neither did she like to be referred to as a 'naive' painter which she felt labelled her 'an illiterate peasant'. Ruhrmund agreed and felt her work possessed grace and skill and that the term 'natural painter' was more appropriate.

Margo Maeckelberghe, another Cornish-born artist, knew Mary at one stage as a very sophisticated lady who wore clothes designed by Alec Walker of the famous Crysède company, who printed and manufactured silk and linen fabrics with workshops and retail outlets in Newlyn and St Ives.

In 1929 Alec Walker, after the break up of his marriage, left Crysède, deter-mined to pursue painting. He became a resident at the Tregenna Castle Hotel in St Ives. It was here that he created his design *St Ives Bay* for use on silk fabrics. He turned his room into a studio and filled it with new paintings and a panoramic view of the harbour, bay, and out to Godrevy lighthouse. Mary Jewels, and Dod Procter visited him there. Mary was impressed with the work, which she roundly declared better than Alfred Wallis or Van Gogh, and wanted to take away the huge mural painting which decorated the walls of the hotel room. Instead, she invited Alec to live at Vine Cottage with Cordelia and Mrs Tregurtha, where they cared for him until he decided to leave Cornwall for London and set up his studio in Fitzroy Square. Alec's daughter Polly said the mural was decorated over after he left.

Some time later Mary and Dod Procter fell out and the rift was never mended. At that time Dod was a much admired painter of the female figure. Her picture *Morning* was exhibited at the Newlyn Gallery and bought for the nation by the *Daily Mail*, shown at the Royal Academy in 1927 and acclaimed 'painting of the year'. She was elected a Member of the Royal Academy in 1942. Dod was a

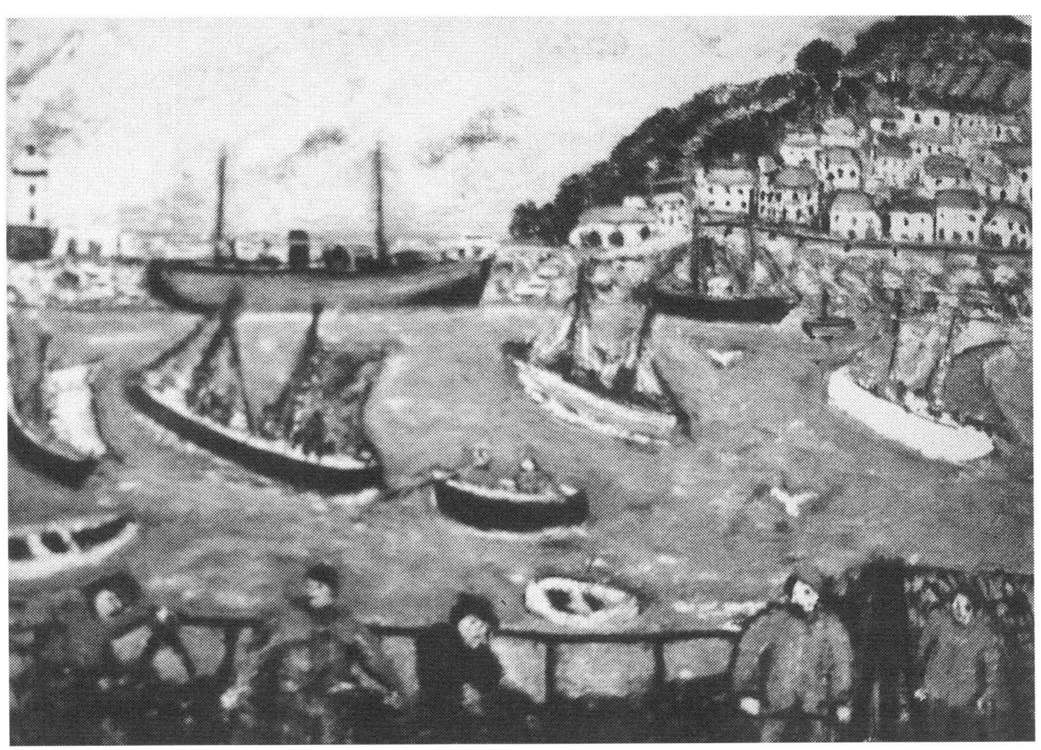

Mary Jewels: *Newlyn Harbour*.

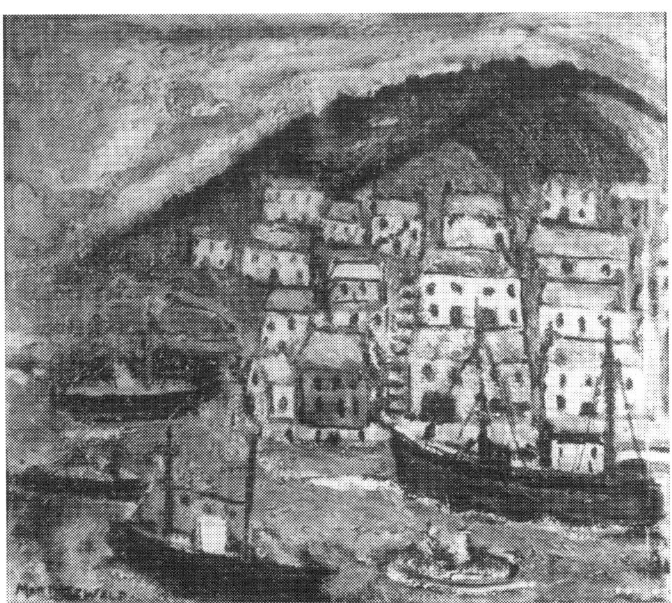

Mary Jewels: *Polperro*, 1962.
[courtesy Reg Watkiss
Collection]

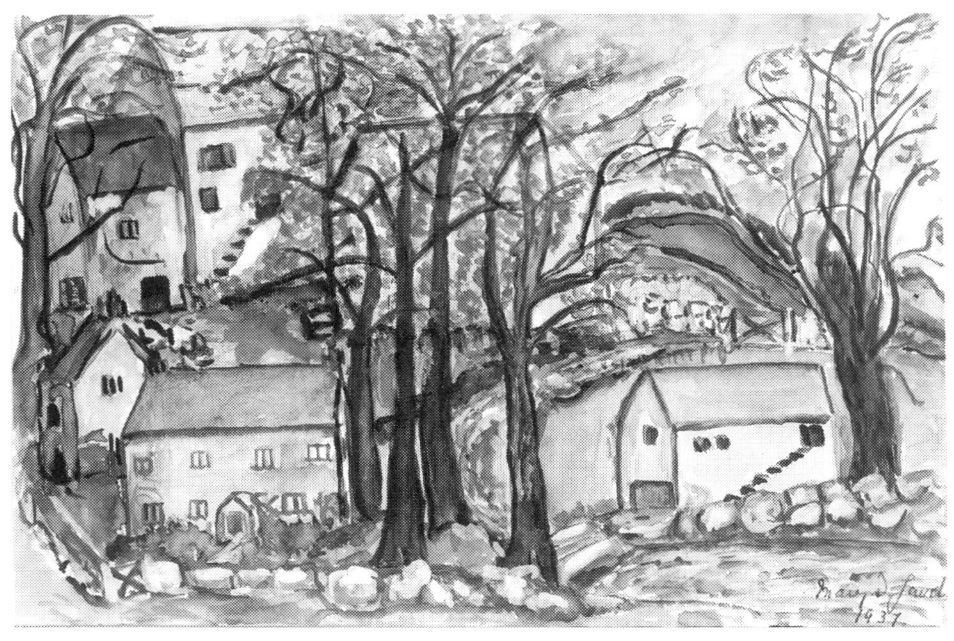

Mary Jewels: *Cottages with trees*, 1937. [courtesy Phillips Auctioneers]

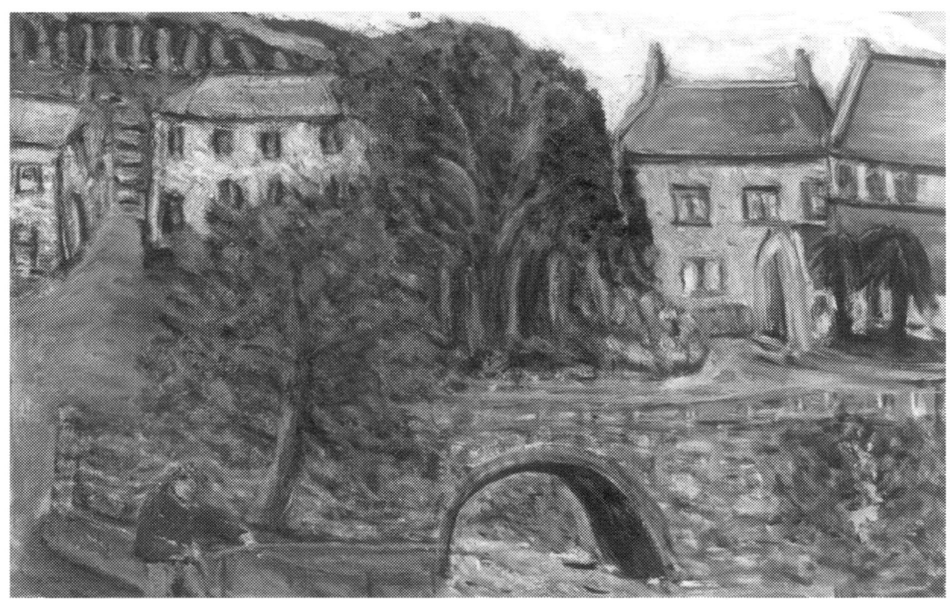

Mary Jewels: *Untitled*, oil on canvas. [courtesy Austin/Desmond Fine Art]

dedicated and hard working artist while Mary's output was slow and sporadic and she was not ambitious to exhibit. Probably neither agreed with the other's way of working. Mary's work was colourful with a dense impasto finish. Dod restricted her use of colour and her figures – sculptural and hardly touched by colour – seem cool compared with Mary's bright vibrancy. Even so, painting for Dod was a passion: 'Her devotion to truth was absolute and ruthless,' noted Noel Welch. Both women were outspoken and would have voiced their opinion of each other's work whether it pleased or offended.

Mary was involved with both the early and later Newlyn school of painters. She lived so long that she spanned the generations and exhibited with both, although she was not greatly interested in the work of other painters, as is often the way with artists of natural talent.

Mary possessed no studio but painted at Vine Cottage, in every room of the house, wherever it was warm and comfortable. She painted largely from memory, when the mood took her, but referred to the occasional small sketch or drawing. Her subjects included landscapes, portraits, the local population, and Cornish cottages, in a wealth of colour, seeming always to be climbing a steep hill. Her canvases were covered with thick textured oil paint, liberally applied with untoned colour. As Sven Berlin wrote, 'She painted the things loved by the Cornish Celts.' She loved to record the fishing fleet of Newlyn going in and out of the harbour about its business of which, as a native, she had a deep understanding. Although better known for her oil paintings, she also worked in watercolour, keeping that vibrancy of colour for which she was so distinguished.

In 1945, the war over, Sven Berlin – sculptor, painter, and first biographer of Alfred Wallis – along with former doctor lately turned artist, John Wells, visited Mary Jewels in Newlyn to see her work. Mary smiled with pleasure at their interest and showed the paintings stored in the back room of the cottage. Writing in his autobiography, *The Coat of Many Colours*, Berlin said that 'she understands the beautiful proportions of the cottages in which her people have always lived, built out of stone and everywhere to be found; also the little fields bordered by stone hedges; and the grotesque armies of corn stooks; the figures of men shaped by centuries of work; the incandescence of light on water, boats that float and do not get stuck in a sea of paint; yet boats seen from the land and not ships articulated at sea. All largely unconscious.' John Wells, on looking at her painting *Cornfields with Peasants*, dubbed her the English Van Gogh. Sven Berlin recalled in the 1990s that 'it was through Augustus John that I knew about Mary Jewels. I met Augustus in Mousehole. I used to go and see her because I got on with her and had one of her paintings for a time.'

In 1946 Sven wrote to Augustus from Porthgwidden Studio, The Island, St Ives, that he had written an article on Mary for *Horizon* magazine, quoting from

Augustus' article in *Vogue* in 1928, and asking him to show some of Mary's paintings to the editor, Peter Watson, who had not heard of her. He also wrote that he was hoping to arrange an exhibition and would have some of the work photographed. 'I think the self portrait may be one to include. The other day I met Mary on Newlyn Bridge. She told me she was working hard.' Unfortunately, the article wasn't published.

In 1949, as is well documented, the St Ives Society of Artists was thrown into disarray at an acrimonious meeting, which led a breakaway group of artists of the more modern outlook to form the Penwith Society of Arts and Crafts in Cornwall. The new society was inaugurated at a meeting held in the Castle Inn, St Ives and Mary Jewels, although not a founder member, was invited to take up membership in that same year. She resigned in 1952. Of one of their first exhibitions Patrick Heron wrote that Kate Nicholson's and Mary Jewels' work was 'in sympathy with the full blooded French use of colour.' In the 1950 spring exhibition of the Penwith Society Henry Trevor reported that 'Mary Jewels, Tom Early, Ben Nicholson, Peter Lanyon and John Wells are obviously painters with the serious purpose of capturing the Cornwall that is felt, rather than seen.'

In the early 1950s Mary visited friends in St Ives and painted a harbour scene titled *Gathering Storm*. She painted it in a day and presented it to her friends when she called round for tea. It was a very busy painting of clouds, seagulls, boats, the pier, harbour and her distinctive feature of cottages piling up as if on a hill. Her particular dark blue colouring was very much in evidence to lend drama to the subject. Nearly half a century later it still has that freshness of vision as on that single day in St Ives when she began and completed it. Alan Bowness also knew Mary about this time. 'I got to meet Mary in the fifties. I supplied her with canvas and paints to encourage her.' He found her work 'gentle and humorous [opening] our eyes to a world that is delightful in its freshness and charm.' He believes her output was not very prolific although her painting life spanned over fifty years, whereas Wallis painted for the last seventeen years of his life and produced work in a frenzy of activity, and W J George worked on hundreds of paintings for twenty years until his death at the age of 94.

Graham Binns became a friend when he was with the Arts Council and visited Mary and Cordelia in their cottage over many years. 'Tea was always taken in the parlour. They were very Cornish, and such fun. I bought several paintings from Mary by going round to tea.' The painter, Adrian Ryan, who lived in Mousehole at various periods in his life and once had a studio known as The Owls Nest over a net loft, recalled that Mary liked to be paid for paintings at £5 a month. He bought two in the sixties, *Lily of the Valley* and *Cornish Cottages, Newlyn*. He noted that Augustus John's children also bought Mary's work.

Artist Alethea Garstin was a friend of both William George and Alfred Wallis and tried to promote their work, to the point of including a representation of one of Wallis's pictures in the background of her painting *Molly by Gaslight*. She also knew Mary Jewels and owned two of her paintings of trees, later owned by the writer Eric Quayle. At a meeting of the Newlyn Society of Artists in 1956 – the year that Michael Canney took over as curator of the gallery there – Alethea proposed that they invite Mary to send a group of four to six paintings to the summer exhibition. In 1957 Peter Lanyon, Cornishman, artist, maker of constructions, supporter and defender of all things Cornish, wrote to fellow artist, Patrick Hayman, 'You will be pleased to hear that Mary Jewels has been showing lately in the Gallery at Newlyn. She is doing very good work with no paint and very little hope while the big guns roar and batter at Art. I am supposed to be going to a party tonight in St Ives, full of artists, but I can't trust myself to be good.' Her work was shown in a mixed exhibition at Newlyn in 1958.

In 1960 the City Art Gallery, Plymouth, mounted an exhibition organised by Michael Canney, *Painters from Cornwall*, in which Mary was represented along with 40 artists from West Cornwall. This was the exhibition from which the Gallery purchased Mary Jewels' *Salt Boat*, Alan Lowndes' *A Street in St Ives* and a Cornish landscape by Michael Canney. In the early 1970s the artist Sheila Cavell-Hicks organised an exhibition at the Queens Hotel, Penzance, which showed the work of Ithell Colquhoun, Bryan Lawrey Warren, Matthew Eddy Rowe and Mary Jewels.

John Halkes became director of the The Newlyn Gallery in 1974 and offered Mary a solo show in May, 1977. Showing in that exhibition was the painting *Cornubia* which Mary painted in the 1940s. It is an unusual picture of a woman with her back to the viewer, head in profile, against a backdrop of the rising landscape of Newlyn; Cornubia is from the Latin for Cornwall, and the picture supposedly represents the county's fertility.

In 1977 Mary was ninety one years of age, eccentric and somewhat forgetful. John Halkes recalled that 'she sat downstairs in the gallery with her hands in her lap, wearing a pair of bright yellow gloves.' They afterwards discovered that they were yellow rubber kitchen gloves. In June of that year John Halkes wrote to the sisters.

Dear Mary and Cordelia,

As you know, the Ikon Gallery at Birmingham are anxious to have a Mary Jewels in their exhibition of *British Primitive and Naive Painting* this summer. Now I *know* you do not like the title but I think the exhibition would be incomplete without one of your paintings, Mary.

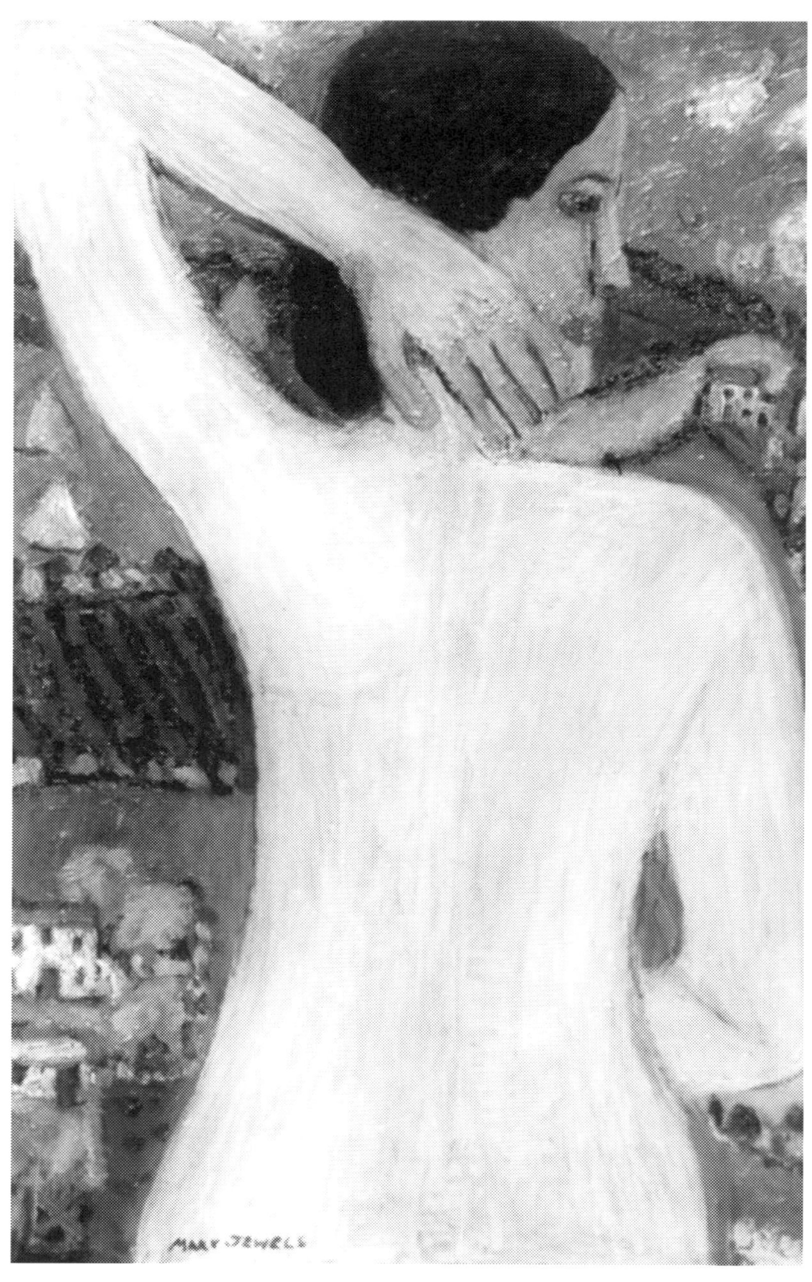

Mary Jewels: *Cornubia*. [courtesy Penlee House Art Gallery & Museum, Penzance]

> If you agree to take part – I would be pleased to collect the chosen
> piece, insure and dispatch it to Birmingham – you would have to do
> nothing more than agree (you could even register your disapproval of
> the exhibition title while taking part!).

Whether Mary did indeed register her disapproval by *not* taking part is
unknown. She disliked showing with painters labelled as naive or primitive. She
is not listed among the exhibitors and may have decided that at the age of 91 she
simply could not be bothered, or was incapable, or perhaps Cordelia, who
tended to manage their affairs, decided against it. The exhibition took place in
September and Mary died in December of that year. Had she been represented,
she would have shown alongside other painters included in this present book,
Ronnie Copas, Martin Leman, Alan Lowndes, Bryan Pearce and Alfred Wallis.

During the last few months of her life Mary deteriorated mentally and
Cordelia, who found it difficult to look after her, had her removed to the
hospital at Barncoose, near Redruth, where she died. Polly Walker, who used to
take meals to them sometimes, suggested that a home help would be beneficial
but Delia wouldn't hear of it and Polly accompanied Mary to the hospital.

Polly recalled that it was Mary who was the first to visit her mother, Kay
Walker, at Myrtle Cottage, Newlyn, just after Polly was born and as she grew
up she was a frequent visitor at Vine Cottage, as were her own children, and
those of Casper and Mary John. The sisters were fond of children and it seems
they were held in high regard by the evacuees who stayed with them during the
war, and who continued to visit them until a few years before Mary died.

Fellow artist Gay Sagar-Fenton, who had been a good friend and neighbour
since the 1960s, organised a party to celebrate Cordelia's one hundredth
birthday. Cordelia had impressed upon Gay that she didn't want any fuss but at
party time she asked, 'Where's the Mayor?' Cordelia also spent a short time in
hospital where her doctor had sent her for a rest, while trying to make her
cottage more comfortable in her absence. She had managed alone in Vine
Cottage until six months before she died in 1989 at the age of 102. The sisters
are buried in the churchyard at Paul with their mother.

Among those attending Mary's funeral were the artists Paul Feiler, Jack
Pender and Charles Breaker. Frank Ruhrmund wrote in his obituary that Mary
Downing Jewels was 'a true Celtic artist with a Celtic vision'. Paul Feiler got to
know Mary because he had taken over Bryan Wynter's studio, previously occupied by Stanhope Forbes. His children were always welcome at Vine Cottage.

Mary and Cordelia delighted in talking of famous people they had known. They
had been on friendly terms with Stanhope Forbes and the artists of the early

Newlyn School, exchanged visits, letters and Christmas cards. Forbes painted a picture of Vine Cottage and in a letter to Cordelia in April 1943 he wrote:

Dear Mrs Dobson

I have great pleasure in asking you and your sister to accept the photograph of the picture which you both so kindly helped me to paint last summer. You will be pleased to hear it is beautifully placed in the Royal Academy. This morning I have heard the good news that it was sold on the opening day. I shall never forget the happy times I spent in your charming garden. Fondest wishes to you both. I hope to see you ere long. Yours ever, S A Forbes

Harold Harvey, the Cornish-born artist living in Newlyn, used to leave his painting gear in the cottage. It may well be that his picture *Woman Reading in a Garden*, c.1902 was a painting of Vine Cottage, with perhaps Mrs Tregurtha as the sitter. Some years later, 'Vine Cottage,' it was noted by Michael Canney, 'was the communications centre for information about the two colonies. Cordelia was the mistress of total recall, from what Henry Moore was wearing at a nineteen-twenties arts ball, to what Sacheverell Sitwell said to the butler when the Dobsons came to visit.' She was also capable of reciting great swathes of Shakespeare, even at the age of one hundred.

They were very fond of Christopher Wood who was always referred to as 'dear, dear Kit', long after his tragic death in 1930. However, Wood has nowhere stated that he was interested in the paintings of Mary Jewels, in spite of his admiration of the naive style, and having been invited to tea and in turn inviting Mary and Cordelia to tea in St Ives. According to an account by Adrian Ryan, Mary claimed that it was she who taught Christopher Wood to paint. Michael Canney's Newlyn notebook records: 'Mary's pictures I thought less good than her conversation, but at their best they may indeed have influenced Christopher Wood', and Sven Berlin was to write that 'Christopher Wood, through Ben, met Mary Jewels and became a friend and admirer of her work.' This does not appear to be borne out by Wood's comment in a letter to Winifred Nicholson some time in 1928, when he thought the sisters were 'a poor female version of Cedric Morris and Lett Haines'. These are hardly the words of an admirer.

From all accounts the sisters withdrew from society as they got older; both became cantankerous, insulted at the slightest remark, or would break their friendship over something of which they disapproved. There were often personality clashes with guests, but since they both lived to a great age, they attracted

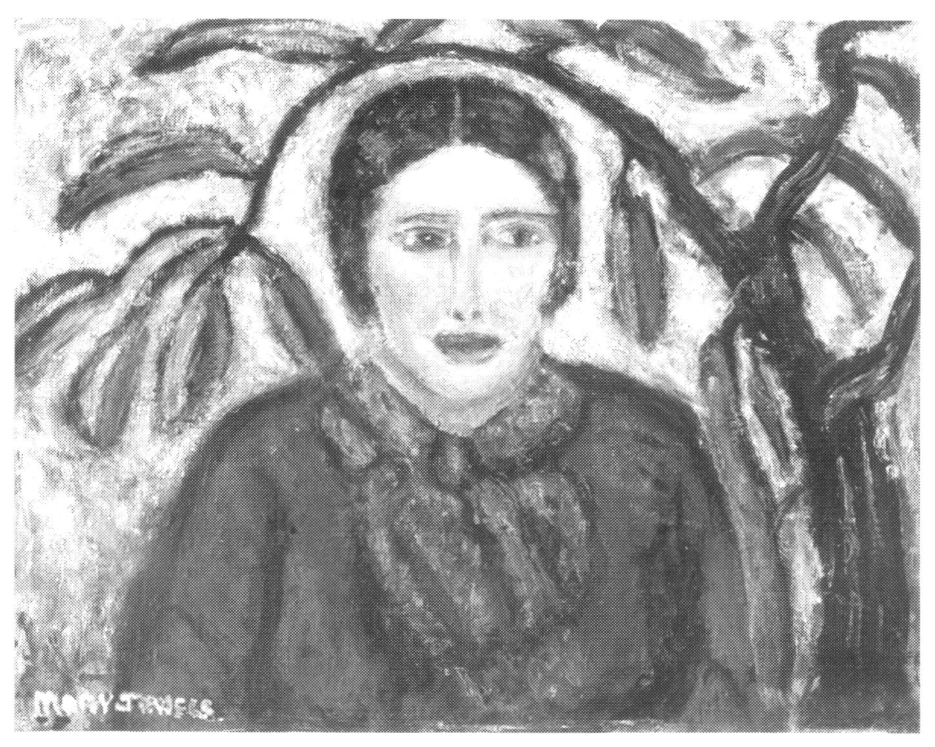

Mary Jewels self portrait, oil on canvas, 1947. [courtesy Austin/Desmond Fine Art]

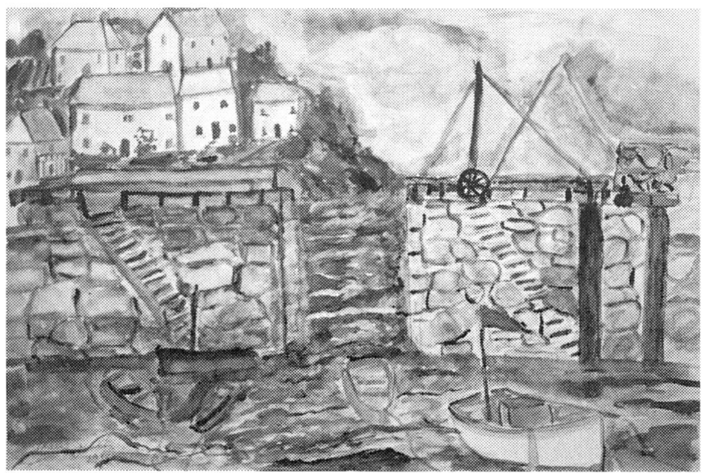

Mary Jewels: *Mousehole*. [courtesy Wills Lane Gallery, St Ives]

many visitors to the cottage for their interesting conversation and independence of mind.

At Mary's death in 1977 there were 30 or 40 paintings in the cottage and Cordelia, short of money, sold these for £50 each in batches to a London art dealer. He also, apparently, negotiated for some work by Alfred Wallis whilst in the West Country. Polly Walker said, "After Mary's death there were a few dealers interested in her work and I warned Delia to be wary of them, but as usual, she wouldn't take any notice."

One of Mary's rare commissions was from Clarks Shoes in Street, Somerset, for a series of small pictures. The company sent a car daily, to drive her to certain spots to paint in the countryside around 1930.

According to one reviewer, 'to Newlyn's shame', Mary was not included in the great retrospective exhibition of Newlyn painters in 1985. She was essentially a Newlyn artist, and Cordelia, who was very proud and protective of her sister's work, never forgave the Newlyn Gallery for this omission.

Two paintings, *Cornubia* and *Cornish Landscape*, were included in the exhibition at the Tate Gallery, London, in 1985, *St Ives 1939–64 Twenty Five Years of Painting, Sculpture and Pottery*, even though she was not strictly a St Ives artist. David Brown, who curated the show said, 'I cast my net very wide and I included Mary Jewels because I think she is a very under-estimated painter and was worth showing.' Her work was represented in Cornwall County Council's Centenary Show, *A Century of Art in Cornwall 1889–1989*, but little has been written of an interesting talent, despite Denis Val Baker's hope, in 1953, that 'Newlyn might well pay greater tribute to Mary Jewels.'

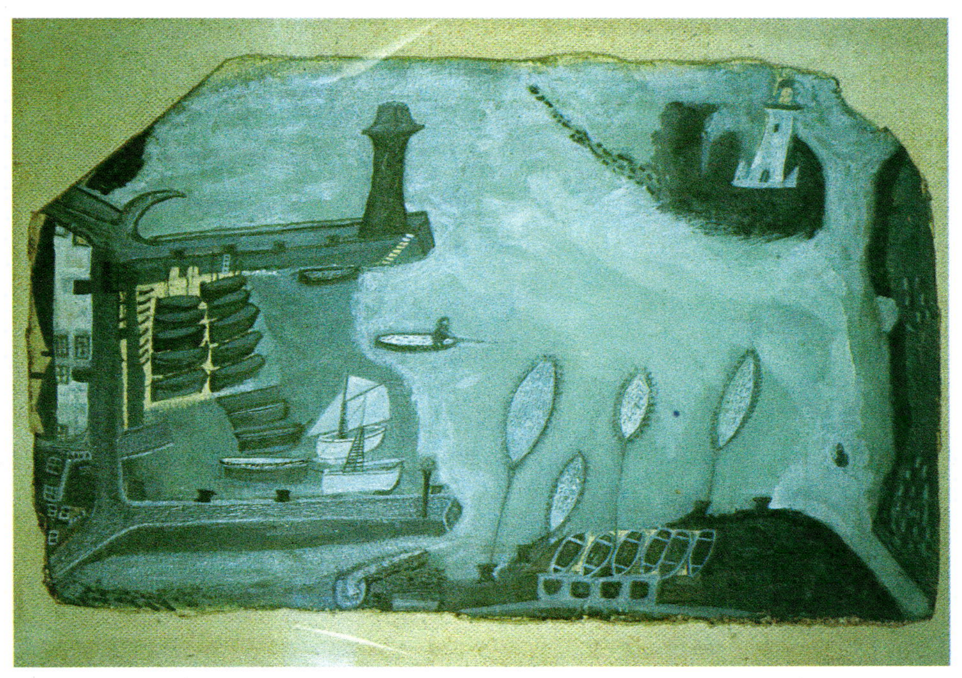

Alfred Wallis: *St Ives Harbour and Godrevy*. [courtesy Dr Roger Slack]

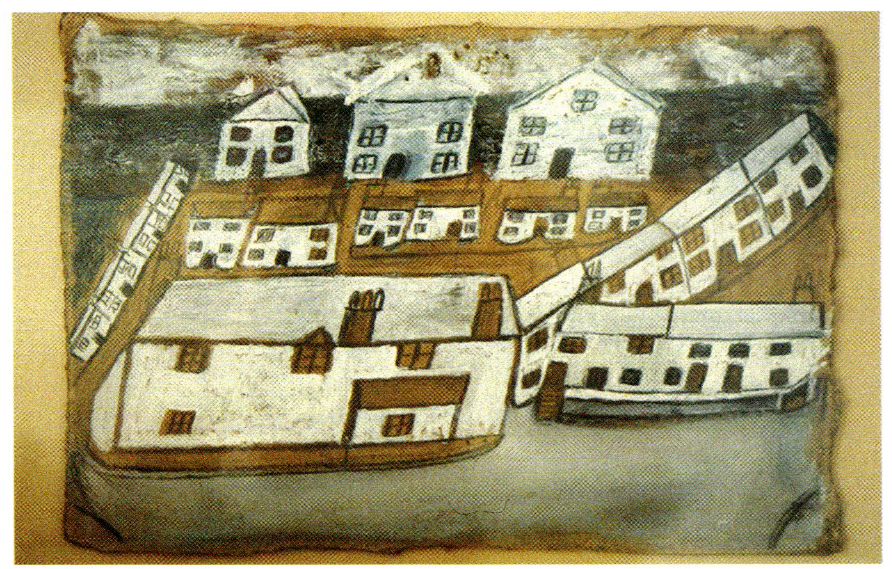

Alfred Wallis: *Houses in St Ives*.

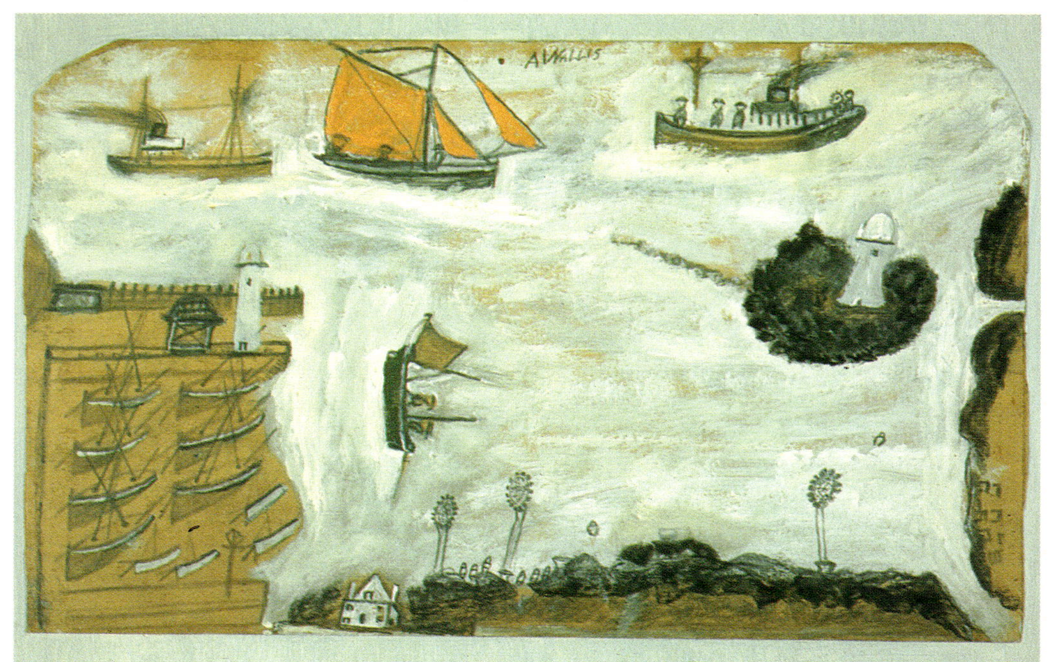

Alfred Wallis: *St Ives sail boats and steamers.*

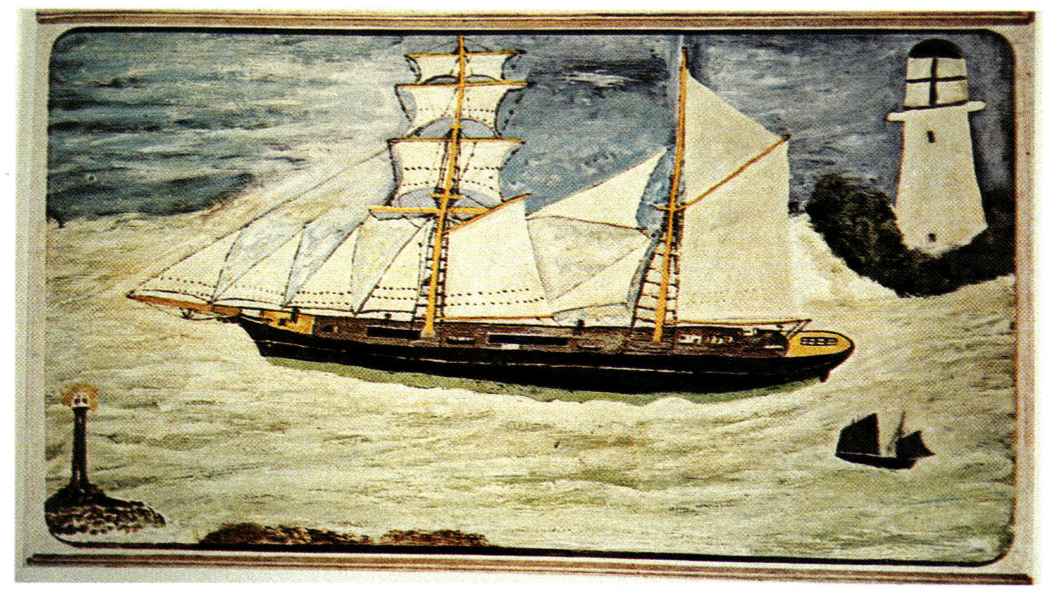

Alfred Wallis: *Full sail with lighthouse.*

114

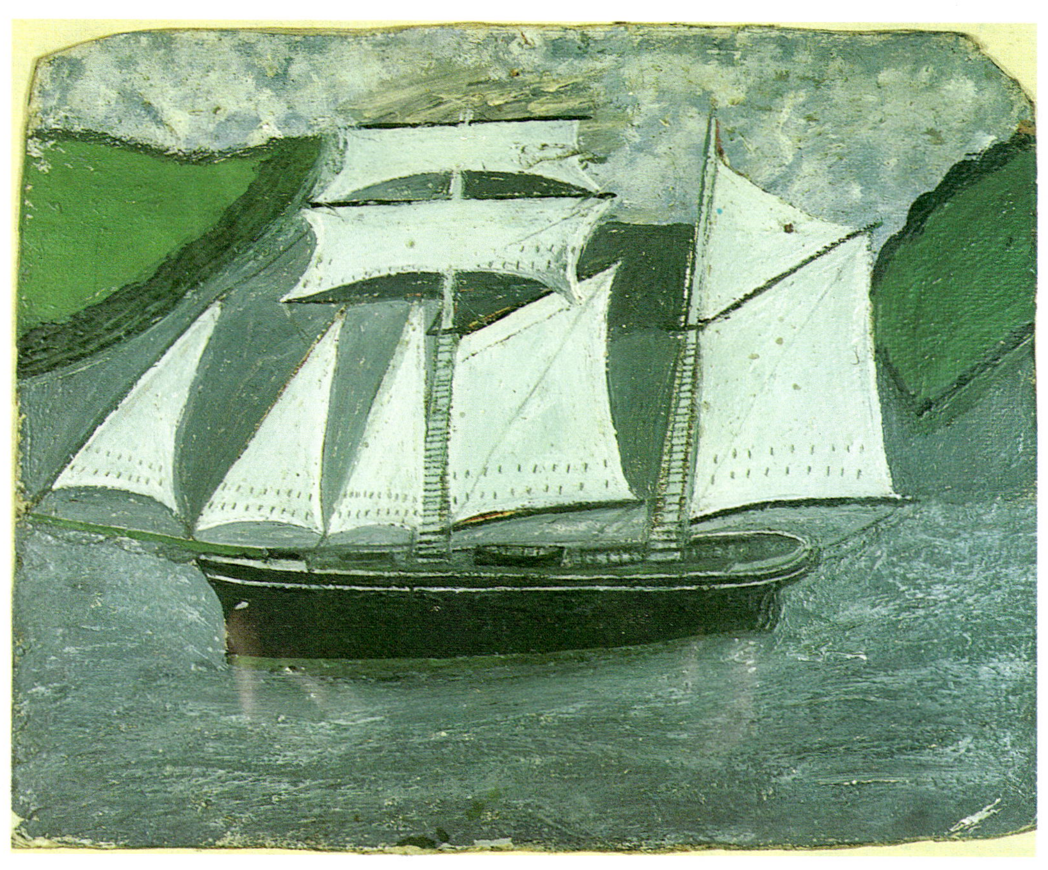

Alfred Wallis: *Schooner in full sail*. [courtesy Dr Roger Slack]

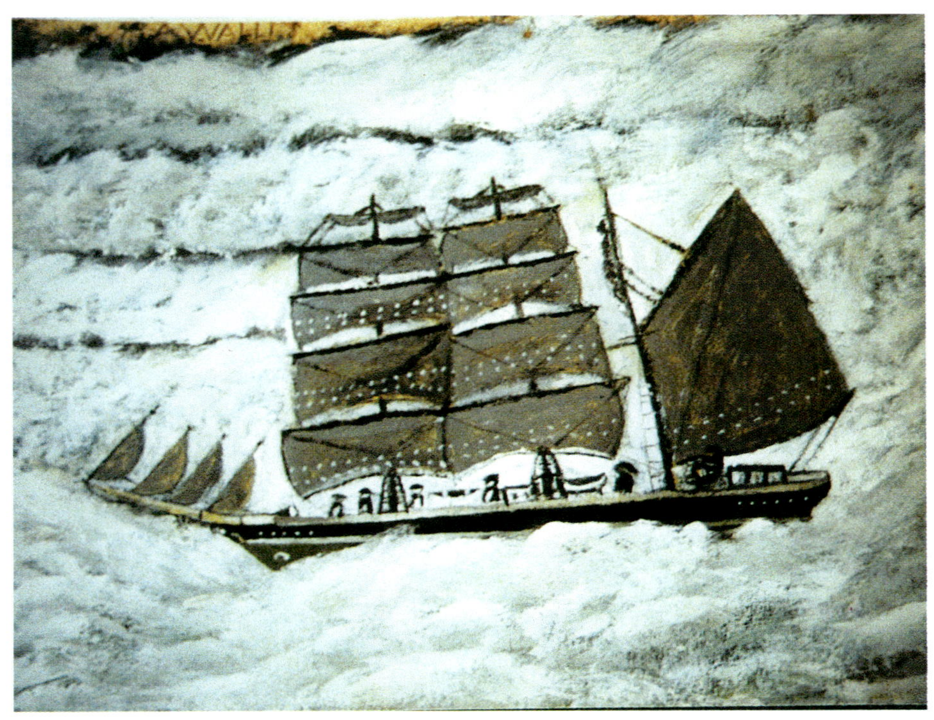

Alfred Wallis: *Schooner*.

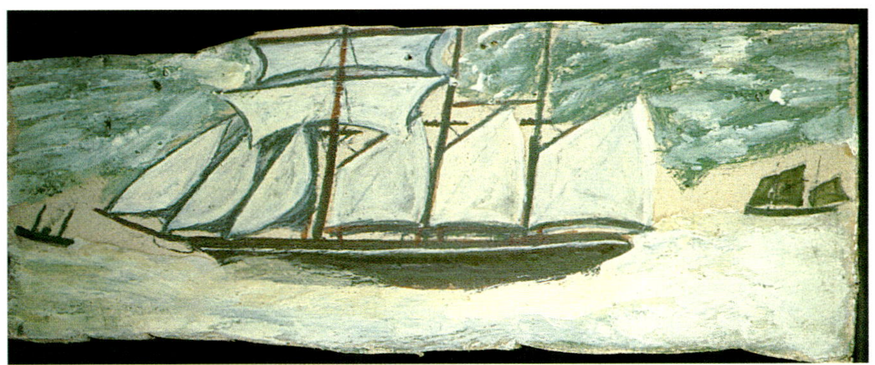

Alfred Wallis: *Full sail*. [courtesy Dr Roger Slack]

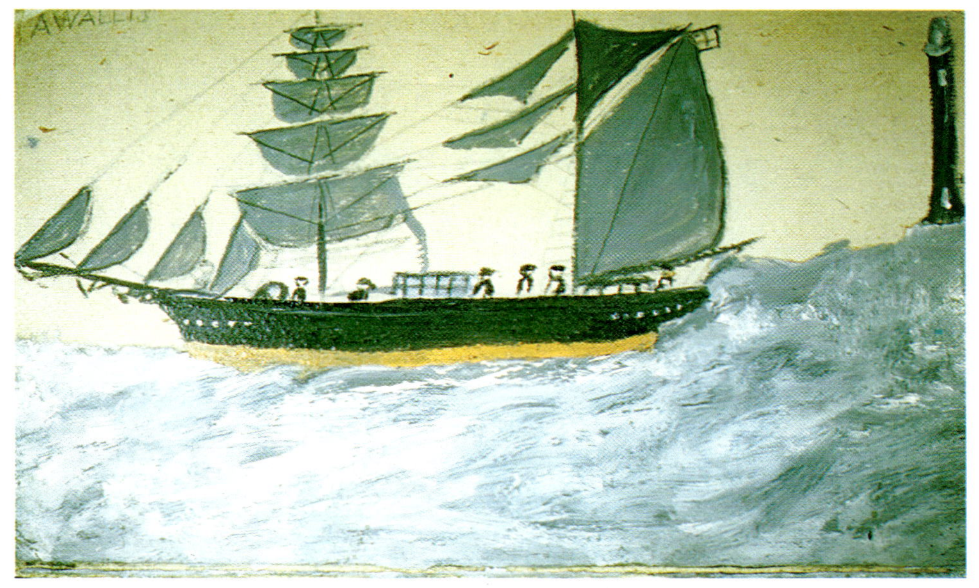

Alfred Wallis: *Full sail*. [courtesy Dr Roger Slack]

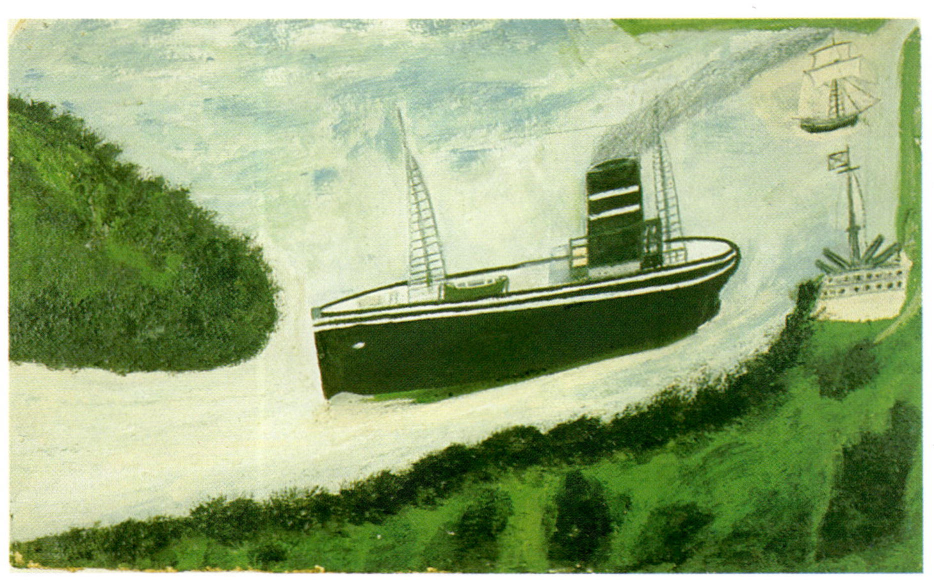

Alfred Wallis: *Steamboat*.

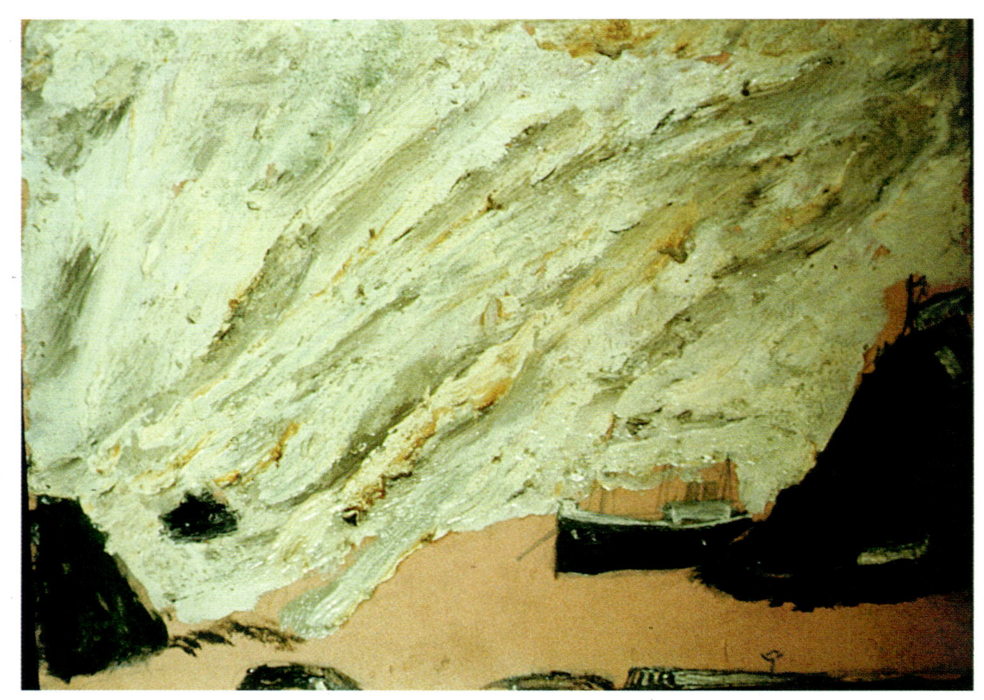

Alfred Wallis: *The Alba*, 1938.

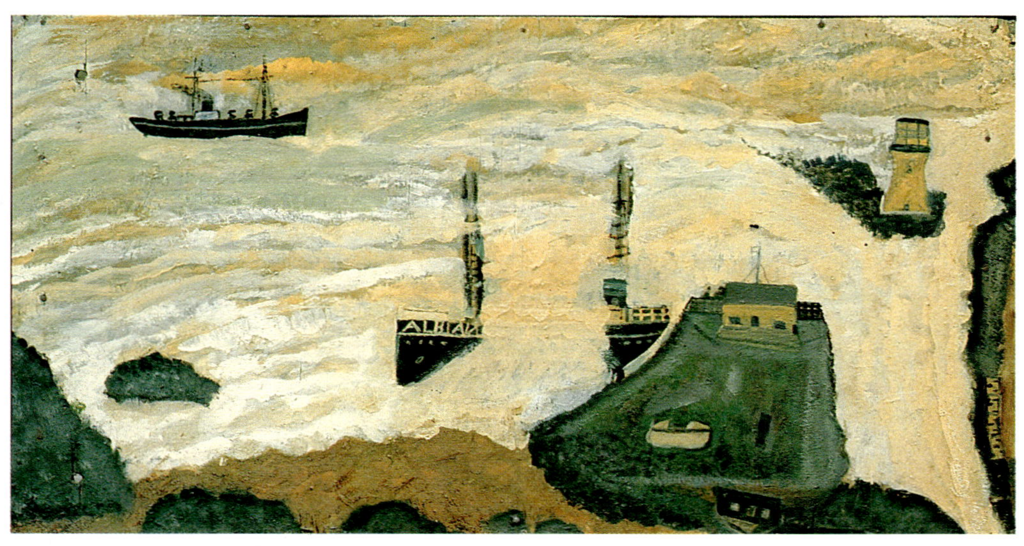

Alfred Wallis: *Wreck of The Alba*. [courtesy Dr Roger Slack]

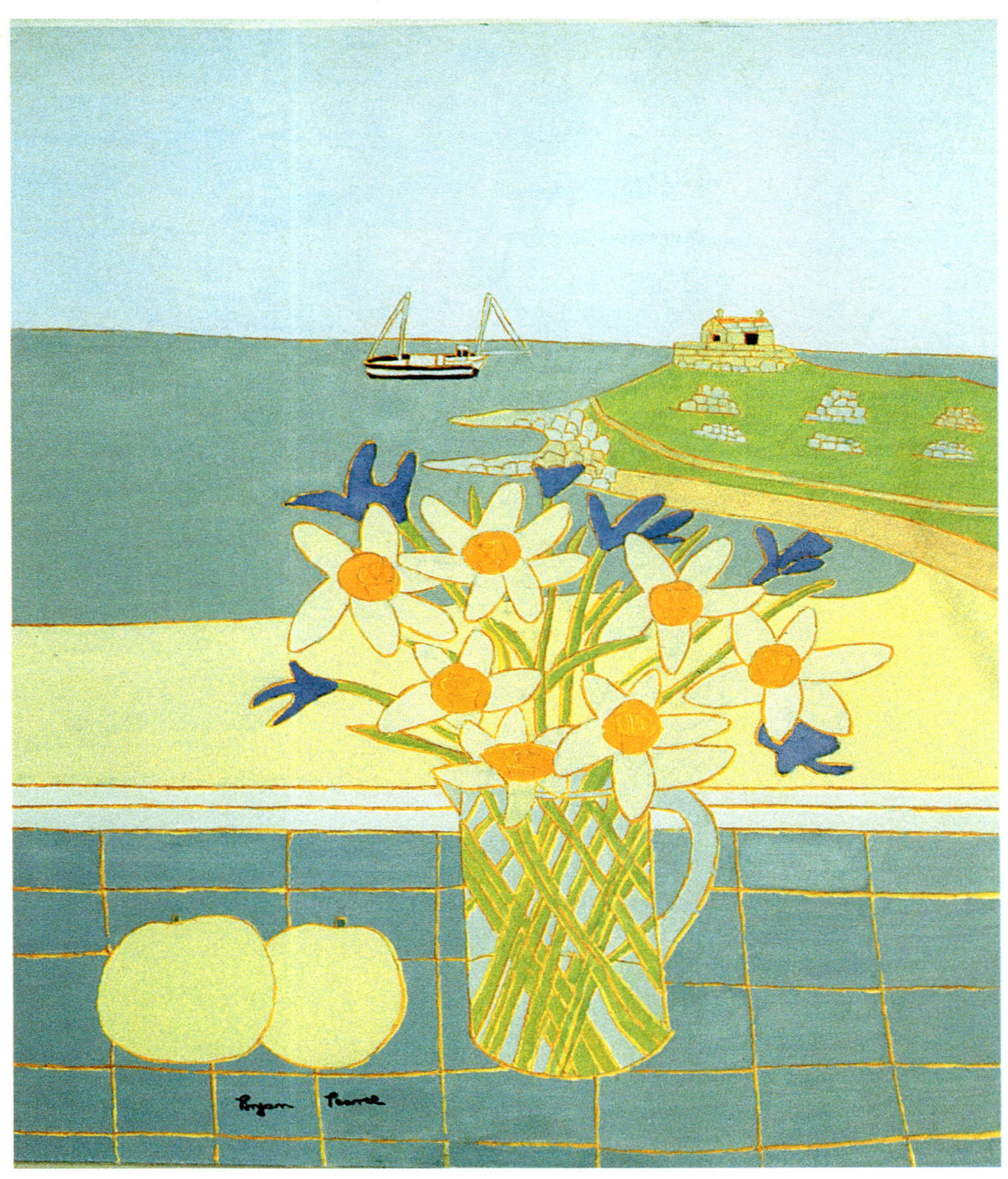

Bryan Pearce: *Daffodils and irises*.

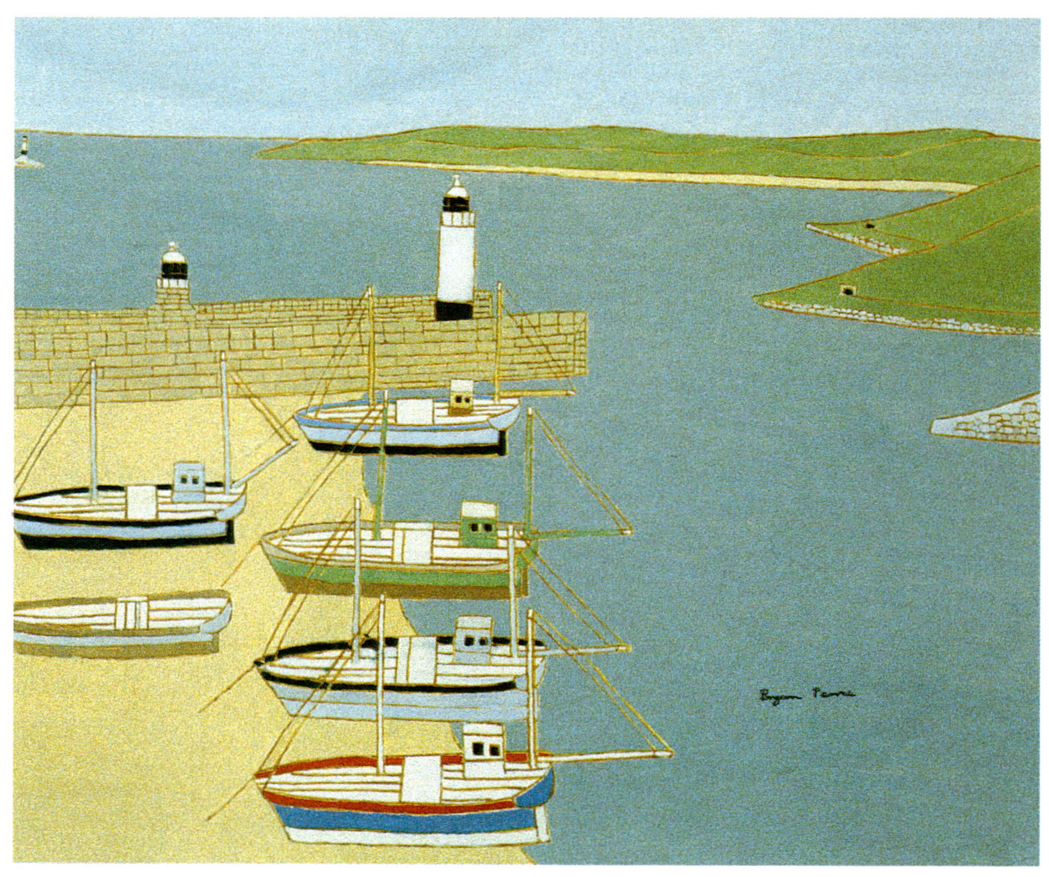

Bryan Pearce: *The Harbour, St Ives*.

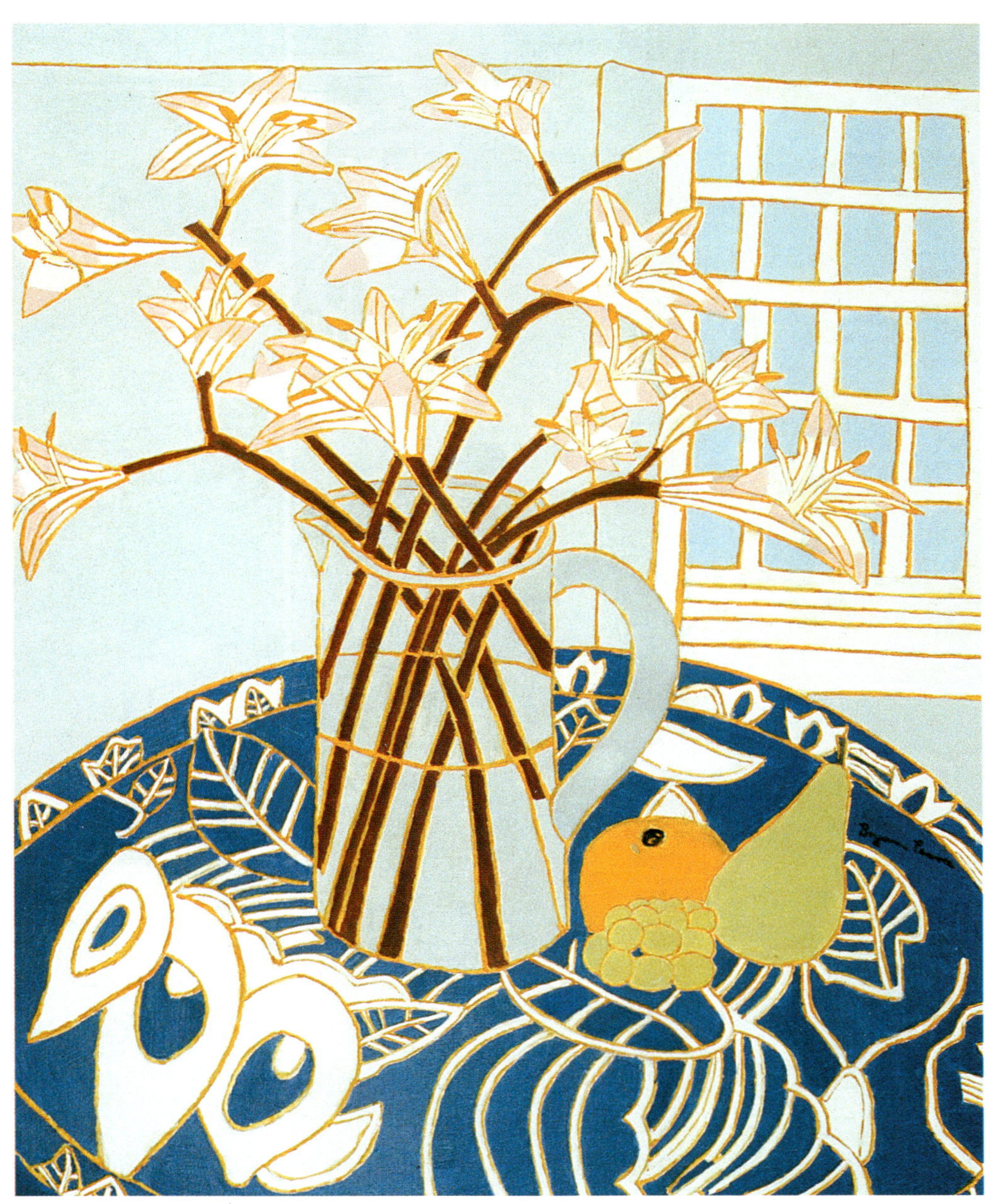

Bryan Pearce: *Lilies with blue cloth*.

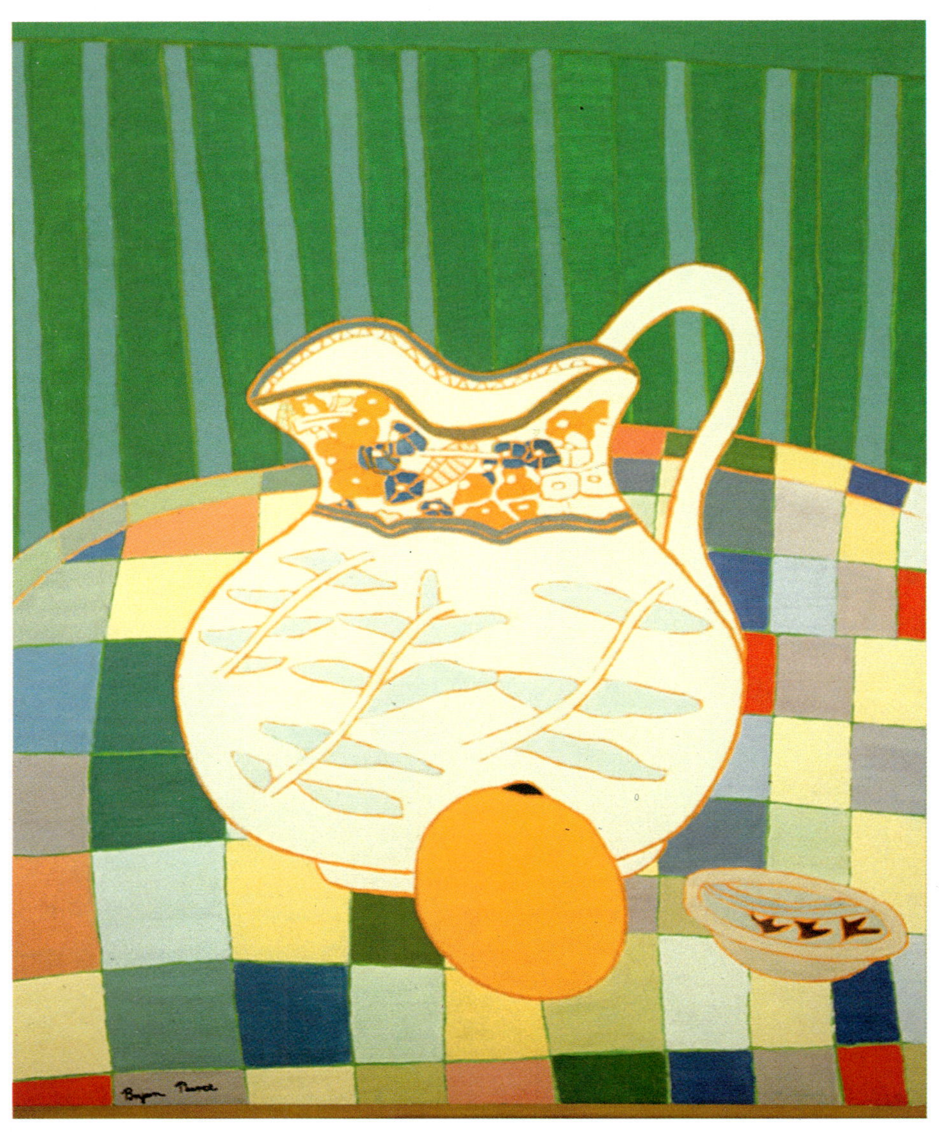

Bryan Pearce: *Jug and orange*, 1967.

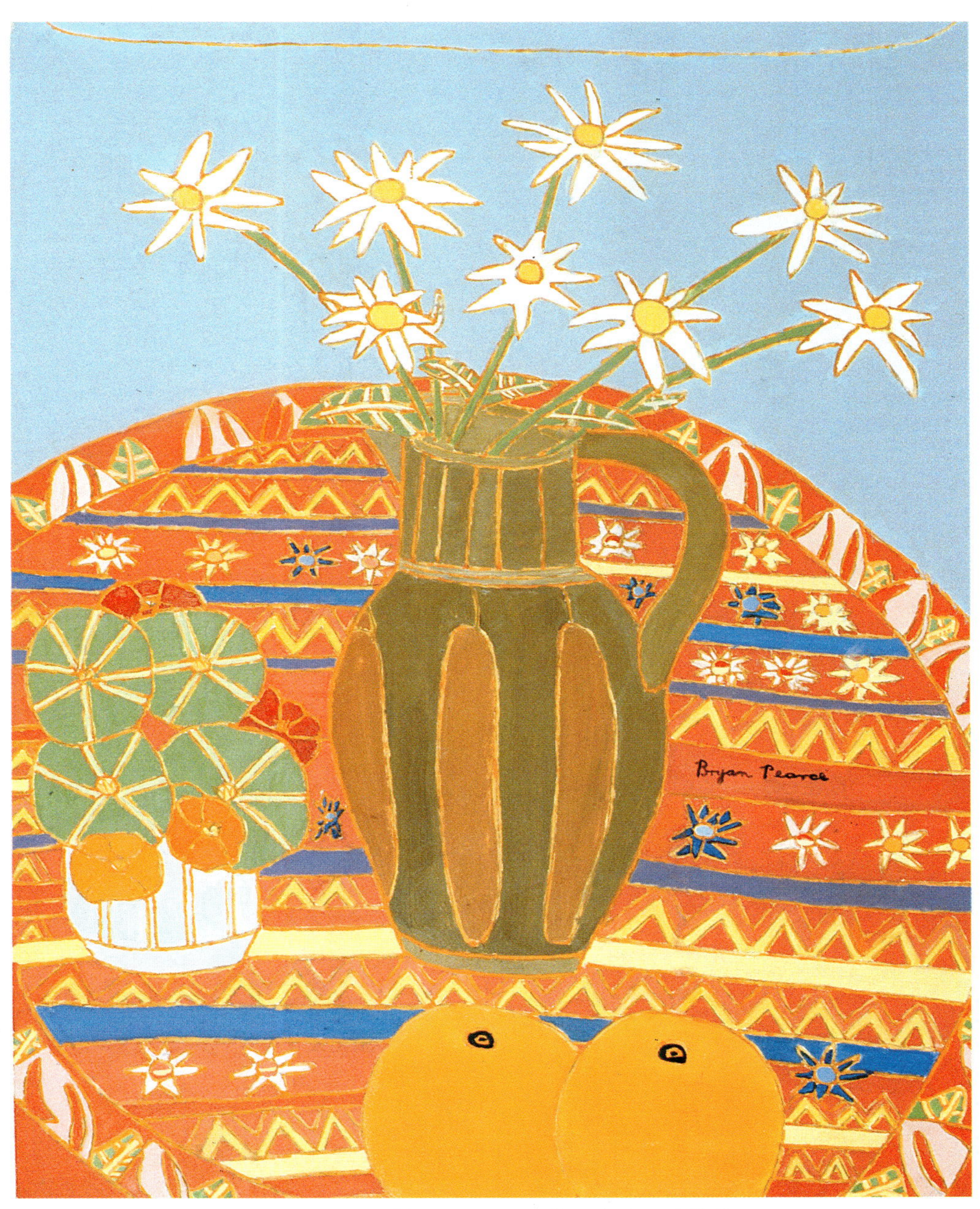

Bryan Pearce: *Marguerites in Greta's jug*, 1986.

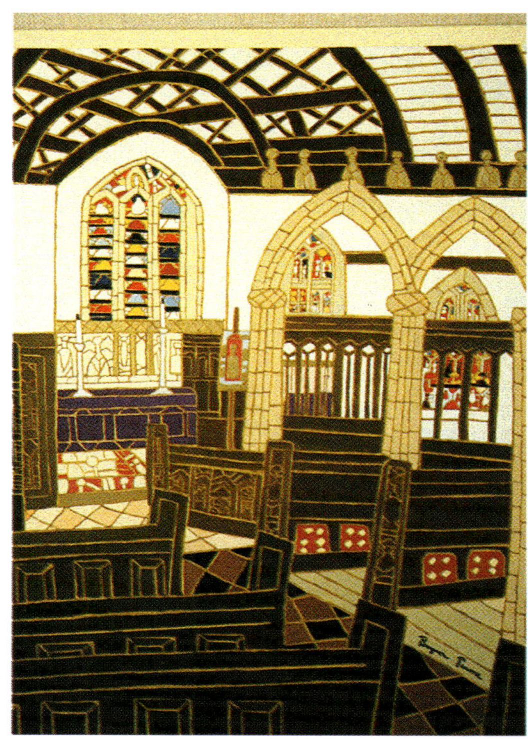

Bryan Pearce: *Parish Church, St Ives.*

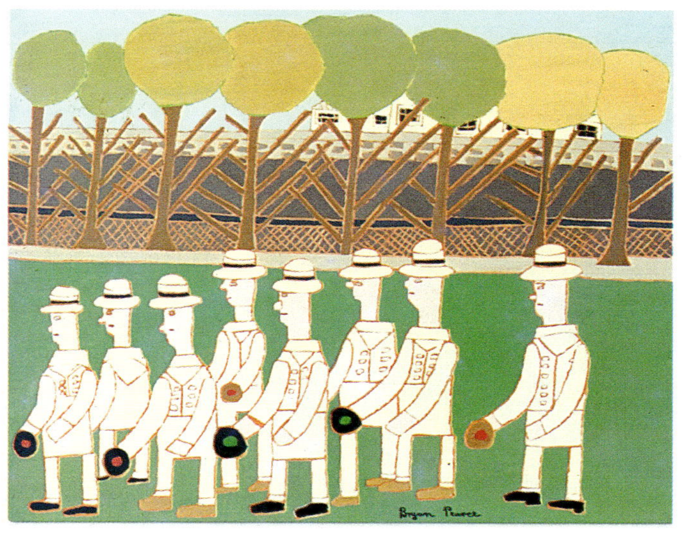

Bryan Pearce: *The Bowling Green.*

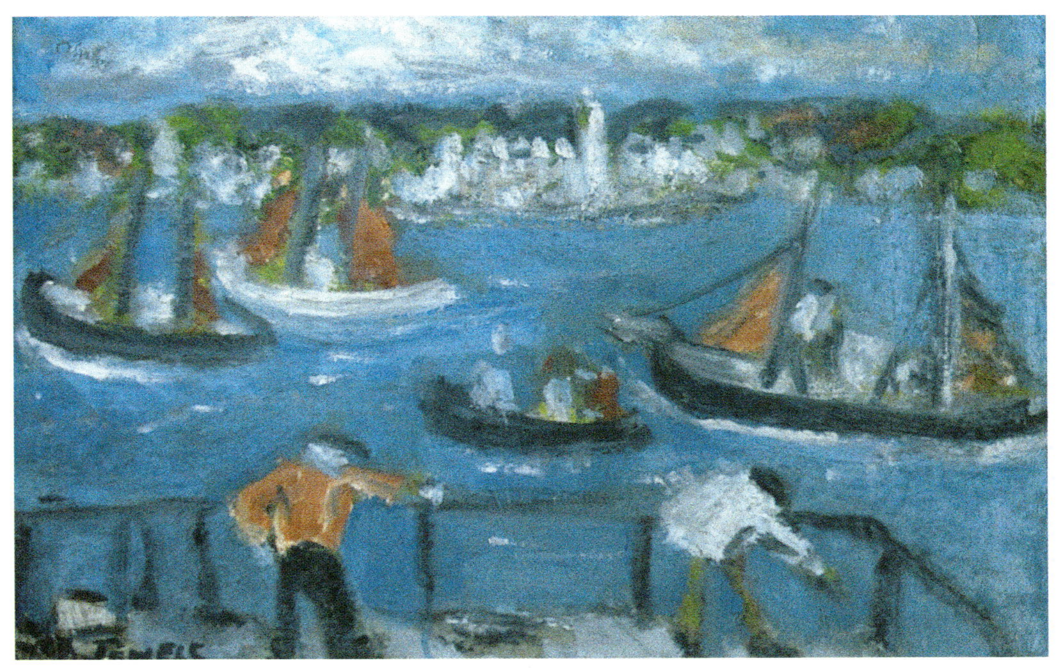

Mary Jewels: *Seascape*, 1971. [courtesy Gay Sagar-Fenton]

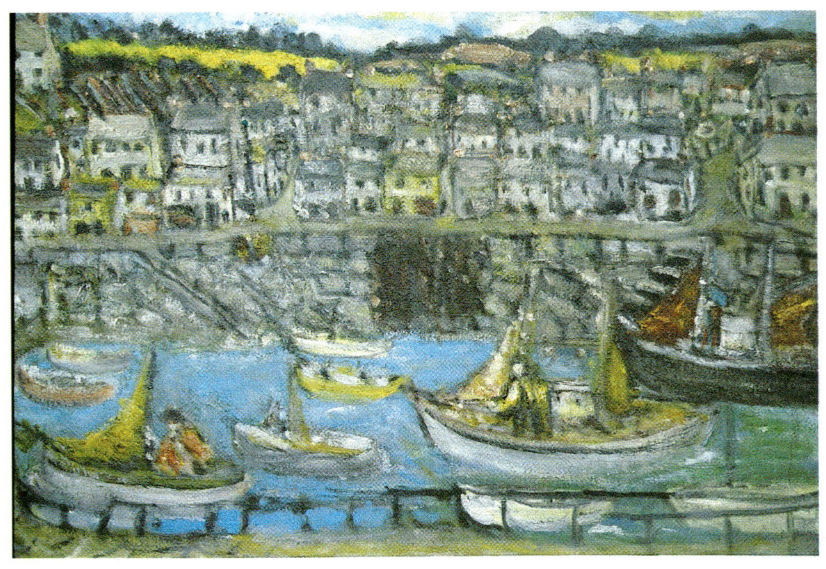

Mary Jewels: *Mousehole*. [courtesy Gay Sagar-Fenton]

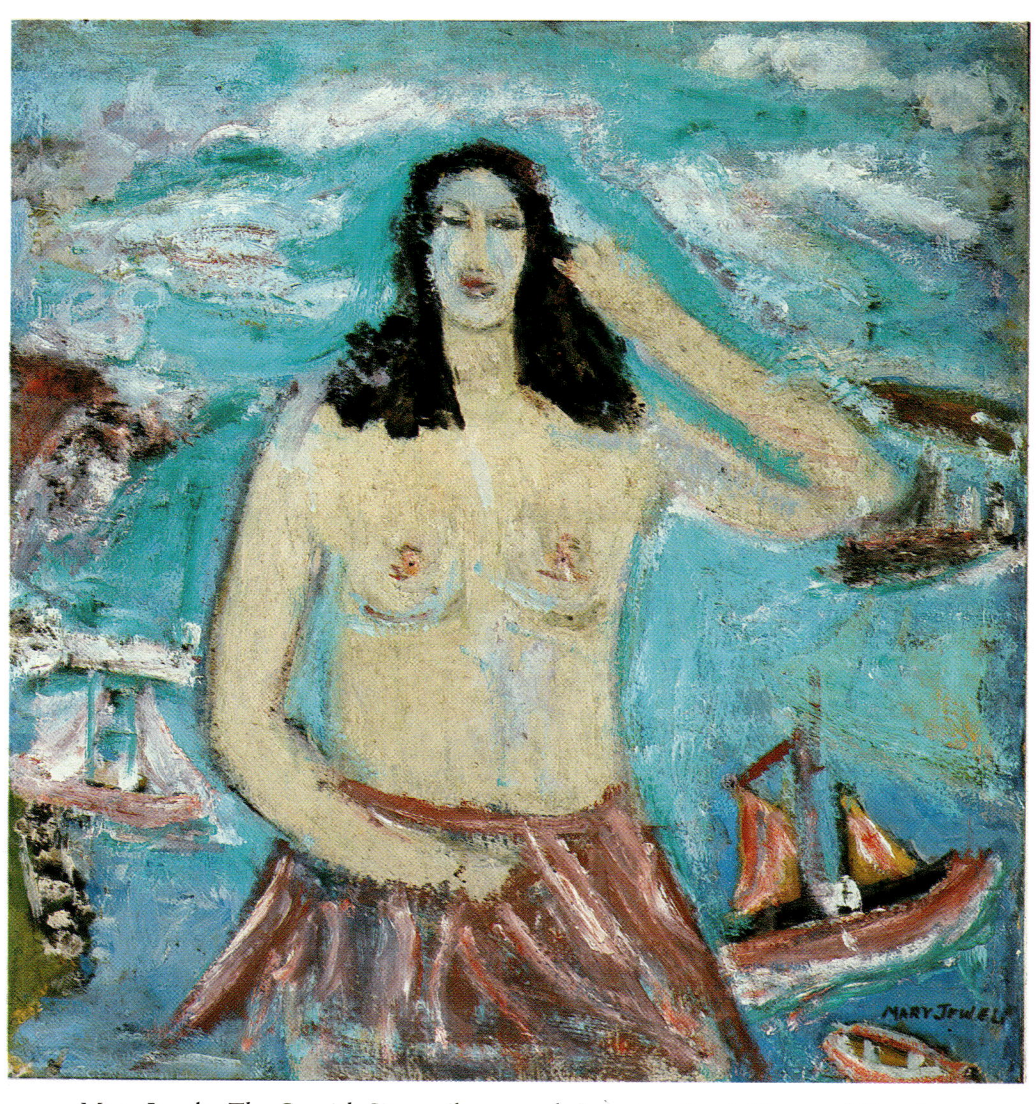

Mary Jewels: *The Cornish Siren*, oil on panel. [courtesy Austin/Desmond Fine Art; photo Colin Mills]

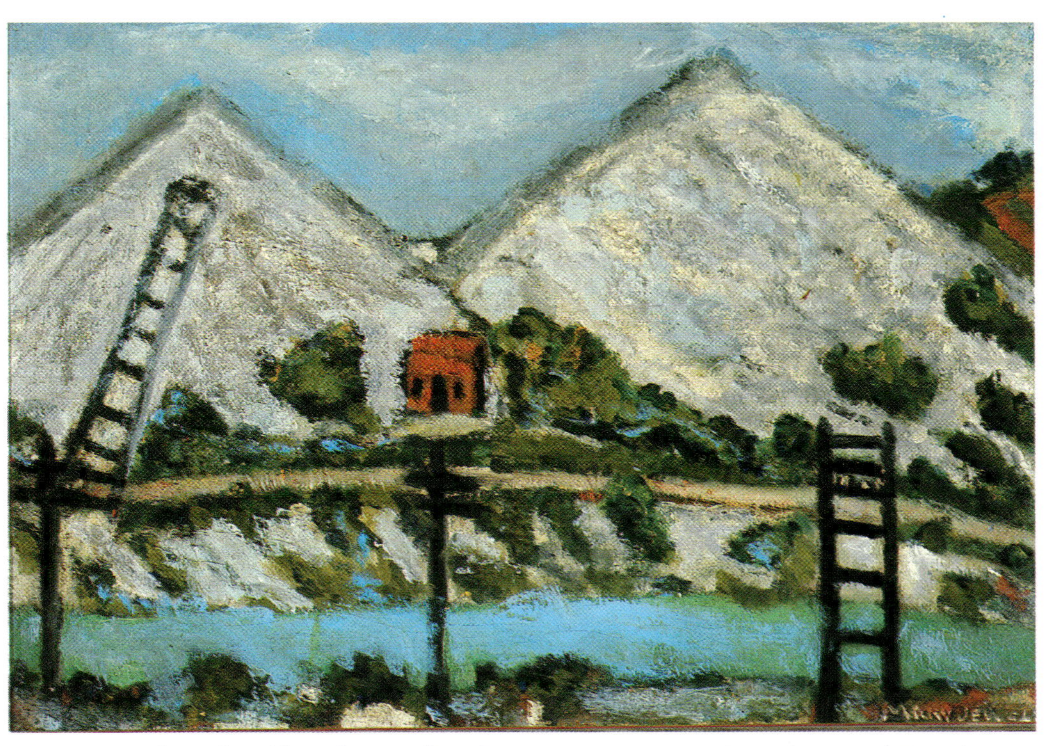

Mary Jewels: *Balswidden Clay Works*, oil on canvas. [courtesy Austin/Desmond Fine Art, photo Colin Mills]

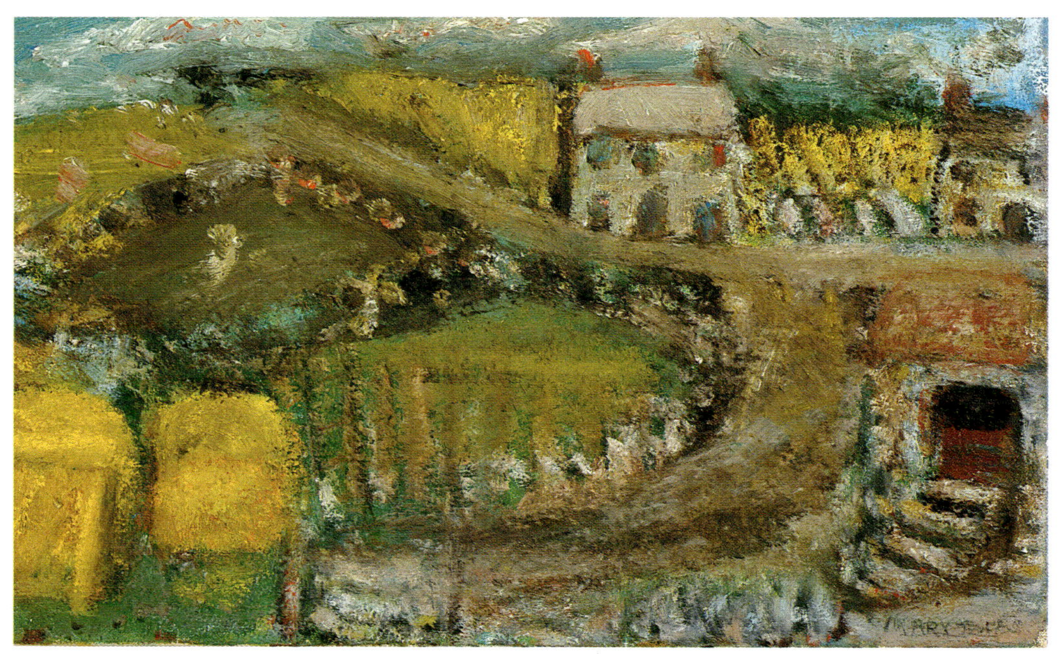

Mary Jewels: *Vine Cottage, Newlyn*, oil on canvas. [courtesy Austin Desmond Fine Art, photo Colin Mills]

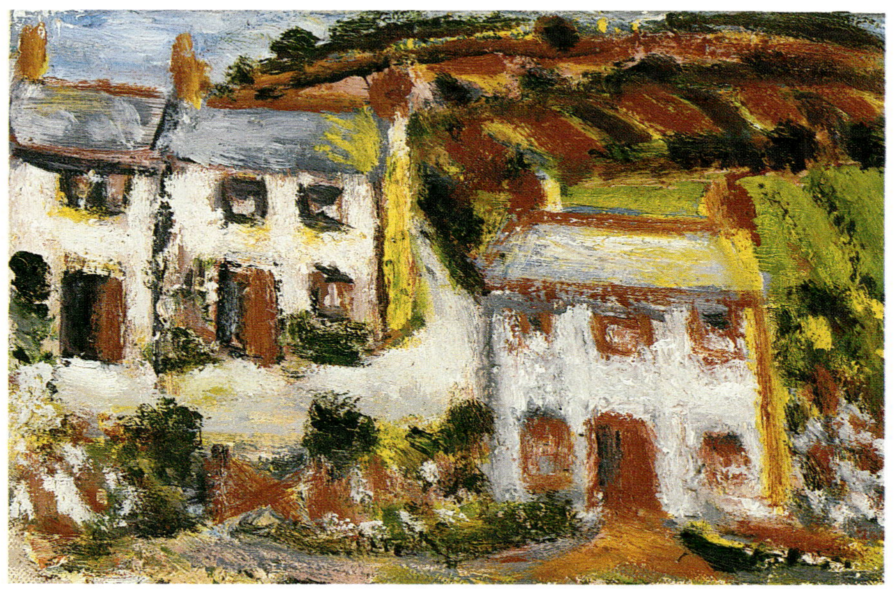

Mary Jewels: *Cottages*, oil on canvas. [courtesy John Austin, photo Colin Mills]

PROFILES
Bob Bourne – Fred Yates

Bob Bourne
b.1931

Bob Bourne is a West Country painter born in Exmouth, Devon, although raised in Brighton, Sussex, who has lived and worked in Newlyn since 1960. He began painting when he was in his early thirties. He is self taught and his work is largely of quiet, thoughtful figures in an interior, but in travelling to Australia and through Europe he became interested in landscape and this has shown itself in more abstract forms.

He was inspired and influenced by the work of Peter Lanyon and Roger Hilton, who were his main reasons for discovering Cornwall. The climate suited him. He worked in hotels to provide a living and in 1967 his mother helped him buy a house in Paul, near Newlyn. In 1973 he exhibited at Tooth's Gallery, London, and became known to Andreas Kalman who bought many of his works in the 1980s. His first solo show in St Ives was arranged by Bob Devereux at his Salthouse Gallery.

His work is composed of large blocks of colour, which make a pattern in themselves, as well as defining the subject of the work, whether in abstract forms or in portraying people in a group relating one to the other. In *Conversation Piece with Roger Hilton*, the mood is intimate, yet restrained. In *Self Portrait* the sitter is remarkably comfortable and composed. He looks out on the world and gives a happy, but ironical, grin in a relaxed manner.

Mike Venning wrote of Bourne's work: 'The paintings do communicate; one's thoughts and feelings are stirred, yet these constitute interpretations, valid in themselves . . . they capture the fleeting and non-quantifiable nuances of human inter-action. This is even apparent in the landscapes which always contain evidence of human existence.'

A member of the Newlyn Society of Artists, Bob Bourne was included in the Newlyn Group's exhibition in Pont-Aven in 1978. Ten years later, in collaboration with the National Trust, *Looking West* was an exhibition designed to raise funds for the Penwith Coastline, and in 1989, *A Century of Art in Cornwall*, celebrating the county council's centenary, embraced both Newlyn and St Ives artists. Bob Bourne was represented in all these group shows.

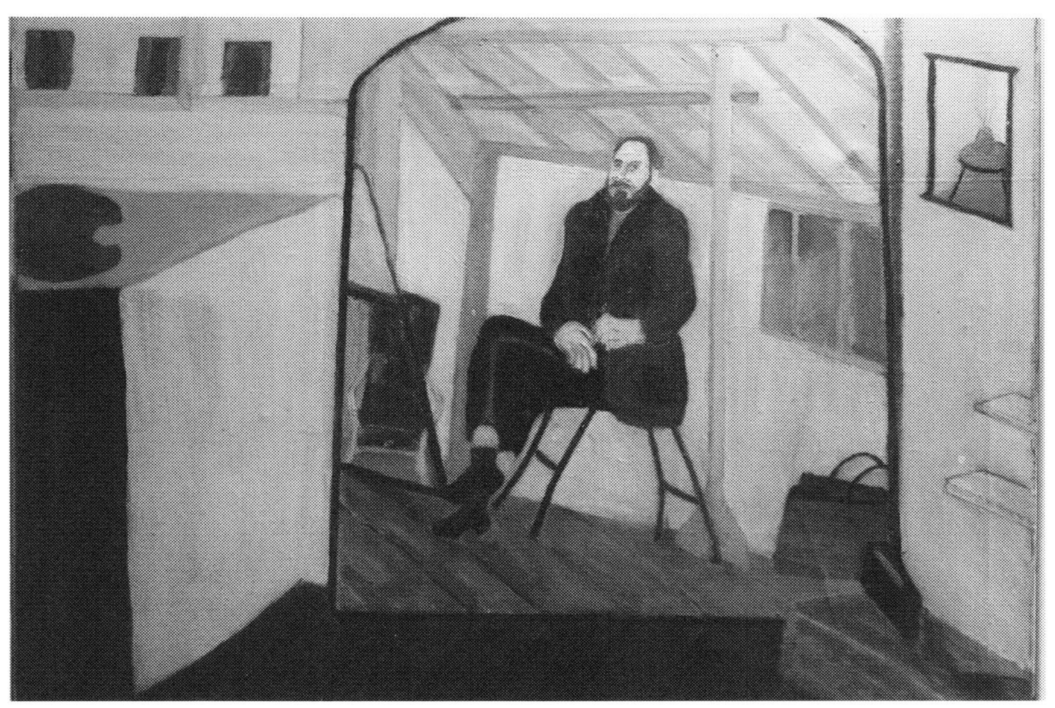

Bob Bourne self portrait.

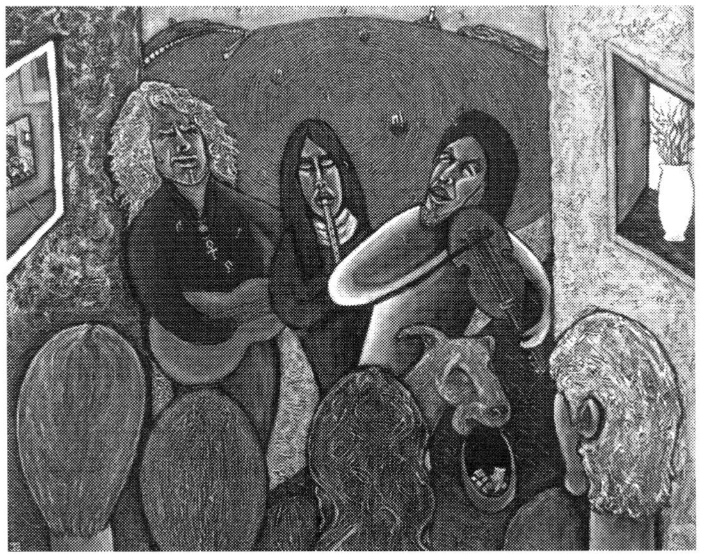

Joseph Clarke: *A merry jig*.

Joseph Clarke
b.1976

Joseph Clarke first came to Cornwall as a boy and says it is a dream fulfilled to be living and painting in the town of St Ives. He is self taught as an artist. Although he is attracted by the landscape, his inspiration reflects the way he lives; who he meets in the street, walking with his family, standing outside the pub or at the sea's edge with his body board – just normal things that life entails, but interpreted with a sense of humour.

His paintings show the feeling for place. They are narrative, 'rather like the Newlyn School paintings in the way that they capture everyday life. Each painting tells a story. People don't feel they have to understand art when they look at my pictures. That's the nice thing about it for me. I like to amuse people.'

Joseph does not sketch or make direct drawings of happenings but works in his studio. 'My brain is my sketch book.' He has a vivid memory and can capture the moment, the way people react to each other, how they stand, their body language, their shape and look. His work is about observation and making people notice what is around them. His pictures are diary entries of daily happenings in his life. He paints with acrylic, on board, a medium which helps record those brief fleetings of life.

A Merry Jig with its flowing musical notes, reflects the street life of St Ives with its roving musicians and its holiday makers. The town is confining but the backdrop is spacious showing the swirling sea, the harbour, the island and Godrevy lighthouse in the far distance. On the easel is the painting shown in a room. He says he sees Cornwall not as someone who has lived here all his life, nor as a summer visitor, but as a person who has chosen to live within its creative ambience.

Working in the Sloop Craft Market he is in direct communication with visitors and is open to their comments. He does not shut himself away in a studio but welcomes people's observations on his work. People are his inspiration. 'Some of the characters in the paintings turn out to be their aunt Hilda, or Roger who lives next door to them, or that old boy they saw eating his ice cream earlier that morning. I love the fact that my work gets people talking and often puts a smile on their faces.'

Ronnie Copas
b.1936

Ronnie Copas was born in the London borough of Lambeth. The best thing that happened to him, he now reckons, was that he never went to art school, although at the time he felt disadvantaged, having so early to earn a living to help support the family. However, he worked as a scene painter and was also involved with graphics: two jobs which helped him discover techniques in design and the application of paint.

In 1969 Ronnie and his wife left London for Cornwall. He gained work as a ferry man, taking boat loads of visitors from Marazion, near Penzance, to St Michael's Mount. They had a cottage on the island and were cut off from the mainland, even with a boat, when the weather became treacherous. Here Ronnie learned the ways of the sea, befriended the local fishermen and came to admire the work of the lifeboat men.

Cornwall inevitably became the subject of many of his paintings. *Grace Over Starry Gazy Pie*, painted in 1976, features a group of four people sitting at table with a great dish of pie with fish heads poking through the top; a particular Cornish recipe. The four Stanley Spencer-ish figures avert their gaze from the subject, the meal. Indeed there is a certain holiness-cum-roguishness in his figures.

In his painting, *Icarus Revisited*, there is a topsy-turviness about his groupings of figures which whirl outwards from the centre of the picture, giving life and vitality. His work is lyrical, the movement free and fluid with grace and freedom in the figures as though the painter had truly brought them to life. Like many other self-taught painters, Copas shows with the Portal Gallery, London.

In 1994 Ronnie Copas was commissioned to paint a mural of scenes from the plays of Shakespeare for Sheila and Robert Pennant Jones. This huge undertaking eventually produced thirty seven very lively, colourful scenes. An associated book, *The Poet and the Painter*, showed his wonderful depiction of the events, in fine detail, alongside the Shakespearean text.

William George
1851–1945

William George was born in Mousehole, fisherman and son of a fisherman. He was grandfather to the more celebrated painter, Jack Pender. For a man from such a background he was well read and comparatively well educated. William took up painting late, at the age of seventy five, using children's water colour paints and scraps of card and paper. The back of a print of John Wesley preaching was one of the first to be used and rehung on the wall with a painting signed 'Will George'. When he did acquire the knowledge of materials and could afford paints and canvas he became a prolific painter. His subject matter was the sea, boats and Mousehole harbour.

Like his contemporary, Alfred Wallis, William George knew the dangers of a fisherman's life from the age of nine, when he went to sea in a Mount's Bay sailing lugger, travelling to Ireland, Scotland and down the East Coast, working as cook and general factotum for five Cornish fishermen as they searched for herring. Another connection with Wallis was through Alethea Garstin, who befriended the two artists, although there is no record of George and Wallis ever meeting. She visited Wallis in the poorhouse and used to drive William about the countryside in her car and take him home to tea at Zennor. She was also responsible for introducing his work to the Newlyn Art Gallery.

Until his death, Jack Pender still painted from his Mousehole home overlooking the entrance to the minute harbour, working in the very room that William George painted from. The views from that window were the inspiration for both painters. Jack wrote about the subject of his grandfather's paintings in the *Cornish Review*, Spring 1971: 'Granite walls and whitewashed walls, slate roofs, grey or lichen coloured, calm harbours, boats running or at moorings. His brush, finger and rag caressed the images out of his simple materials.' When he died at the age of ninety-four he had produced a great number of paintings of intricate design and detail. It was the local custom in Mousehole to ask William George to paint a picture for a wedding present.

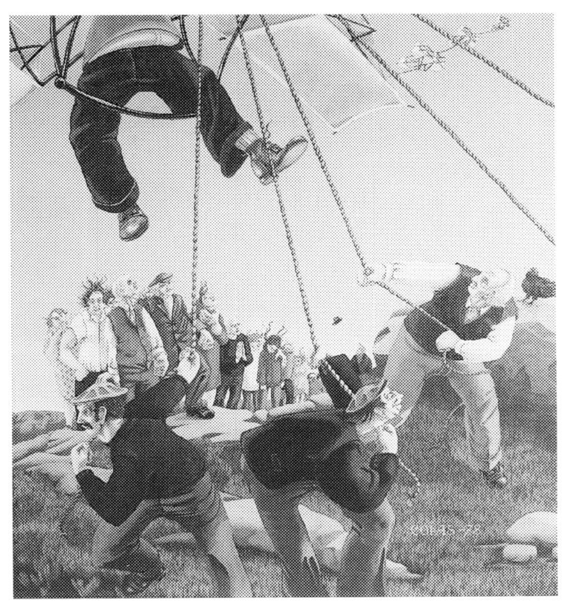

Ronnie Copas: *Icarus Revisited*, egg tempera/panel,
1978.

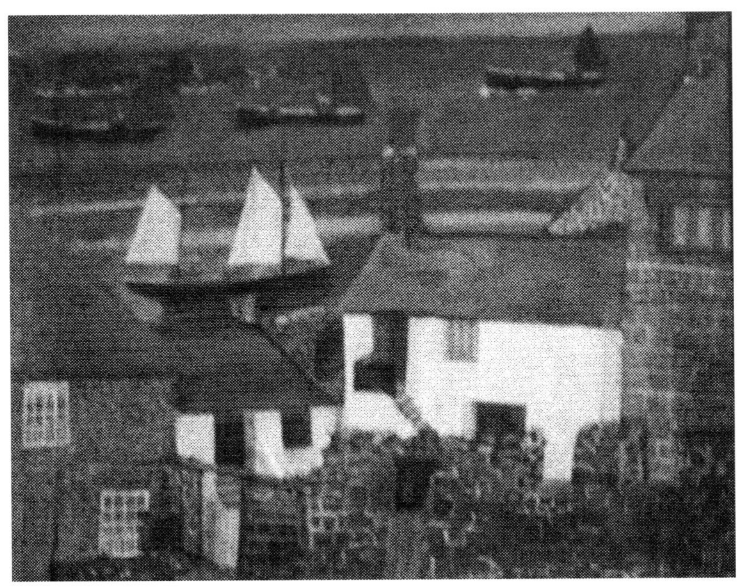

William George: *The Morwenna*.

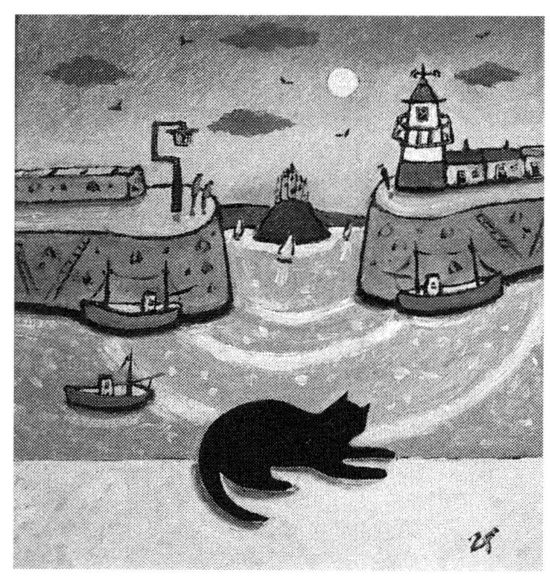

Joan Gillchrest: *Mousehole Black Cat.*

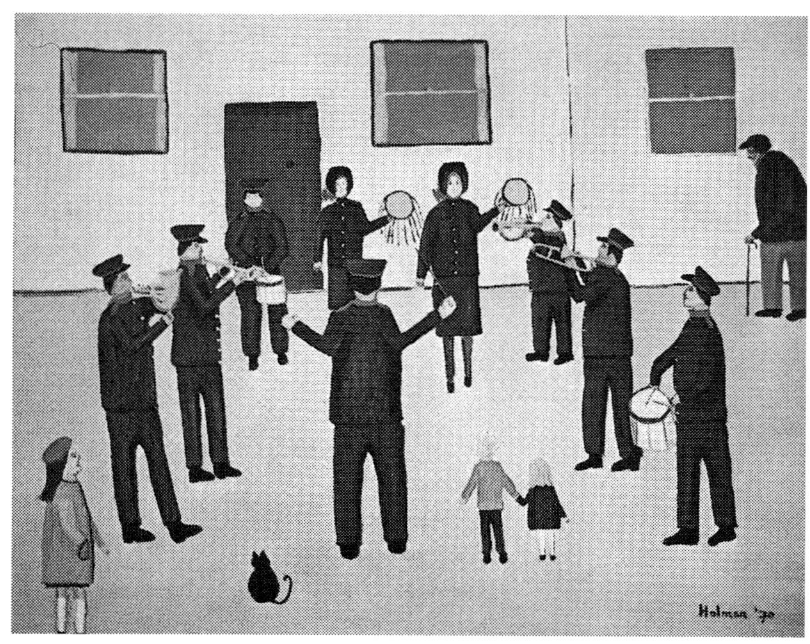

Betty Holman: *The Salvation Army.*

Joan Gillchrest
b.1918

Joan Gillchrest was born in London in 1918, moving to Cornwall forty years later. Since then the harbour at Mousehole has been the subject of her paintings. The harbour's embracing arms contain many boats, merrily engaging in the life of boating and fishing. Her people are energetic onlookers of the harbour scene with its busy craft and the distant St Michael's Mount. The people are busy, chatting, exchanging pleasantries, observing and enjoying the activities of life.

The painter creates the scene with her brush, generating a great liveliness and feeling of being part of some wonderful animated happening. She is so involved with the life around the magic circle of the harbour that she would like to make her exit from this desirable place in a Viking ship, burning its way through the narrow entrance and out to sea; probably to the applause of spectators.

In *Mousehole Cat*, the cat sits on the quay eyeing the entrance to the harbour, which is the mouse hole. Mousehole is probably the smallest harbour entrance in Cornwall. Joan is noted for the humour in her work. Usually she is a close observer of people meeting and talking, inviting the viewer to carry on the story in our heads; we are invited by the groupings of figures, the animation of the characters on canvas who indicate that there are several stories to be told. Mostly it is the visitor to Mousehole whom she fixes with her sardonic eye and features in her pictures.

Frank Ruhrmund wrote that 'although she may make it all seem easy, to achieve these finely-honed and humorous paintings, she has dissected and distilled her material; sorted and shifted her subject matter to somewhere beyond the banal or ordinary, to a point as refined, as delicate and dangerous, as that of the sharpest steel.'

She has exhibited at the Royal Academy, other galleries in London, and widely in the West Country. Although she studied at the Grosvenor School of Art and afterwards in Paris, she has retained that clear-eyed vision which is uniquely her own and which no amount of training has erased.

Betty Holman
b.1911

A Cornish woman, Betty Holman was born in Camborne, a daughter of the famous engineering family. She married Jim Shackell and moved to Australia where her daughters, Caroline and Victoria, were born. Twenty years later, in 1957, she returned to England before going to live on the island of Ibiza. It was here that she started to paint when she found a discarded canvas belonging to her sister-in-law, Linden Holman.

At first she borrowed paints and brushes from Douglas Portway, who gave her encouragement. She showed him her first painting: the lifeboat house in St Ives. He looked at it and said, 'I think you should paint another.' He kept her working to solve her problems, never telling her how to do it. She was then aged forty-nine. Five years on she was ready to exhibit her work. Betty lived in Ibiza from 1958 to 1967 and then returned to England, to live in Salubrious House in St Ives with Douglas Portway and family. This was a second home: summer months were spent in France where they continued to paint.

In *The Salvation Army*, the grouping of the figures radiate from two female figures central back, to the conductor at the front. The band could be playing for their own enjoyment, facing each other and attracting only an old man passing by, some curious children and a cat. It is a fine composition of figures in a self-absorbing occupation.

Her subject matter includes scenes in Spain, family portraits, the Cornwall of her childhood with street scenes of houses mounting in tiers on a flat canvas, the piers and harbours, and children playing games in remembered scenes from childhood. 'I make up the pictures, that is, I never go out and copy something. For one thing I can't draw, and the picture only seems to come alive when I start the painting.' Betty has exhibited widely and was included in Britain's first International Naive Art Exhibition at the Hamilton Gallery, Mayfair in 1979.

Betty's work is included in the book *Twentieth Century British Naive and Primitive Artists*.

Judy Joel
b.1946

Judy Joel grew up in an environment which encouraged her to explore with paint and collage and to make pictures. She provided a similar creative atmosphere for her own children. It was while she was nursing one child through an illness, and unable to leave the house, that she took up painting as an adult. Her first picture was a present to her mother, a wedding scene.

Having started she began to paint more pictures. A friend was impressed with the freshness of her work and suggested an exhibition, and on the day her daughter was born she learned she had sold four of those paintings. Over the next ten years she painted steadily, not exhibiting, choosing her subject, and collecting a body of work.

Friends and family made requests for paintings and she began to take commissions. She paints compilations of people's lives. This creates a design problem to be solved and is tremendously challenging, but exciting. She starts with a collection of photographs of people, houses, pets and the ephemera of their every day happenings. The finished picture gives an insight into the history of their family life over a number of years.

Judy paints on a flat surface, whether on the dining room table, on a board on her lap, in the garden, or on the harbour in Mousehole, where she lives. She loves painting when the sun is shining. 'I can paint anywhere.' She works with acrylic and gouache and is entirely self taught. She enjoys watching her work take shape. 'I set up the paper and it takes time to get the feel for the subject. Sometimes I paint throughout the night if I get into a painting.'

Having designed what is going to happen she includes the background and foreground and the subsidiary subjects. 'I love putting in the people. It's then it comes to life and I can relax. I like doing small figures best.' The people go into the picture nude. Then she dresses them, deciding what they will wear and choosing the colours. 'And I end up with two eyes and a smile.'

Mousehole is the joyful subject of many of her works. Everything is in the picture – houses, boats, sea, the surrounding fields – and of course the essential element, the people. She captures it all. Since the death of her mother, Katie, ten years ago, she has included her in each of her pictures, where she is accompanied by one of the family dogs. Judy signs her paintings alongside the figure of a mouse.

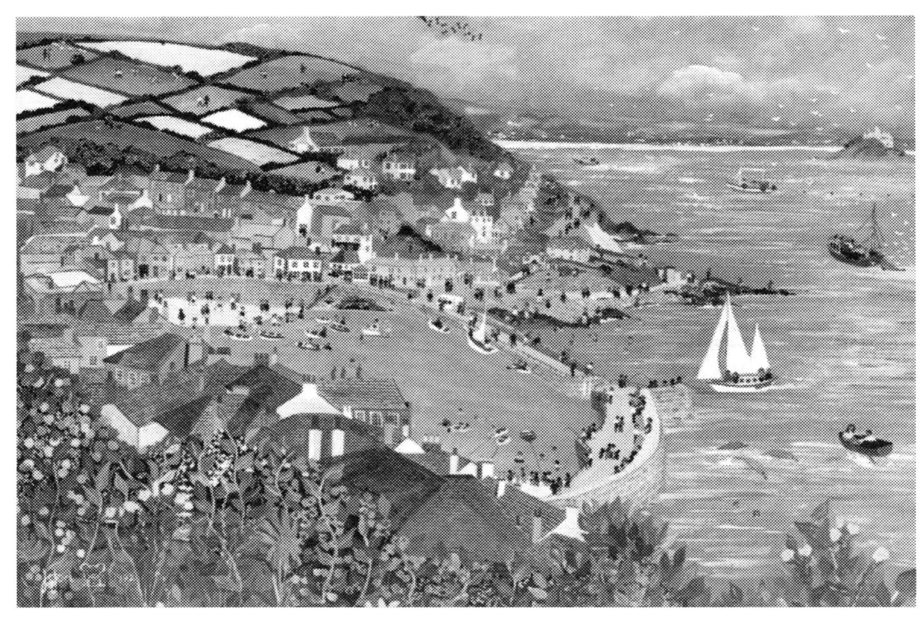

Judy Joel: *Mousehole.*

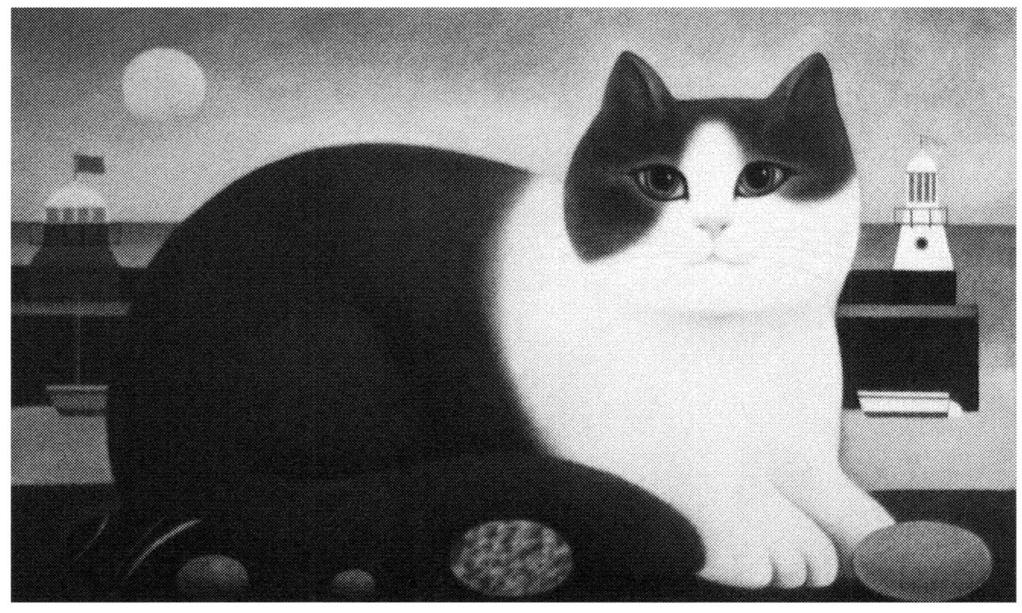

Martin Leman: *Pier Cat, St Ives (Smeaton's Pier)*, 1996.

140

Martin Leman
b.1934

Martin Leman was born in London, son of a Covent Garden market trader. Since childhood, Martin has paid regular visits to Cornwall and now has houses in London and St Ives. After a short time in the army he studied graphic design at the Central School, London, and after a spell in advertising taught at several art schools. In 1979, after publication of his first successful book, *Comic and Curious Cats*, he gave up teaching for full-time painting and to produce more books.

He began painting in his late twenties. His paintings of the nude or semi-clad female figure in interiors are seen as humorous portrayals of the intimate details of a woman's world. Another pre-occupation became cat portraits. This developed still further to the unidentified cat, except that it could only be a Leman cat, in the way it sits or lies, or stares out from the canvas, and in the delicacy with which he applies his paint.

In *Pier Cat St Ives*, Leman's palette is colourful and controlled. The smooth surface of the canvas leaves not a trace of a brush mark. The picture planes are hard edged, illustrative, yet have an essential painterly quality. Smeaton's Pier, Godrevy lighthouse and the Island appear as regular features in Martin's paintings.

Early in his career he was offered two solo shows at the Portal Gallery and has since exhibited widely throughout this country and on the continent. In St Ives he has shown at Wills Lane, Sims Gallery (later at Marazion) and the New Craftsman. In the early 1990s, a painting of Martin's, showing a white cat sitting amongst a group of famous St Ives works of art, was sold as a print, with other artists' work, to help raise money for the building of the Tate Gallery in St Ives.

Martin has gained a reputation for his prints, calendars and greetings cards of cats. With his wife Jill, who studied graphic design at the Central School of Art and Design, London, they have produced a number of highly successful books. *A World of Their Own* features a selection of British twentieth-century naive artists, with an illustration of a still life by Bryan Pearce on the front cover. Martin works both from his house in Islington, London, and from his St Ives studio.

Alan Lowndes
1921–1978

Alan Lowndes was apprenticed to a decorator after leaving school at 14. He took up painting classes part time in Stockport, where he was born, after leaving the army in 1945 and while continuing to work. In the late 1950s he moved to Cornwall where he lived for part of each year in the Italianate barn at Tremedda Farm, near Zennor, getting to know other artists in the area and painting full time. In 1959 he married and with his wife Valerie, bought a house in the Digey. In the following year *A Street in St Ives*, which featured the Digey, was purchased by Plymouth City Art Gallery for their permanent collection. He shared a Piazza studio (now demolished) in St Ives with the painter Michael Broido and later took a Porthmeor studio. In 1964 the family moved to Halsetown, a village just outside St Ives, staying until 1970 when they moved to Gloucester.

Lowndes was inspired by rugged Cornwall and, in complete contrast, by the industrial landscape of the north of England. Everyday scenes and the goings on of ordinary life were attractive: seaside holiday activities in St Ives yielding a rich vein of subject matter, people, colour and texture. The painting *Coconut Shy* displays his observation and celebration of people holidaying. A boat in the harbour provided a look-out from which to observe, and from which he also caught fish for the family. However, he never forgot his northern roots, earning *The Times*' description as a painter of northern life.

One of his finest portraits was of the sculptor John Milne, a neighbour and friend of Barbara Hepworth; it depicts a young man in the prime of life, dressed in blues, set against a textured red background, a confident stance proclaiming his place in the world. In 1959 Lowndes and Milne exhibited together at Crane Kalman's gallery in Manchester, where Lowndes had had his first solo show in 1950. The gallery paid him a stipend to retain his work and he exhibited with them over many years. In 1964 he had a one-man show in New York, and a retrospective exhibition of paintings from 1948–72 at Stockport Art Gallery, the poet, W S Graham, writing a poem for the catalogue.

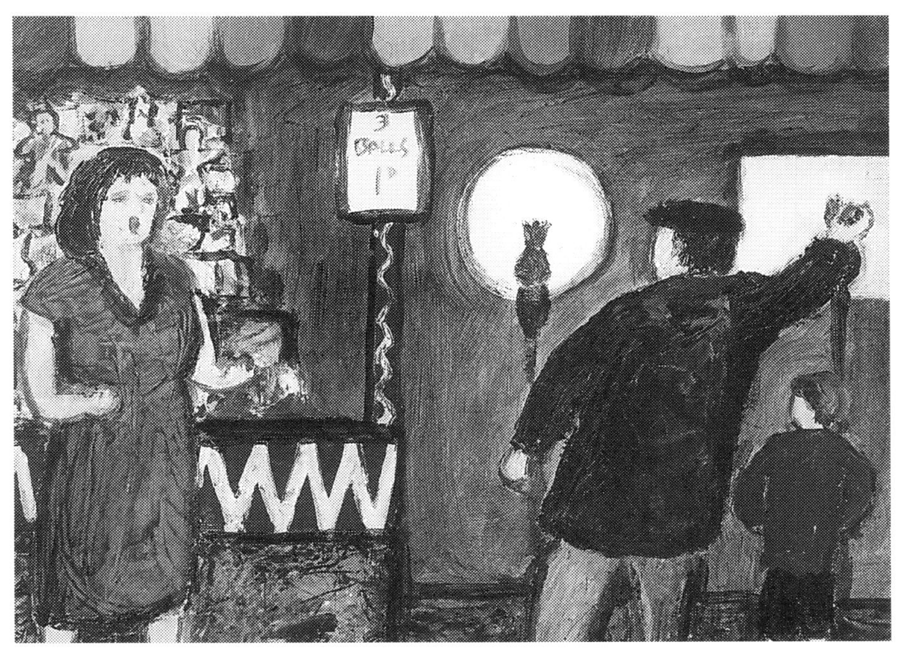

Alan Lowndes: *Coconut Shy.*

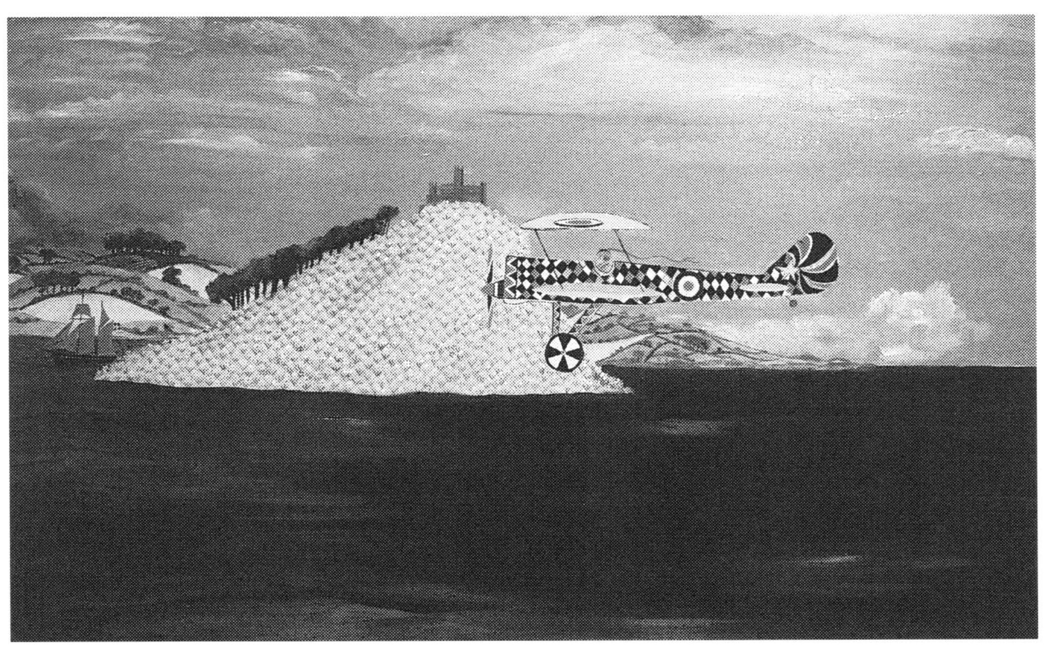

Lewes Mitchell: *Aeroplane by St Michael's Mount.*

143

Lewes Mitchell
b.1932

Lewes Mitchell is a Cornishman, born in Penzance, son of a carriage cleaner working for the Great Western Railway at Penzance Station. He left school at 15 and began work on a farm overlooking Mount's Bay. It was, he said later, a marvellous training, working in the landscape he would later capture and paint. 'I saw St Michael's Mount every day. I couldn't help but be affected by this landscape, where most of the space was taken up by the sea and sky. All under that special light in this last ten miles of England jutting out into the Atlantic.'

He started painting when he was nearly 40 years old, totally self-taught, combining this activity with farm work to earn a living. He admits to a debt to artist Alexander Mackenzie, who came to teach art in Cornwall and encouraged him to continue to work in the way he felt represented what he wanted to say, and how he wanted to say it in paint. He was inspired by a dazzling Picasso painting of a Mediterranean landscape. His own brilliant colours, and richness of detail, give out his message of hope, love and joy which he trusts will operate on the viewer long after he has ceased to paint.

In *Aeroplane by St Michael's Mount*, the love of pure colour shows an obsession with paint and its tactile application. The evenings are a time when he realises his fantastical paintings of ships, balloons, planes, Mount's Bay, with St Michael's Mount as a jewel in the ocean, and the idyllic back drop of sea, farms and field patterns, with hay, daffodils, cauliflowers.

His colours are pure and untoned. He loves the vibrancy of primary colours and uses them vigorously, the work bold and bright. His paintings glow with joy and optimism and have been well described as 'an expression of his simple beliefs in the goodness of life'.

Win Oatway
1921–1997

Win Oatway was born in South London. From serving in the Civil Service she joined the ATS during the war, becoming a lance corporal. She eventually moved with her family to Somerset, where she lived for the rest of her life.

After developing her acute observation of life in journalistic skills for local radio and newspaper articles, she later took to painting, using her sense of humour and memories of happy scenes from childhood as inspiration for her paintings. Although the street culture of city children's games has died out, she recorded shops, people and their dress in true-to-life style. The amount of detail in her work betrays her complete absorption in her painting activity. She enters completely into the world she is creating with her brush. Her minutely detailed scenes are always peopled, her subjects' expressions a guide to what they are doing in the painting. Even her animals are joyfully active.

In *Children Dancing* she shows the man with the organ barrel, and the monkey, providing the music for the dancing children. She recalls the services provided by the butcher with his striped apron and cart, the muffin man ringing his bell, the delivery boy with his bike, the balloon seller, and the coalman with his horse and cart. The memories evoked, and the sense that her paintings are historical records, must give pleasure to the people whose childhoods are echoed here. The tenement buildings either side are occupied by working class families, but the open gate signifies the freedom to escape to nature, and the park.

Win first showed at the Portal Gallery, London in the 1970s and began an association with the painters of St Ives. She considered St Ives, where she gained much respect and support, her spiritual home. Commissions in later life included one for Lord Bath of Longleat. Although plagued by ill health, she continued to paint pictures which glowed with vitality and joy. Her son comments, 'Her paintings may be naive in style, but never in content or execution.'

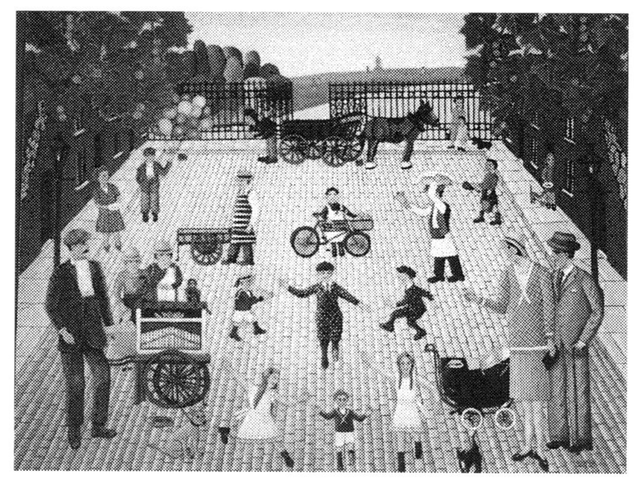

Win Oatway: *Children Dancing*.

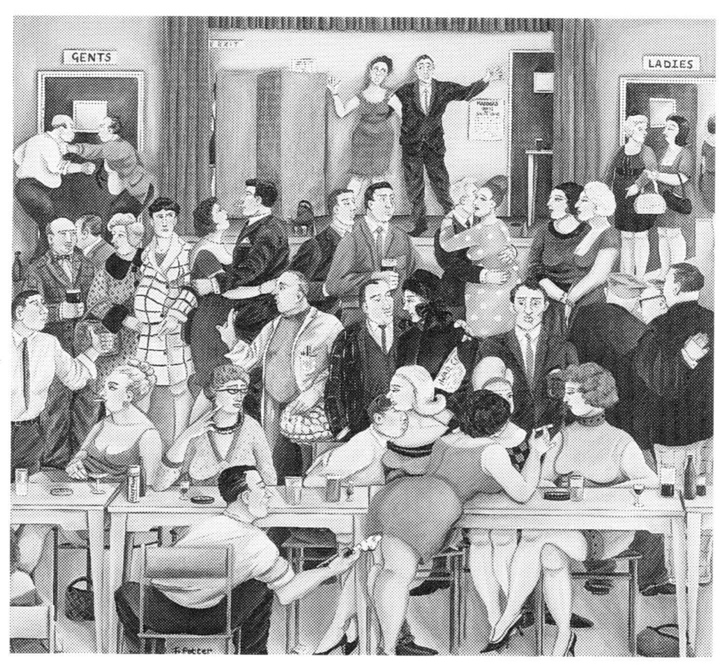

Toni Potter: *Maddox's Club*.

Toni Potter
b.1960

Born in Shrewsbury, Shropshire, Toni Potter studied speech and drama at Middlesex University and worked in theatre in education, children's theatre, the fringe, and with touring companies for ten years. She also wrote and performed her one-woman show around the country. All this time she was drawing and observing people and earned a little by illustrating; the comic style of her painting started to develop, revealing a perceptive, kindly humour that empathised with human nature.

'I see my painting as an extension of the way I look at people, the kind of observations I make of their lives, their relationships and insecurities. Their physicality interests me, how they started out quite perfect and how they have developed.' Toni's first paintings in oils were based on imagination and fantasy. She now works in acrylic and focuses on reality, basing her work on her large extended family and her childhood memories of how that family operated. As an only child, she was a quiet observer of the lives of her aunt and uncle who ran a pub and of the gatherings of her family in the club and pub atmosphere.

Maddox's Club is a lively pub scene with figures animated in dance or talk. The man and woman on stage struggle to capture the attention of the crowd, who are more interested in following their own self-absorbing activities. It is a faithful memory of childhood when sheer enjoyment and good fun shaped people's lives; or perhaps a desperate need to capture the moment and hold it for as long as possible.

In 1988 Toni arrived in St Ives and her paintings matured. She starts with an idea, makes sketches, doesn't draw from life except to make a figure anatomically right. In working from scenes of childhood she uses family photographs as a guide for the layout of the painting, makes a detailed line drawing, traces that on to the canvas or paper and starts to paint. It is a fairly lengthy process, during which the painting can develop quite differently from how she first saw it in her mind's eye, although her memory ensures truth to the event she portrays.

Ben Tobias
1901–1985

Ben Tobias (Hiam Galutsky), born in Montreal, Canada a son of Russian/Polish immigrants, was granted British citizenship in the early 1950s. In 1918 he studied at Ontario College of Arts and painted extensively throughout Canada and the USA, while working as ranch hand and miner. In the 1920s he visited Paris, still combining painting and working in menial jobs. Raoul Dufy became a friend and, some time later, through an introduction, helped Ben exhibit at the Lilienfeld Galleries, New York. He showed alongside Utrillo, Chagall, Dufy, Braque, Courbet and others, and also exhibited in Germany. His painting *Café Zeus* was bought for the Ben Uri Gallery in London.

In the early 1930s he first visited St Ives and met his wife. Two sons were born in the town. He exhibited in group shows and painted extensively throughout Cornwall. He later returned to Canada with his family and he and his wife worked in cafés, earning just enough to survive. His wife supported him in his desire to continue painting, 'giving him her undying love'.

In *The Pier, Normandy*, the elongated length of the pier structure diminishes to infinity, so also do the figures on the pier. The figures to the fore of the picture are large with free flowing movements. The central figures take the eye further to a line of ladies, mostly dressed in yellow and all wearing white or yellow hats, and getting smaller with distance. The painting shows the artist's skill in playing with perspective.

In St Ives Ben often worked with the local fishermen, to help out with money problems, while his wife looked after the children. A local family, the Hicks, started collecting Ben's pictures and this was both a moral and a financial support. A son recalled that when they left St Ives many of his father's paintings remained in their cottage, but no record has been found of them.

In the 1960s his work was exhibited in Paris and London to good reviews. In London he painted 'Frumah pictures': portraits of Rabbis and Jewish scenes from life. The Frumah family were a main support. 'They not only acquired his paintings but helped in every way so he could continue to create his life's work.'

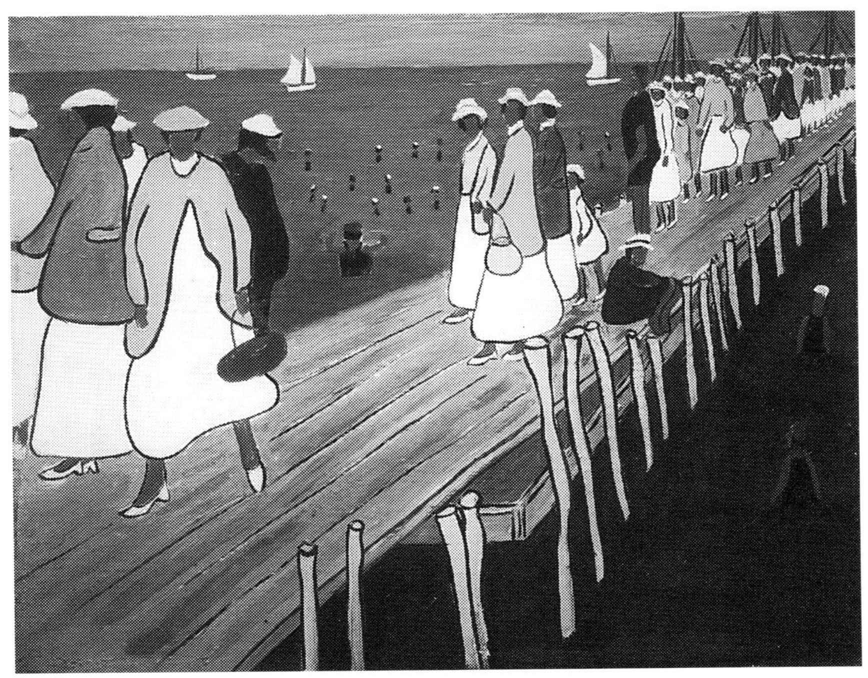

Ben Tobias: *The Pier Normandy.*

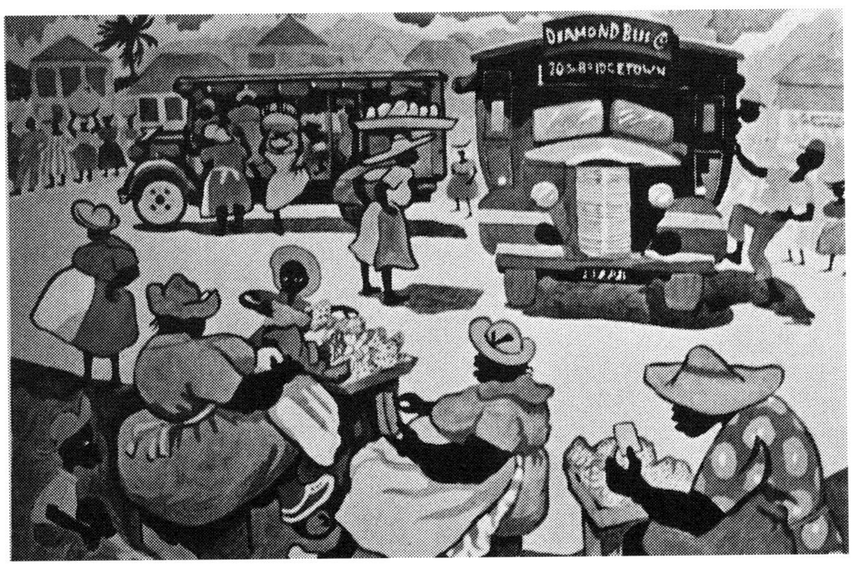

Clare White: *Hallo Sunshine.*

Clare White
1904–1997

Clare White had a rare sense of humour. By the age of five she had already decided to be an artist. Although born in Sidmouth, Devon, she spent her adult life in St Ives from where she explored the world. Her first solo exhibition at the town's Salthouse Gallery showed a range of work from countries in which she had travelled, Paris, Venice, Brittany, Egypt, Turkey, Sicily and throughout Europe. But most pleasurable of all, were the islands and folk of the West Indies. She always sketched, noting the activities of people, their attitudes, their way of life and their relationship with others. She once said to Dame Barbara Hepworth, 'Look at all the famous works you have produced, while I have only done little things.' The famous sculptor replied, 'Yes, but you have lived.'

Clare's paintings are full of humour, spirit and personality. As in *Hallo Sunshine*, everything is colourful and joyful in the lives of the unwitting models for her great sense of life being lived to the full. She wrote to the author, 'I always wanted to inspire people to be happy and courageous.'

She reviewed other painters' exhibitions for the local paper, wrote and produced plays and made scenery for the St Ives Arts Club. Scenery painting, she thought, had a profound effect on her approach to painting on canvas. In 1954 she served as the Club's first woman president. Her memories of serving the Club were enriched by knowing such artists as the potter Bernard Leach, painters Peter Lanyon, Jean and Malcolm Haylett, the novelists Mary Williams and Phyllis Bottome, and Father Delaney, who collected a number of pictures by St Ives artists, to display in the Catholic hall. Her posters for the local parish church events and St Ives festivals were a joy.

Clare spoke several languages and even in frail old age she regularly went into St Ives by train from her private nursing home in Lelant to teach Italian to a friend, and was still determined to be part of the intellectual life of the town. Of her paintings she said, 'I hope still to produce things which, though small, may live on after me and generate a little happiness.'

Fred Yates
b.1922

Although working at it full-time since 1969, Fred Yates confesses that painting is still a complete mystery. 'I don't ever think of colour, or balance. In any case to me, *thinking* means control and I like to paint free and happy, like a jazz pianist.' Ask him what his secret is and he'll say, 'Oh it comes, in time; with hard work.'

Born in Manchester, he studied art at Bournemouth College of Art as a mature student, after serving as a Grenadier Guardsman during the war years. At art school the principal, wisely, allowed him to go his own way. 'There were occasions when I felt out of my depth,' but he survived the experience, not knowing whether it enriched him or not. Fred is always to be found painting in some Cornish village or other, or on the coast, or looking for a location in the surrounding countryside, with a huge canvas strapped to his back. He paints largely out of doors, whatever the weather, and allows himself to get carried away with the smell, the dream, of paint: the activity of layering on those areas of magic and singing colour.

In *Lamorna Woods*, the flowers, foliage and trees merge with the colourful beings who walk through the luxurious and luscious flora. The painting is a depiction of the glorious life that Fred sees all around him, in landscape and in people. He is a solitary character, self possessed, who indulges in a vicarious world quite outside his own existence, involving himself in the happiness of others through the medium of paint and canvas.

He enjoys working freely with colour and paints straight from the tube to create the impasto finish and larger-than-life image of his work. People, patterns and life to the full are portrayed liberally in his pictures, all revealing his love of being a painter. His work is often full of people, reflecting his Manchester background, with workers swarming out of factory gates, and the crowds who take their holidays in St Ives.

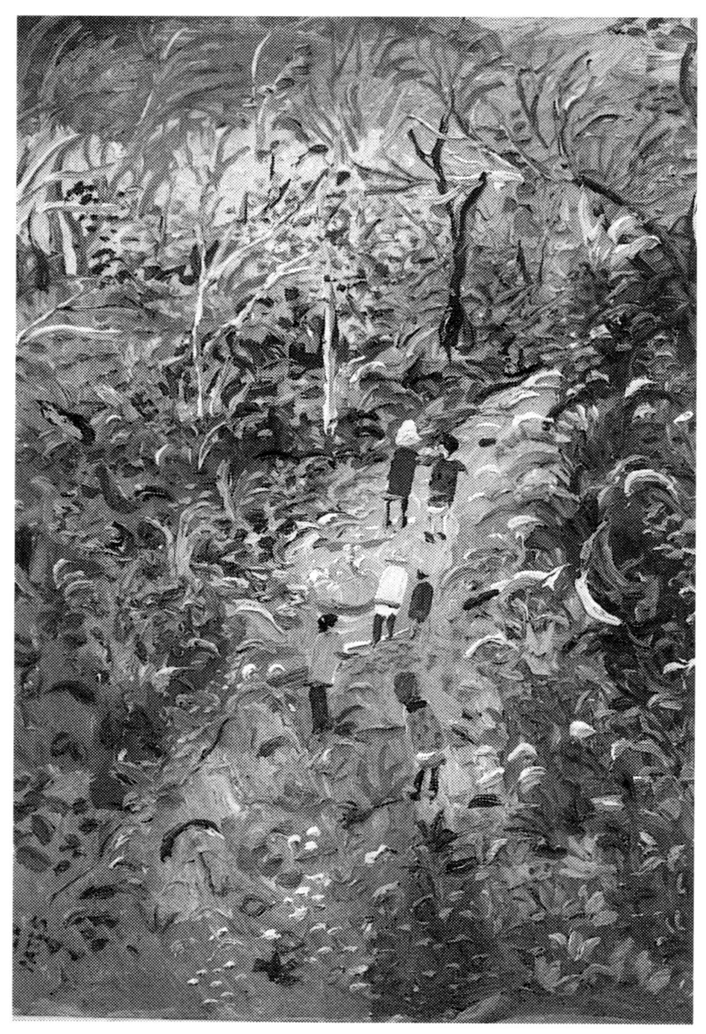

Fred Yates: *Lamorna Woods.*

BIBLIOGRAPHY

Books

Berlin, Sven *Alfred Wallis, Primitive* Nicolson and Watson 1949, reprinted and updated by Redcliffe Press Ltd, Bristol, 1992

Berlin, Sven *The Coat of Many Colours* Redcliffe Press Ltd, 1994

Berriman, Hazel *Crysède The unique textile designs of Alec Walker* Royal Institution of Cornwall, 1993

Berriman, Hazel *Arts and Crafts in Newlyn 1890–1930* Newlyn Art Gallery, 1986

Bihalji-Merin, Oto *World Encyclopaedia of Naive Art: A Hundred Years of Naive Art* Muller, 1984

Canney, Michael *Norman and Alethea Garstin* Dowrick Design & Print, 1978

Davies, Peter *The St Ives Years: essays on the growth of an artistic phenomenon* The Wimborne Bookshop, 1984

Davies, Peter *St Ives Revisited – innovators and followers* Old Bakehouse Publications, 1994

Ede H S *A Way of Life: Kettle's Yard* Cambridge University Press, Cambridge 1984

Hardie, Melissa *100 Years in Newlyn, Diary of a Gallery* Patten Press, New Mill, Penzance, 1995

Harrison, Charles *The Modern, The Primitive and the Picturesque* Scottish Arts Council

Havelock-Allan, Lucy *The Pier Gallery* Stromness, Orkney, 1978

Heron, Patrick *The Changing Forms of Art* Routledge and Kegan Paul, 1955

Hill, Polly & Keynes, Richard *Lydia and Maynard Letters between Lydia Lopokova and John Maynard Keynes* André Deutsch, 1989

Ingleby Richard *Christopher Wood An English Painter* Allison & Busby, 1995

Jakovsky, Anatole *Naive Painting* Phaidon Press Ltd, 1979

Jason, Neville & Thompson-Pharoah, Lisa *The Sculpture of Frank Dobson* Henry Moore Foundation and Lund Humphries, 1994

Jones, Ruth *The Path of the Son* Sheviock Gallery Publications, 1976

Lanyon, Peter and Andrew *Cornwall* with introduction by William Feaver, Alison Hodge, 1983

Leman, Jill & Martin *A World of Their Own – 20th Century British Naive Painters* Pelham Books, 1985

Lewison, Jeremy *Ben Nicholson* Phaidon Press Ltd, 1991

Lister, Eric *Portal Painters – A Survey of British Primitive Fantasists* Alpine Fine Arts Collection Ltd, New York, 1982, Portal Gallery, London

Lister, Eric & Williams, Sheldon *Naive & Primitive Artists, 20th Century British* Astragal Books, London, 1977

Melly, George *A Tribe of One, Great Naive Painters of the British Isles* Oxford Illustrated Press Ltd, 1981
Melly, George *Alfred Wallis* (boxed cards) Kettle's Yard, Cambridge, 1990
Morphet, Richard *Cedric Morris* Tate Gallery Publications, 1984
Mullins, Edwin *Alfred Wallis, Cornish Primitive* Macdonald & Co. Ltd, 1967, Pavilion Books Ltd, 1994
Nicholson, Winifred *Unknown Colour* Faber & Faber, 1987
Portal Painters, A Survey of British Idiosyncratic painters Alpine Fine Art Collection, 1992
Rona Guide to the World of Naive Art, RONA Register of Naive Artists, 1978
St Ives 1939–64 Twenty Five Years of Painting, Sculpture and Pottery, Tate Gallery Publications, 1985
Three Hundred Years on Penwith Farms Penwith Local History Group, 1994
Val Baker, Denys *Britain's Art Colony by the Sea* George Ronald 1959
Val Baker, Denys *Paintings From Cornwall* 1950s
Vann, Philip *Patrick Hayman: A Voyage of Discovery* The South Bank Centre, 1990
Whybrow, Marion *Bryan Pearce – A Private View* St Ives Printing & Publishing, 1985
Whybrow, Marion *St Ives 1883–1993, Portrait of an Art Colony* Antique Collectors' Club, 1993
Whybrow, Marion *The Leach Legacy, St Ives Pottery and its Influence* Sansom & Company Ltd, Bristol, 1996

Articles and Catalogues in date order

'The Woman Artist', Augustus John, *Vogue*, 18 April 1928
Letter to Ben Nicholson from Alfred Wallis, December 1928, Tate Gallery Archive 8717.1.2.5258
The notebooks of Margaret Mellis 1939
'Alfred Wallis', Ben Nicholson, *Horizon*, Vol. 7, No 37, 1943
'Alfred Wallis', Sven Berlin, *Horizon*, Vol. 7, No 37, 1943
'Two Painters in Cornwall, Alfred Wallis & Christopher Wood', H S Ede, *World Review*, March 1945
'Penwith Society Spring Exhibition', *Cornish Review*, Summer 1950, No.5, 1950
'The Boy and the Painter', A W Rowe, *St Ives Times & Echo*, December 1957
'Mary Jewels and Naive Painting', Alan Bowness, *Painter and Sculptor*, Vol. 1, No.3 Autumn 1958
'Bryan Pearce', Charles Causley, BBC broadcast 1962
'Bryan Pearce', feature film on BBC TV 1962
'Bryan Pearce', excerpt from foreword for catalogue, St Martin's Gallery, London 1964
Letter from Barbara Hepworth to Dr Roger Slack 1964
'Bryan Pearce, Rooftop Painter', Michael Williams, *Cornish Magazine*, Vol.7 No.9 January 1965

'The Old Man of the Sea-Piece', David Sylvester, *Sunday Times Magazine*, January 1965

'Alfred Wallis', exhibition catalogue, Waddington Galleries, Cork Street, 1965

'A Group of Primitives and Naifs', Peter Lanyon, *Studio International*, November 1966

'Alfred Wallis: the poetry of "what used to be"', Edwin Mullins, *Studio International*, November 1966

'Icons of the Sea – recollections of Alfred Wallis', *The Listener* 20 June 1968

'Alfred Wallis', BBC radio programme, May 1968

'An Arts Council Exhibition of Alfred Wallis', Tate Gallery, with introduction by Alan Bowness, 1968

'Alfred Wallis', Frank Ruhrmund, *Cornish Review* No.9, 1968

'Bryan Pearce', feature film, ITV Westward Diary, 1969

'Grandpa Was a Painter', Jack Pender, *Cornish Review* No.17, Spring 1971

John Stevens Wade, interview with Mary Pearce, *Western Humanities Review*, Autumn 1973

'The Newlyn School of Painters', Lorraine Craig, *Cornish Review* No.27, Winter 1974

'Bryan Pearce', *Aquarius*, ITV, 1974

'Bryan Pearce' catalogue introduction, Alan Bowness, Museum of Modern Art, Oxford, 1975

'Arts & Crafts in Cornwall, Mary Jewels', Frank Ruhrmund, *Cornish Life*, Vol.3, 1976

'Bryan Pearce', BBC TV *Nationwide*, 1976

'Still Life, Bryan Pearce', Dudley Doust, *Sunday Times Magazine*, 24 July 1977

'British Primitive & Naive Painting', catalogue, Ikon Gallery 1977

'Bryan Pearce Paintings and Drawings' catalogue introduction, Alan Bowness, Victor Waddington, London, 1978

'Alfred Wallis' catalogue, Penwith Galleries, St Ives, 1983

'Primitive Visions, Painters of Cornwall', Denys Val Baker, *Country Life*, 16 August 1984

'Tate Showing for St Ives Artists', John Halkes, *Western Morning News*, February 1985

'The Magic of Bryan Pearce', Frank Ruhrmund, *St Ives Times & Echo*, October 1992

'Alfred Wallis', Margaret Mellis, Royal West of England Academy/Redcliffe Press Ltd, 1992

'Alfred Wallis: Reflections on an After-Life', *St Ives Times & Echo*, August 1992

Letter from the late Michael Holloway to Bryan Pearce 1992

'The Ancient Mariner of St Ives', Martin Gayford, *The Sunday Telegraph*, October 1992

'The Old Man of the Sea', Sven Berlin, *Art Review*, May 1995

'Ancient Mariner', Richard Ingleby, Kapil Jariwala Gallery, *The Independent Tabloid*, February 1997

'Around the Galleries, Alfred Wallis', John Russell Taylor, *The Times Arts*, March 1997

'Alfred Wallis & His Family, Fact and Fiction', Peter Barnes, St Ives Trust Archive Study Centre, St Ives, 1997

Excerpts on Mary Jewels and Cordelia Dobson from Michael Canney's Newlyn Notebook (date not known)

ACKNOWLEDGEMENTS

Many people have helped in my researches, with special thanks going to Dr Roger Slack for his generous support and interest, the late Mary Pearce for her kind and supportive interest and for access to all Bryan's archive material and slides, and to Peter Tregurtha for information on the family of Mary Jewels.

I want to thank my editor, John Sansom; Sir Alan Bowness for permission to quote from articles on Wallis, Pearce and Jewels; Peter Barnes for permission to draw on his new research on Wallis; The Book Gallery, Bedford Road, St Ives, for access to letters; Del Castagli for access to her collection of catalogues, articles, photographs of Bryan Pearce; Patrick Heron for permission to quote from articles on Wallis; Margaret Mellis for permission to quote from her writings on Wallis; Frank Ruhrmund for consent to quote from his many articles; St Ives Archive Study Centre; and the West Cornwall Archive for helpful information, and access to material and photographs; Penlee House Art Gallery & Museum; St Ives Library staff Greta, Liz, Jenny, Sue and Jane. Quotations from the letters of Lydia Lopokova are by kind permission of the Provost and Scholars of King's College, Cambridge.

Many thanks also for information and/or photographs to Austin/Desmond Fine Art, Wilhelmina Barns-Graham, Sven Berlin, the late Hazel Burston, Graham Binns, Michael Canney, Valerie Dobbs, Peter Evans, Paul Feiler, Ander Gunn Collection, Bret Guthrie, John Halkes, Melissa Hardie, Joanne Johnson, Sheila Lanyon, Tom Lugg, Margo Maeckelberghe, Jane Mitchell, Denise Morris, Richard Morphet, Bryan Pearce, Portal Gallery, Eric Quayle, Donald Rawe, the late Adrian Ryan, St Ives Times and Echo, Gay Sagar-Fenton, Leon Suddaby, Polly Walker and Geoffrey Wollaston. Sources of illustrations are also indicated in picture captions. The author has made every effort to trace copyright holders and owners; any errors or omissions will gladly be put right in future editions.

INDEX

Index of names other than Bryan Pearce, Mary Jewels and Alfred Wallis. Page numbers in bold refer to illustrations.

Aldridge, John 65
Armfield, Stuart **72**

Barnes, Peter 53, 54
Barns-Graham, Wilhelmina 17, 68, 89
Baughan, -. 11
Bennett, David 86
Bennett, Sheila 86
Berlin, Sven 54, 63, 65, 66, 71, **72**, 73, 97, 98, 105, 110
Berlin, Helga 65
Binns, Graham 106
Birch, S.J. ('Lamorna') 94
Blow, Sandra 27
Bottome, Phyllis 150
Bourne, Bob 130, **131**
Bowness, Sir Alan 7, 21, 28, 33, 85, 86, 100, 106
Bowness, Lady Sarah 85
Bramley, Frank 27
Braque, Georges 148
Breaker, Charles 109
Broido, Michael 142
Brown, David 93, 112

Caddick, Arthur **96**
Canney, Michael 49, **96**, 100, 107, 110
Castagli, Del 85
Cavell-Hicks, Sheila 107
Causley, Charles 86, 89
Chagall, Marc 98, 148
Clarke, Joseph **131**, 132
Colquhoun, Ithell 107
Copas, Ronnie 109, 133, **135**
Cothey, Win 78, 85
Courbet, Gustave 148
Craig, Lorraine 100

Dacre, Winifred (Nicholson) 65
Delaney, Father -. 150
Devereux, Bob 130
Dexter, Peter 85
Diaghilev, Sergei 101
Dobson, Cordelia see Tregurtha, Cordelia
Dobson, Frank 94, 100–102, 110
Dodds, Valerie 85
Dowling, Jane 93
Dufy, Raoul 148

Early, Tom 106
Ede, H.S. ('Jim') 9, 12, 17, 21, 33, 35, 45, 46, 65–67, 82, 86
English, Mrs -. 85
Epstein, Jacob 6

Falconer, David 89
Farrell, George 54, 71
Farrell, Jessie 59
Feaver, William 21
Feiler, Paul 109
Forbes, Elizabeth 27
Forbes, Stanhope 27, 94, 109, 110
Frost, Sir Terry 89
Frumah family 148
Fuller, Leonard 23, 24, 49, 78

Gabo, Miriam 65
Gabo, Naum 65
Galutsky, Hiam see Tobias, Ben
Gardiner, Margaret 21, 65, 67
Garnier, G.S. 94
Garstin, Alethea 49, 67, 71, 107, 134
Garstin, Norman 27
George, William J. 98, 106, 107, 134, **135**
Gilbert, H.C. (Gillie) 85

Gillchrest, Joan **136**, 137
Gotch, T.C. 27
Graham, W.S. 142
Grier, Louis 27
Grigson, Geoffrey 65
Guthrie, Brett 71

Halkes, John 107
Harvey, Harold 94, 110
Haylett, Jean 150
Haylett, Malcolm 150
Hayman, Patrick 66, 107
Heath, Isobel 23
Hepworth, Barbara 6, 16, 17, 21, 27, 28, 45,
    53, 59, 63, 65, 67, 73, 89, 142, 150
Heron, Patrick 7, 27, 68, **70**, 71, 89, 106
Hicks family 148
Hilton, Roger 130
Hodge, Alison 21
Hodgkins, Frances 27, 98
Holloway, Michael 89
Holman, Betty **136**, 138
Holman, Linden 138

Jakovsky, Anatole 91
Jewels, A.O. 93
Joel, Judy 139, **140**
Joel, Katie 139
John, Augustus 94, 97, 98, 100, 105, 106
John, Casper 109
John, Dorelia 97
John, Mary 109
Jones, Ruth 90

Kalman, Andreas **140**
Kirman, Dr Brian 75
Knight, Laura 27, 97
Knollys Eardley 63
Lander, Carrie 61
Lander, Thomas 54
Langford, Sarah 61
Langley, Walter 27
Lanyon, Andrew 11, **15**
Lanyon, Peter 21, 24, 27, 28, 66, 75, 106, 107,
    130, 150
Lawrence, T.E. 101
Leach, Bernard 63, 65, 73, 150

Leach, David 68
Leah, Father -. 81
Leman, Jill 141
Leman, Martin 109, **140**, 141
Lett-Haines, Arthur 98, 110
Lewison, Jeremy 12
Lindner, Moffat 27
Lopokova, Lydia 101
Lowndes, Alan 107, 109, 142, **143**
Lowndes, Valerie 142
Lowry, L.S. 91

Mackenzie, Alexander 144
McWilliams, John 38
Maeckelberghe, Margo 71, 102
Mannings-Sanders, George 65
Mellis, Margaret 21, 28, 40, 49, 63, 65, 68
Melly, George 7
Milne, John 142
Mitchell, Denis 12, 17, 21, 27, 68
Mitchell, Lewes **143**, 144
Moore, Henry 6, 110
Morris, Cedric 12, 94, 98, 100, 110
Mostyn, Margery 75, **76**
Mullins, Edwin 16, 73
Munnings, Alfred 94, 97
Muntz, Elizabeth 94, **95**, 101
Myers, Leo 101

Nicholson, Ben 7, 11, 12, 16, 17, 27, 28, 40,
    59, **62**, 63, 65–68, 73, 89, 100, 101, 106
Nicholson, Edith 101
Nicholson, Elizabeth (Penny) 101
Nicholson, Kate 17, 106
Nicholson, William 12, 101
Nicholson, Winifred 11, 12, 16, 21, 59, 60, 66,
    67, 110
Noszlopy, George T. 89

Oatway, Win 145, **146**
Olsson, Julius 27

Park, John 27
Pearce, Margaretta 75, **76**, 77, 90
Pearce, Mary 23, 24, 27, 33, 41, 46, 49, 75,
    76, 78, 81, 82, **83**, **84**, 85, 86, 89, 90
Pearce, Walter 75, **76**, 78, 86

Peile, Misome 49
Pender, Jack 109, 134
Pennant Jones, Robert 133
Pennant Jones, Sheila 133
Phillips, Gerry 73
Picasso, Pablo 66, 144
Portway, Douglas 138
Potter, Toni **146**, 147
Procter, Dod 102, 105

Quayle, Eric 107

Rawe, Donald 21, 37, 73
Read, Herbert 59, 65, 68
Reddihough, C.S. 65
Ritman, Lieke 85
Rousseau, Henri (Douanier) 7, 8, 12
Rowe, Albert 45, 49
Rowe, Matthew Eddy 107
Ruhrmund, Frank 67, 86, 100, 102, 109, 137
Ryan, Adrian 106, 110
Ryan, Vivien **96**

Sagar-Fenton, Gay 109
Sagar-Fenton, Penny **96**
Shackell, Jim 138
Sitwell, Edith 101
Sitwell, Osbert 101
Sitwell, Sacheverell 110
Slack, Dr Roger 16, 49, 53, 54, 59, 60, 61, 71,
    72, 73
Smart, Borlase 27
Smith, Jean Kennedy 90
Snell, William Arnold 94
Snell, W.H. and Son, 94
Spencer, Stanley 133
Stokes, Adrian 17, 28, 40, 49, 60, 61, 63, 65
Summerson, John 65
Sutherland, Helen 65

Tobias, Ben 148, **149**
Tregurtha, Cordelia (Dobson) 93, 94, **96**,
    100–112
Tregurtha, Jane (Downing) 93, 98, 102, 110
Tregurtha, John 93, 94
Tregurtha, Peter 94
Tregurtha, Thomas 93, 94

Tregurtha, Weymouth 93, 94
Trevor, Henry 106
Tribe, Barbara **74**, 81

Utrillo, Maurice 148

Val Baker, Denis 112
Van Gogh, Vincent 66, 105
Vann, Philip 66
Venning, Mike 130
Vibert, John Paul 93
Vogler, Felicitas 12

Waddington, Victor 33
Wadsworth, Edward 101
Walker, Alec 102
Walker, Anna **96**
Walker, Holly **96**
Walker, Polly 102, 109, 112
Walker, Sarah **96**
Wallis, Charles (father) 53
Wallis, Charles (brother) 53, 54
Wallis, Emily 54, 57
Wallis, Jane (mother) 53
Wallis, Jane (sister-in-law) 54
Wallis, Susan (also Ward) 11, 49, 53, 54, **55**,
    57, 59, 60
Walton, William 101
Ward, Jacob 54
Ward, Nancy 53, 59, 61
Warren, Bryan Lawrey 107
Watkins, Kathy 85
Watson, Peter 106
Wells, John 89, 105, 106
Wesley, John 134
White, Clare **149**, 150
Whybrow, Marion **72**, 73, **80**, 90
Williams, Mary 150
Wollaston, Geoffrey 93
Wood, Christopher 11, 12, 16, 17, 60, 65, 66,
    68, 110
Wood, Gwen **96**
Woodard, Dr -. 75
Woolcock, Emily 16, 59, 61
Wynter, Bryan 109

Yates, Fred 151, **152**